A Hunter of Peace

No one may know
I went among those hills with a broken heart
and only on the high places could I learn
that I and mine
were very close together.
We dare not tell those beautiful thoughts,
they like to say "explorer" of me,
no, only a hunter of peace.
I found it.

from a letter,
Mary Schäffer Warren

A Hunter of Peace

Mary T. S. Schäffer's

Old Indian Trails

of the Canadian Rockies

Incidents of Camp and Trail Life, Covering Two Years' Exploration Through the Rocky Mountains of Canada.

with photographs by the Author
and by Mary W. Adams and Others

including a previously unpublished account

The 1911 Expedition to Maligne Lake

and

Yahe-Weha — Mountain Woman

a portrait of Mary Schäffer Warren

by E. J. Hart who has edited and
annotated the texts

The Whyte Foundation   Banff, Alberta, Canada

1980

Most of the extant material on Mary Schäffer Warren resides in her collection housed in the Archives of the Canadian Rockies. We would, however, like to thank several other people for their assistance in providing additional research and pictorial materials. They are: Mr. and Mrs. Charles Reid of Banff, Mrs. Vera McGinn of Banff, Mr. Humphrey Toms of Vancouver, Mr. George Vaux of Philadelphia, and Mrs. Barbara Whyte of Medicine Hat.

We would also like to extend our sincerest appreciation to the Alberta 75th Anniversary Commission for its generous grant which has made the production of this book possible.

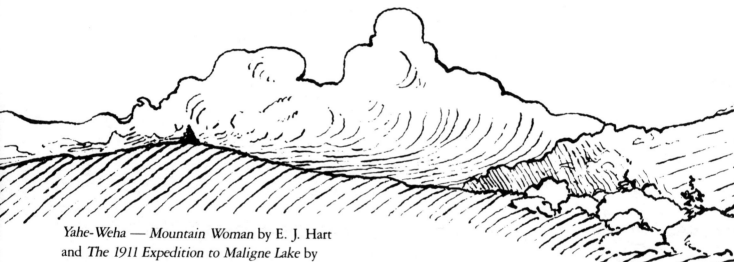

Yahe-Weha — Mountain Woman by E. J. Hart and *The 1911 Expedition to Maligne Lake* by Mary T. S. Schäffer are copyright © 1980 by the Peter and Catharine Whyte Foundation, Box 160, Banff, Alberta, Canada, and may not be reproduced in any form except by reviewers who may quote brief passages (not to exceed one hundred and fifty words) without the written permission of the Whyte Foundation. The photographs are also © copyright by the Whyte Foundation.

Second Printing, 1983
Third Printing, 1986
We have endeavoured to locate the ownership of the copyright to Mary T. S. Schäffer's *Old Indian Trails* without success.

Old Indian Trails of the Canadian Rockies was originally published by G. P. Putnam's Sons, New York, in 1911.

The design of this edition is by Jon Whyte Alex Emond of Banff executed the drawings for the title pages

The colored photographs reproduced in *A Hunter of Peace* were, with two exceptions, coloured by Mary T. S. Schäffer Warren. The portrait on the cover and the photograph on page 133 are black and white photographs from the Schäffer collections coloured by Carole Harmon and Edward Cavell respectively.

ISBN:0-920608-06-X

A Hunter of Peace is printed by D. W. Friesen and Sons Ltd., Altona, Manitoba. Distributed by Altitude Publishing Ltd., Box 490, Banff, Canada, T0L 0C0

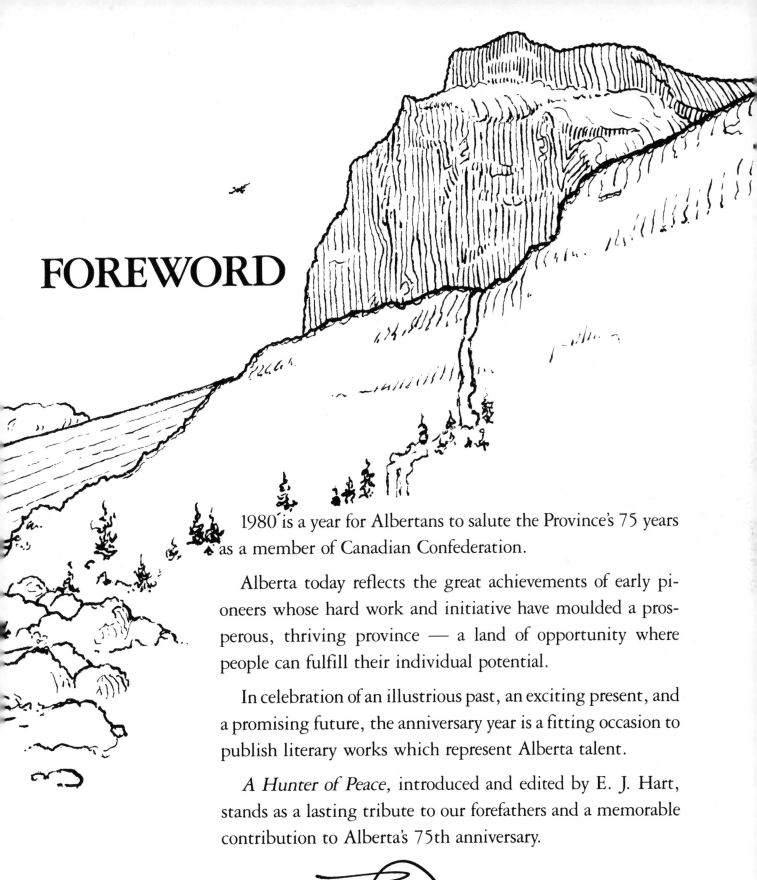

FOREWORD

1980 is a year for Albertans to salute the Province's 75 years as a member of Canadian Confederation.

Alberta today reflects the great achievements of early pioneers whose hard work and initiative have moulded a prosperous, thriving province — a land of opportunity where people can fulfill their individual potential.

In celebration of an illustrious past, an exciting present, and a promising future, the anniversary year is a fitting occasion to publish literary works which represent Alberta talent.

A Hunter of Peace, introduced and edited by E. J. Hart, stands as a lasting tribute to our forefathers and a memorable contribution to Alberta's 75th anniversary.

R. W. Dowling
Commissioner
Alberta 75th Anniversary Commission

Yahe-Weha — Mountain Woman
The Life and Travels of Mary Schäffer Warren, 1861-1939

E. J. Hart

During a carriage drive to view the incomparable beauties of Emerald Lake on a fine summer's day in August, 1907, Rudyard Kipling observed an interesting spectacle. Later, in his book *Letters of Travel 1892-1913*, he described the incident and a sequel to it at Mount Stephen House that evening:

> As we drove along the narrow hill road a piebald pack-pony with a china-blue eye came round a bend, followed by two women, black-haired, bare-headed, wearing beadwork squaw jackets and riding straddle. A string of pack-ponies trotted through the pines behind them.
>
> "Indians on the move?" said I. "How characteristic!"
>
> As the women jolted by, one of them very slightly turned her eyes, and they were, past any doubt, the comprehending equal eyes of the civilised white woman which moved in that berry-brown face.
>
> "Yes," said our driver, when the cavalcade had navigated the next curve, "that'll be Mrs. So-and-so and Miss So-and-so. They mostly camp here-about for three months every year. I reckon they're coming in to the railroad before the snow falls." . . .
>
> The same evening, in an hotel of all the luxuries, a slight woman in a very pretty evening frock was turning over photographs, and the eyes beneath the strictly arranged hair were the eyes of the woman in the beadwork jacket who had quirted the piebald pack-pony past our buggy.
>
> Praised be Allah for the diversity of his creatures!

Unwittingly, Kipling had described the dichotomy of the lady he had observed. In the drawing rooms of Philadelphia she was to her acquaintants the cultured, charming and talented Mrs. Mary Townsend Sharples Schäffer; in the wilds of the Canadian Rockies she was to the Stoney Indians *Yahe-Weha*, "Mountain Woman."

Mary Sharples* was born at West Chester, Pennsylvania to wealthy Quaker parents on October 4, 1861. Her father's family had arrived in America from England in 1644 and from that time forward its offspring had only married among "the English group." During the War of Independence, when most loyal British subjects had emigrated to Canada as United Empire Loyalists, members of the Society of Friends chose to remain in the Colonies, but retained their attachment to the mother country. The family home at the corner of Church and Dean Streets was all constructed from and furnished with English materials. Her father Alfred's intense love for England and things

---

* Various members of the Sharples (pronounced sharp' less) family spelled their name with one or two s's. Although her father used the Sharpless form, Mary always used Sharples.

English Mary felt at a young age, and in later years she sometimes balked at being called an American.

By her own admission Mary lived a pampered childhood. Alfred Sharpless, the former Superintendent of the Schuylkill Navigation Company, became a gentleman farmer in 1870 and also served as a bank director and a member of the borough council. In addition to his own considerable funds he had the benefit of his wife's (née Elizabeth Cope Sharples) large inheritance. Given these circumstances, the Sharpless household was well staffed with maids and servants, and Mary could devote her time to traditional handwork, such as embroidery and needlepoint, and to being educated in the proper manner. The Quaker approach to education was an empirical and practical one, and she excelled in mathematics and languages at school, likely the Friends' Select School in Philadelphia. Apart from her schoolwork and handwork her main interest was art and she was undoubtedly taught by a private tutor as was the fashion for young ladies.

From the age of nine one of Mary's few responsibilities was "overseeing" her younger brothers, Fred and Herman. With this task began her affection for young boys that would remain with her for the rest of her life. She later stated that "at age 16 I took a motherless boy, educated him and set him on the road to success," perhaps an allusion to an adopted family child. However, he was to be just the first of many, including nephews and other young men met throughout her life, who benefited from her unrequited maternal instincts. Despite the care and attention lavished on the boys, her domestic abilities languished and she later admitted that "I did not know how to make a bed at the tender age of 18."

If she lacked the homemaker's skills, Mary made up for them in other ways. A precocious child, she often secretly listened to her parents' conversations and learned many interesting things, particularly about science. Her father was an avid mineralogist and one of his great friends was the Swiss geologist, Dr. Joseph Leidy of the Academy of Natural Sciences of Philadelphia. When Mary was about six Alfred Sharpless began to allow her to accompany him on his drives into the country with Dr. Leidy and she began to absorb a good deal of "the story of stones, grasses and the small things people attach no importance to." Quaker education tended to foster an interest in natural history and it is not surprising that these influences eventually led to a study of botany.

Mollie Adams, Mary Schäffer, Billy Warren and Joe Barker in camp

Another influence on her life awakened when as a young girl Mary listened, her ear pressed to the dining room door, to her "Cousin Jim," an officer in the United States Army, whose brass-buttoned uniform and clinking spurs were a wonder to a child. "Cousin Jim" related details of his life in the west — of prairie schooners and buffalo hunts, but most of all of Indians and how Uncle Sam's army was slowly pressing back the western tribes for the advancing tide of white settlement. One story he told was of the destruction of an Indian village that had been so complete even the women and children had been killed. Examining the carnage, he had made a heart-rending discovery, a live baby peeping out from under the shelter of its mother's dead body. Hearing this was too much for Mary and she let out a sob that led to her discovery and subsequent banishment to her bedroom never to hear of the poor babe's fate.

Quaker teaching stressed quiet introspection, and for her part young Mary gave this particular incident more

than its due share. It gave rise to what she described as her "fever," which manifested itself in a love for the Indian race that had received such unfair treatment at the hands of the white interloper.

> The baby face, the dead mother, the smoking tepees remained in the child's mind forever after and governed many an act as she grew older. She never spoke of what she heard that night, but the shadow of the story always hung on her horizon. She asked for "Indian stories," she tramped the Pennsylvania hills after the heavy rains looking for the old Indian arrowheads, dreamed daydreams over the Indian stone battle-axes, basins, anything which referred to the people who had once owned the continent which she and hers called "ours."

Even with all the opportunities and attractions available to a girl of her background, it was an insistent desire to actually see the people of the plains which remained uppermost in Mary's mind. Finally, when she was in her mid-teens, a train trip with her family to California provided the fulfillment for that longing.

Rubus parviflorus

Mountain Raspberry

Having created her own romantic vision of the west to the extent that she carried a small revolver with her on the train, she was a little disappointed. Her first encounter with Indians occurred in the middle of the Mohave Desert where the engine stopped to take on water. Some rather pathetic Indian women gathered to receive scraps of tainted meat thrown out from the dining car. Shocked at the reality of the situation, she nonetheless kept up her spirits and at Lake Tahoe met an Indian family which better fit her preconceived notions. From the "handsome squaw" she purchased a beautiful hand-made basket, the first of what was to become a fine collection.

A second visit to the west soon after the first trip included a voyage on a freight steamer up the west coast to Alaska. Since the captain of the vessel was in search of a cargo of fish, he penetrated many bays and inlets and Mary was able to observe numerous Indians in a more or less untouched setting. At one stop she chanced to befriend a beautiful young Indian woman who gave her a pair of soft, doe-skin moccasins, a gift she would treasure all her days.

At the completion of the second trip, Mary had assuaged her initial "fever" to acquaint herself with the aboriginal inhabitants of the west. Nevertheless, she had kindled an interest in travel that would see her make several other trips over the following few years. At the same time she attempted to take on some responsibilities around the home. Her first attempt to bake a pie was so disastrous it was fed to the chickens, but it provided the impetus for her to begin to learn more than just languages, art, and mathematics.

In 1889 Mary took a trip on the Canadian Pacific Railway from Montreal to Vancouver which changed the course of her life. One reason for the trip was to visit Glacier, high in the Selkirk Range of British Columbia, which she had been told about by a friend. The friend, Mary Vaux (pronounced Vox), was a woman Mary's own age with similar interests in art and botany. Beginning in 1885 she had accompanied her father, George Vaux, and her younger brothers, William Vaux jr. and George Vaux jr., on trips to the western United States, including Yellowstone Park and the California coast. Returning from their excursion of 1887, the Vaux family travelled through Canada and chanced to stop at Glacier House, the CPR's newly opened hostelry in Rogers Pass. They were highly impressed with the surroundings, particularly the magnificent Great (Illecillewaet) Glacier. Keenly interested in the natural sciences, the Vaux brothers marked the terminus of the glacier and took various photographic views of it. In 1894 the family would return to the area to begin an annual measurement of the movement of both the Illecillewaet and Asulkan Glaciers, using a system of metal plates placed in a line on the glaciers, supplemented by photographs from fixed reference points.

Meanwhile, the Vauxes had talked with Dr. Charles Schäffer, an acquaintance made through their common membership in the Academy of Natural Sciences of Philadelphia. Schäffer, who had graduated with an M.D. degree from the University of Pennsylvania in 1859, was at this time in private medical practice, but his real interest lay in the field of botany and he was anxious to examine the flora at Glacier described to him by the Vauxes. In 1889 he did so and during her brief stop at Glacier House Mary was introduced to the charming, albeit much older, doctor. Their acquaintance was renewed on returning to Philadelphia and soon afterward she became his bride.

Life with Dr. Schäffer was a continuation of what it had been in her own family. Schäffer too was wealthy and could never resist giving his pretty, auburn-haired wife whatever her heart desired. At times her health was not particularly good as she began to suffer the first effects of a life-long battle with neuritis. The doctor pampered her even further, though he too suffered from bad health in the form of heart disease. Despite these afflictions, in 1891 he decided that they should return to the mountains so he could make further investigations into the botanical discoveries he had made during his initial visit.

The 1891 trip was the first of more than a decade of annual excursions the Schäffers made together to Glacier, Field, Lake Louise and Banff in the course of the doctor's studies. Investigation into the literature available on the flora of the region led to his realization that, apart from the brief studies of John Macoun, virtually nothing was known about it. This the doctor meant to rectify, although his heart problem necessitated that his investigations be neither too strenuous nor too far from the railroad line. For her part, Mary accompanied the doctor on his rambles and then returned with him to the comfortable confines of one of the CPR hotels for the night, where she carefully dried and pressed the specimens gathered.

The couple had been at this task for quite some time before they realized Mary's talents could both aid Dr. Schäffer in his work and make it more interesting for her. Preoccupied with his own work, he had only a "dim idea" of Mary's skill in art and when she finally made him aware of it "we both got quite a shock." Her ability to capture the gorgeous colouring of the plants they had gathered became a valuable adjunct to his efforts, although the correctness of detail he needed did not come easily. Mary's artistic training; which included tutelage under the great American flower painter, George Lambden, was geared toward groupings. It was not what the doctor required:

> He was emphatic that every petal, every stamen should be correct to the last and *I* was much more interested in grouping . . . . This last is the very essence of being wrong and many a sketch had to be destroyed for what was to me a mere kink. But I learned my lesson and any sketch that passed his eagle eye simply HAD to be correct.

Complementing her abilities as an artist was her newly-found interest in photography, a skill gained from both her husband and the avidly photographic Vaux family. Utilizing a technique she called "vertical photography," she photographed specimens next to a measuring device to produce the proper scale. The negatives could then be used for prints or for the lantern slides she carefully hand-coloured to capture the original shades and hues of the subject. Her skills in both art and photography ultimately led Dr. Schäffer to appreciate his younger wife in a new way, strengthening their marriage.

The halcyon days which the Schäffers experienced both in Philadelphia and in the mountains abruptly ended in 1903. Never particularly well in his later years, Dr. Schäffer passed away in November, 1903, apparently from a heart attack, although substantial losses in the stockmarket may have exacerbated his poor health. In an incredible turn of bad luck Mary's mother had passed away only a few months before and her father was to die less than a month later, their money too either frittered away or spent on the requests of importuning relatives. These events and their subsequent effect on her life she later described:

> I lived my earlier life among the dreamers of my world. They were dear people but absolutely the most impractical ones you could conceive. My father, a scientist of high order; lots of money today, all spent on poor relations the next. My mother a little dark-eyed heiress many times over and her impractical husband spending it for gay horses or whatever came into his mind, tho the poor relations were forever to the front. Later I married the most wonderful scientist of my acquaintance. He could never resist giving me anything money could buy and tho his mind was so remarkably keen for science, he had no business acumen. Again I had to stand by and see this and that inconsequential getting solid lumps of money for the mere making of a poor mouth. The Dr. really died of a broken heart when one of the world's crashes came and I was left to stare the future in the face with very little.

Mary summoned up the fortitude to meet the situation: "All this taught me such a bitter lesson, to count my pennies, to lean on no one and make the best of the crumbling fortunes." She proved equal to the task, recouping enough of the losses to remain financially secure for the remainder of her life. Aiding her in this endeavour was a Calgary lawyer and member of the Legislative Assembly of the North West Territories, Richard B. Bennett. Having become a good friend of both her husband and herself during earlier trips and as a member with James Lougheed of one of the foremost legal firms in western Canada, "R. B." was in a good position to recommend some investments. One in particular in which he had a personal involvement was the E. B. Eddy Company and it immediately began to pay excellent dividends.

Fending for herself after her husband's death left Mary little time to grieve, but the pain of his loss became more acute after she had set her financial house in order. Realizing she required something to fill the void in her life, she decided nothing was more important than completing his work.

Several obstacles stood in her path. Her initial problem stemmed from a lack of necessary knowledge in botany to carry on with the classification. Although always keenly interested in the subject and able to press, sketch, or photograph any botanical specimen, she could only classify the very ordinary species. Faced with this situation, she enlisted the aid of Stewardson Brown, Curator of the Herbarium of the Academy of Natural Sciences of Philadelphia, a well respected botanist. To interest him in the project she promised the credit for the work would be his, since its completion was more important than whose name it appeared under. Brown agreed, and over the ensuing three years worked his way through both existing and new collections.

It was in the making of these new collections where Mary's second difficulty stood. Dr. Schäffer's health had precluded his collecting very far from the railway, but her completion of the work required examination of more remote areas. For this her background had inadequately prepared her, for most of her travels in the mountains had been "within sound of the shrieking engines and passing trains of the mountain division," and she had a deathly fear of horses. Her first experience with camping and travel on horseback had been in 1893

The Schäffer camp at Lake Louise, 1893

when Dr Schäffer approached pioneer outfitter and guide Tom Wilson to outfit a small party for Lake Louise. Wilson had provided the necessary horses from his ranch at Morley and appointed two Stoney Indian guides, William and Joshua Twin, to escort the party and set up camp on the lake's shore. Although she found the ride to Laggan on top of a CPR boxcar exciting, Mary was less than enamoured with horses and camping. From their tent door they had "looked out upon that magnificent scene with chattering teeth and shivering bodies and vowed never again to camp in the Canadian Rockies." Wilson, who was to become a most treasured friend, did not take her statement at face value and over the next few years "simply dragged a poor little delicate tourist to points she would not have reached." Nevertheless, by her own account her only experience with the real wilderness was a long carriage ride and hike taken in 1898 from Revelstoke to view the wonders of the canyon at the Big Bend of the Columbia.

Notwithstanding fears of horses, bears, and the wilderness in general, Mary's resolve led her back to Wilson's door in 1904 to request someone who could

gradually toughen her up for longer trail trips into the mountain fastnesses. Wilson assigned to her a young guide he had recently hired, William "Billy" Warren, or "Chief" as she soon affectionately called him, a handsome, twenty-two year old veteran of the Boer War when he arrived at Banff in 1902. A native of Harlow, Essex, he had attended St. Mary's College and learned accounting from his father before enlisting in the Imperial Yeomanry. Discontented with a clerk's job in London after the war, he decided to emigrate to Canada, where on arrival he faced difficulty in finding employment. So many Englishmen were appearing on the Canadian scene at that time that the sign "No Englishman Need Apply" was everywhere, and he headed west to test his fortune in Banff. Wilson, who had succeeded with Bill Peyto, Jimmy Simpson, Harry Lang, and numerous other Englishmen he had hired, immediately gave him a position on his crew. By 1904 Warren had demonstrated sufficient skills as a guide, and his pleasant disposition made him an ideal candidate to accompany Mrs. Schäffer. Her assessment was flattering:

Julia Henshaw and Mary Schäffer near Glacier House

"there are older ones [guides], there are better hunters perhaps, with wider experience in forest lore, more knowledge of the country, but for kindness, good nature (such a necessary adjunct), good judgment under unexpected stress, he had no superior."

Mary's first season with Warren she spent in areas such as the Yoho and Ptarmigan Valleys, locations both rich in botanical specimens and not requiring long trips. The following year, 1905, the horizon stretched to the fascinating country bordering the North Saskatchewn River. On one trip she allowed three lady acquaintances to accompany her, a decision which was partly a mistake but in another way quite fortunate. Problems arose a few days out: two of the ladies made no bones about the fact that they were not impressed with trail life and wished to return to 'civilisation' as quickly as possible. The third lady took to the experience immediately. She was Mary "Mollie" Adams, originally from Boston, a teacher of geology at Columbia College

in New York. This "new and understanding friend" agreed that two was an optimum number for any trip. Thereafter they never broke this rule, travelling thousands of miles together in the wilderness without a riffle of disagreement.

Upon returning from the trip to the North Saskatchewan, Mary took part in what was her most exciting adventure to date in the mountains. Charles Deutschman, the former trapper who had discovered and begun to develop some interesting caves in the Cougar Valley near Glacier, invited Mary Schäffer and Mary Vaux to a personal tour. They were the first ladies to view the subsequently famous Nakimu Caves, and, in awe of their splendour, Mary wrote an article for the Calgary *Herald:*

> At 9:30 our real work began — the descent into the cavernous unknown. For the work good ladders have been placed and any danger lies entirely with the explorer . . . .

—8—

Few of the chambers, or corridors, are named, but one called the auditorium stands out alone. A great vaulted gallery burst upon us from out of the gloom, hundreds of gallons of water were rushing down, sweeping by us with an angry roar, and as the red candle lit it up, the dashing spray was dripping blood, the deep walls were crimson and one felt such a small, helpless bit in nature's plan . . . .

The tour forced the ladies to follow their guide through a hole "that looked about large enough for a marmot." Other hazards followed: "She wiggled through minus the sinuous grace and plus a goodly amount of soil, and tumbled gently into a pot-hole, another gentle slide, a pay-out of rope, a sensation of growing into the waist-like proportions of a wasp, and she found herself in a taller pot-hole with a tiny river running gently down her back, while before her lay nothing." When the time came to leave the caves she admitted she was "glad to slip back into daylight."

Her 1905 collecting completed Dr. Schäffer's work, and Brown soon finished his analysis and writing. G.P. Putnam's Sons published *Alpine Flora of the Canadian Rocky Mountains* in 1907 and it sold for $3.00. Highlighting the edition were thirty full-page coloured plates and ninety-eight other illustrations, all made from Mary's watercolour drawings and photographs. Although Brown's name appeared as the author, the book's dedication revealed the source of its inspiration: "Offered To The Lovers Of Alpine Florae In Memory Of Dr. Charles Schäffer Of Philadelphia, Who Was Among The Pioneer Botanists Of The Canadian Rockies, And Who Early Recognized This Region As A New And Interesting Field For Study."

The work of Canadian botanist Julia Henshaw, *Mountain Wildfowers of Canada*, preceded *Alpine Flora* by one year. Henshaw had encountered the Shäffers several times at Glacier House and discussed the doctor's work and Mary's method of photography with them. Later Mary would make some veiled references to someone's having stolen their work and would express disappointment at Mrs. Henshaw's book appearing first.

The impetus of her initial inspiration for riding the trails of the Canadian Rockies now satisfied, Mary found new challenges toward which to direct her efforts. Her negative attitude to travel and camping in the mountains expressed in 1893 had now been completely reversed. As well, a fortuitous meeting in 1903 with one of the earliest explorers of the Canadian Rockies had fired her imagination. Sir James Hector, the

Dr. James Hector, 1903

indefatigable geologist of the Palliser Expedition of 1857-60, had returned as an old gentleman to view the location where in 1858 his horse had kicked him senseless, giving rise to the names of Kicking Horse River and Pass. Mary overheard him speaking of the incident at Glacier House, introduced herself and learned at firsthand details of many of his explorations of the region. Dreams that she too might have opportunities to see the mountain wilds the hand of the white man had not yet touched grew from this chance encounter.

With Mollie Adams she discussed both her idea and the information about the mountains brought back by contemporary scientists, alpinists and tourist-explorers such as A. P. Coleman, J. Norman Collie, Walter D.

Wilcox, Professor Charles E. Fay, and several others. Mary and Mollie realized it was not thought proper for women to take part in such exploits, to encroach upon the sole preserve of men. But Mary's Quaker background, which stressed the equality of the sexes, came to the fore in this instance and finally their "cups splashed over," leading to a momentous decision: "Then we looked into each other's eyes and said: 'Why not? We can starve as well as they; the muskeg will be no softer for us than for them; the ground no harder to sleep upon; the waters no deeper to swim, nor the bath colder if we fall in,' — so — we planned a trip." Not rejecting the idea as they thought he might, the faithful Warren encouraged them and "cheerfully assumed the leadership." For the season of 1906 their destination lay north to Wilcox Pass and included an examination of the Alexandra River and Pinto Lake areas. In 1907 their objectives were broader: to penetrate the headwaters of the North Saskatchewan and Athabasca Rivers and, time permitting, to search for a lake known to the Stoney Indians as Chaba Imne (Beaver Lake), lying somewhere to the north of Brazeau Lake.

The trips of 1907 and 1908 Mary recounts fully in *Old Indian Trails*. All that needs adding is Mary's attitude and philosophy about the rather amazing accomplishments of the two expeditions. While she insisted that it was a woman's right to make them, both she and Mollie regarded them as pleasure trips and were quite willing to let the men do the work: "I have never insisted on my woman's rights when it came to laying the bacon and flour, the kitchen utensils and blankets slap up against the sides of the patient beast which is to bear the burden, or to throw the tarpaulin over all, then adjust a tangle of ropes that holds everything in place until the next stopping place, with not a sore shoulder from a shifting saddle. At this point I have always resigned my rights as a woman." To Warren and his assistant, fellow Englishman Sid Unwin, she gave all credit for their success in reaching Maligne Lake and the Yellowhead country, stating that it was due to "Mr. Warren's long outlook and Sid's determination." Her and Mollie's part she described as "like the tail to an active horse."

An interesting sidelight to Mary's participation in the trips was her inspiring a novel by the popular English author, Mrs. Humphrey Ward. The CPR brought Mrs. Ward to Canada by way of promotion in 1908, and she met Mary at Field just prior to her renewed quest for Maligne Lake. After the successful conclusion of her search, Mary sent a description of the trip and some photographs from it to Mrs. Ward and then gave the matter no more thought. Surprisingly, in 1910 she received a copy of the book *Canadian Born* (later published in Canada as *Lady Merton, Colonist*), the romantic adventures of a young lady largely set in the Lake Louise area but ending with a honeymoon trip to Elizabeth (Maligne) Lake. Mrs. Ward's accompanying letter stated Mary had been the model for the heroine. Although somewhat flattered, Mary did not think the novel one of Mrs. Ward's better efforts, particularly since "she could never grasp my loved country."

Meanwhile, Mary had herself become involved in writing. There was a strong literary tradition in the Sharples family: her father had been well-known for his contributions to newspapers on agriculture and events of the day under the pseudonym "John Plowshare," and other relatives had written both fiction and journalism. Following in their footsteps, she had her own first article published in the popular magazine *Rod and Gun* in 1904. Based on her old interest in the Indians of the northwest, it was entitled "The Burial of Cher-on-kee," an account, seemingly related by an old fur trader, of the eerie events surrounding the death and burial of an Indian friend. However, her subsequent writings she based on material gathered from her experiences on the trail. These included newspaper stories, such as the aforementioned one on the Nakimu Caves and, more frequently, articles for the journals of two clubs of which she was an active member, the Geographical Society of Philadelphia and the Alpine Club of Canada. Articles entitled "The Valleys of the Saskatchewan with Horse and Camera" and "Among the Sources of the Saskatchewan and Athabasca Rivers" appeared in *The Bulletin of the Geographical Society of Philadelphia* in April of 1907 and 1908 respectively, and two articles entitled "Flora of the Saskatchewan and Athabasca River Tributaries" and "Untrodden Ways" appeared in *The Canadian Alpine Journal* in 1908.

The success greeting these articles undoubtedly fostered an idea that was occupying Mary, a book recounting her adventures. According to her, the original inspiration came when her nephew, Eric Sharples, insisted that the diaries she and Mollie had kept be put into story form. For her friends, whom she could not "enthuse" by merely describing the trips, she wrote "to bring to them the fresh air and sunshine, the snowy mountains, the softly flowing rivers, — the healers of every ill." Finally, her book was a testimonial to her friend Mollie.

On returning from the trail in 1908, she and Mollie departed for a trip to Japan. There they joined Dr. I. Nitobe, a Japanese scientist and worker for peace who had married a friend of Mary's family. The Nitobes introduced the ladies to the wonders of Japan throughout the fall and early winter of 1908. Then the trip abruptly and tragically ended. Mollie died of unknown causes and was laid to rest in Kobe by her friend. The death shook Mary to the very core.

Material for the book she drew largely from the diaries, her own memory and the accounts of others, such as Coleman, Outram and Collie, who had covered some of the country before them. For the answers she could not obtain from these sources she called on Tom Wilson, whose excellent memory and fine library contained historic information on the mountains. Particularly helpful on the subject of early fur traders, he was also able to provide the correct name for the river which emptied the lake they had visited, the Bad or Maligne River according to Dr. Hector in the *Palliser Journals*.

She worked on the book during her continuing annual trips to the Canadian Rockies in the summer months and over the course of winters spent in Philadelphia. Her winter activities also included a series of lantern slide lectures on the subject of her travels given to various scientific groups in the eastern United States. Through her familiarity with the management of G. P. Putnam's Sons, one of the foremost publishers in the country, an agreement for them to publish was soon worked out. *Old Indian Trails of the Canadian Rockies*, a volume of 380 pages containing 100 illustrations from photographs by both herself and Mollie Adams, appeared in 1911 and sold for $2.00 per copy. Its dedication read "To Mary Who With Me Followed The 'Old Indian Trails' But Who Has Now Gone On The Long Trail Alone." Newspaper reviews, particularly in the eastern United States, were highly laudatory. A major review in the New York *Times* opened by stating that "In reading 'Old Indian Trails' by Mary Schäffer it is difficult to decide just what impresses us most: the excellence of the writing, the picturesqueness of the country described or the personality of the author herself."

Before the book was off the press, Mary was involved in planning a second expedition to Maligne Lake. In the three years since her original trip, the Miette and Yellowhead country had changed from a virtually uninhabited wilderness to an area alive with humanity due to the approaching rails of a second Canadian transcontinental line, the Grand Trunk Pacific. At the same time the Canadian government was developing the newly established Jasper Forest Park adjacent to the railway's surveyed route. Late in 1910 D. B. Dowling of the Geological Survey of Canada approached Howard Douglas, Commissioner of Parks at Edmonton, with the idea that Mrs. Schaffer re-visit the lake to survey it. He argued that this would not only provide some much needed information but would also, as a result of her increasing fame, help to advertise the beauties of the area. Douglas agreed and released sufficient funds for cutting a suitable trail for access from the railway tote road to the lake.

Dowling, from his own work familiar with the Athabasca River country and well-acquainted with Mary, experienced no difficulty convincing her to take on the challenge. He took it upon himself to teach her the method of log and compass surveying that she would need to employ in her work. As companions for the trip Mary invited along her sister-in-law Caroline and her nephew Paul, the wife and young son of her brother Fred, a successful metallurgist and mining engineer in New York. Paul had been suffering from whooping cough over the past winter, and his aunt felt that fresh air and sunshine were just what was needed to effect a cure.

The eventful journey of 1911 to reach Maligne Lake, and the happenings in its environs during the survey, Mary recounts in her previously unpublished manuscript which completes *A Hunter of Peace*. The trip marked the end of her active exploratory work in the Canadian Rockies. With the coming of a second railroad she could see that things would never again be the same. She lamented the passing of the days prior to the encroachment of "civilisation," particularly brought home to her the following year when on returning to visit the Big Bend for the first time since 1898 she was able to reach it by motor car instead of the considerable buggy ride and hike that had previously been required.

Mary's life had again reached a turning point. Now fifty years of age, having accomplished all she had set out to do, she little knew what her future might be. Beginning to find Philadelphia a gloomy place over the long winter months, she decided to spend a part of a winter in Banff to see if she could stand the weather. Since her attachment to Billy Warren had grown over the years, it is likely his presence also had something to do with her decision. Her 1912 visit extended into the winter and she found it to be quite acceptable. Accordingly, she asked Warren to look for a piece of property where she might have a suitable residence constructed. In 1913 he succeeded in finding one but when she saw it she "nearly died," for it was at the end of Grizzly Street immediately opposite the Banff cemetery. Recognizing that Warren had done his best, she said nothing, and Warren soon built her a comfortable frame home which, not at all ostentatious from the outside, was beautifully appointed inside. The spacious living room was graced by a magnificent brick fireplace and all the rooms were finished, ceiling and walls, with a fine V-joint fir planking. Once her collection of beautiful eighteenth century antiques was ensconced with an accompanying selection of fine art, needlework and stitchery, and Indian artifacts, she began to feel at ease and named her new home "Tarry-a-while."

Prior to and after her move to Banff, Mary continued to take short summer outings on the trail under Warren's guidance. Probably with her financial assistance, Warren acquired an outfitting business he operated out of Lake Louise and Field. Meanwhile, in the decade she had known him, Mary's admiration of Warren's character and abilities had grown to the point where it knew no bounds. In June, 1915, despite the disparity in their ages, the two decided to marry. While the details are not known, it seems likely it was a match of mutual admiration and convenience. For Mary it was the answer to her prayers and she became completely devoted to her new husband and her new home. These feelings she perhaps best conveyed in a letter to a friend written a few years later: "I want you to see a mountain bungalow, a spot which so many come on unexpectedly and in looking around almost invariably say 'Here is a home.' It's not rustic, but it has a great hearth and great hearts but the best one is mostly busy all summer long — my CHIEF."

Her allusion to Warren being busy all summer long derived from the immediate success he experienced in his business affairs after the marriage. Already possessing "a strong practical character," he utilized his wife's considerable funds to acquire new business interests in Banff. By 1920 he was the owner of the Alberta Hotel and the Cascade Garage on Banff Avenue and the following year he initiated construction of the Cascade Hall and became involved in a new motorized transportation company, Rocky Mountain Tours and Transport. Harkening back to his wife's friendship with R. B. Bennett, he was also a local stalwart of the Conservative Party. Bennett, a frequent house guest, was at the time M.P. for Calgary West, but he was already on the path to becoming his party's leader and ultimately the Prime Minister of Canada.

With her husband deeply involved in his business and political activities, Mary continued to strive to make her life meaningful. For several years her focus was the First World War, as she became very active in the war effort on the home front. One unique project was her hand-colouring a set of lantern slides depicting her trips in the Canadian Rockies and sending them overseas along with a descriptive commentary to entertain wounded soldiers in English hospitals. Entitled "In The Heart Of The Canadian Rockies," the presentation had its desired effect as she received word that "more than one poor lad from Alberta recognized something from home."

Beyond her volunteer involvement, Mary had a personal stake in the war when her favourite nephew, Eric Sharples, decided to enlist. Eric was the son of her brother Herman, a mechanical engineer for whom she found a position with the CPR in Calgary after he had experienced some problems working for a relative in the United States. Eric became the apple of his aunt's eye and spent much of his time in her company. She was able to find him a position in the Fleischman Yeast Company and helped provide him with the means to attend technical school at night. When he expressed a desire to join the army, Eric's parents asked Mary to send him to an expensive school in Pennsylvania instead. She could not bring herself to comply with their request, and when he fell on the Somme she experienced an overwhelming feeling of guilt and loss. Sid Unwin, her old friend of the trail who was also serving overseas, asked for three days' leave to search for Eric's body but was unsuccessful and it was never found. Tragically, Unwin died from wounds three months later, compounding her grief.

After all the other losses Mary had experienced, Eric's death was particularly hard to accept. He was in many ways the son she never had; "I do not think that he ever knew much difference between his mother and me," she later stated, lamenting that boys were often given to women who cared little for them while "those that could love a dozen are left starving for what could be a wealth to them." Partly in reaction, she tended to surround herself with younger people for the rest of her life. To a friend she admitted that "I do love the younger generation much better than the older one," and frequently held dinners and card parties in her home for some of the younger set in Banff. On their part, those she invited attended because of her charm, grace and warmhearted friendliness. Her home was equally allur-

Mary Schäffer Warren
at Tarry-a-while

ing with its beautiful collections and its exotic pet parrot.

As she progressed into her late middle years, Mary maintained an interest in the country she had travelled in earlier days, even though she could no longer visit it herself. In 1924 she became one of the initial supporters of the Trail Riders of the Canadian Rockies, a CPR sponsored organization formed to promote all aspects of trail riding in the mountains. The Trail Riders awarded various grades of buttons to members representing the amount of mileage covered on horseback during their career. At the first annual "Pow-Wow" of the club held in the Yoho Valley in July, 1924, someone mistakenly put down her mileage at 200, a faux pas that made her furious since, as she said, "I have at least 8000 to my credit." The error was quickly rectified and she joined a

select group presented with the 2500 mile and upward button.

Because she was a recognized authority on the wilderness areas of the Canadian Rockies, people often referred to her when they were planning trips of their own. She relished this role and would spend a great deal of time writing to tell people what to avoid and what to see. Often in her letters she became quite outspoken about the mountain exploits of others. Nothing bothered her more than those who sought glory and reputation for adventures similar to the ones she had undertaken solely for enjoyment and peace of mind. As she put it, "my own work was done just for the love of being in the open, not for the largest number of ascents, which seems a fungoid growth here ever since I came to the country." Equally irksome were a few critics who felt that she had claimed the discovery of Maligne Lake when it had obviously been visited previously by others. To them she responded: "We never made any claims that 'we were the first people there.' One need only have followed our footsteps and seen the trapper's old campfires, the fallen wikkiups and many other marks to learn that the lake had been well visited long before the Indians told us of its beauty."*

Mary continued to pursue her other interests as well, including painting, photography, writing and needlework. By no means a recluse, she seldom went out in public except to attend meetings of local organizations, such as the Mount Rundle I.O.D.E., of which she was an active member. Frequently she entertained in her own home both local friends and numerous visitors who called on her from Philadelphia and the eastern United States. In most instances she was glad of the company because her husband continued to be busy much of the time with business and other matters. The other matters included several lady friends whom Mary certainly knew about but never made an issue of, understanding the needs of her much younger husband on this score. As the years progressed, her attachment to Warren increased as did her dependence on him. He responded by treating her with the utmost respect and devotion, making sure that she had lots of company, a chauffeured car whenever she wished to go out, and, in later years, taking her on numerous trips to warmer climes.

During their winter trips the Warrens spared no expense in seeing to their comfort and enjoyment. Even with the onset of the Depression their lifestyle did not alter appreciably. An incident which occurred during a visit to California in 1935 illustrates both this and the fact that Mary's determination had not waned with the passing years. At Catalina they visited an aviary which housed a famous parrot named "Jimmie." Because of her penchant for parrots, and given that "Jimmie" was very talented and talkative, she decided she had to have him:

I asked if anything would buy him, but Charlie Chaplin had offered $5000 for him which the man gave me to understand would outbid anything I could offer. (My clothes were last year.) So I said whatever Charlie would go I would put on another thousand. I was not scared that

* Mary was accurate in her statement; in addition to its being visited by the Stoney Indians, Maligne Lake was reached by the CPR surveyor Henry McLeod in 1875 (he called it "Sorefoot Lake") and was frequented by the Moberlys and other half-breed hunters and trappers of the Athabasca Valley.

I might have to face several thousand for a bird, but I did think he thought me rather shabby. No sum would ever buy that bird.

In 1933 Mary was involved in a minor automobile accident in which she banged her head, an incident which began a slow deterioration of her health. Her neuritis also flared up again, made much worse by worry over the serious heart condition which her husband began to experience. The latter became so severe that Bennett prevailed on Warren to visit a special clinic in Portland in 1937. From that time onward he had to rest and to take a tank of oxygen daily. Meanwhile, Mary's mind, affected by her health and her age, tended to wander somewhat in her final years. Nevertheless she was able to keep up a large correspondence with both old and young friends, remaining young in her spirit and outlook. She died at Banff on January 23, 1939, and Warren followed her four years later. Together they are buried in the cemetery that she came to accept as "a place of rest, kindly neighbours and a harbinger of birds during summer," beneath the mountain peaks she loved.

In the decades since her death, Mary's memory has not faded in the minds of those who knew her either personally or through her work. In an age of growing engagement with the environment which has seen literally thousands travelling her old trails, she has become a source of wonder and inspiration. It is as though her old attraction to young people has maintained itself even after her death. Each year many young people visit the Archives of the Canadian Rockies to read her manuscripts and view her photographs. Invariably they come away impressed by the respect she showed for all things great and small, animate and inanimate that she found in the wilderness, and by her spirit and pluck in venturing into that wilderness to discover them.

In the nineteen-thirties Mary attempted to have Putnam's re-publish *Old Indian Trails*, out of print for many years yet still very much in demand. Unsuccessful, she often lamented that fact. Seeing the wish of this remarkable woman fulfilled some seventy years after her book's original publication we felt an excellent project for the celebration of Alberta's 75th Anniversary. I hope that readers of this work agree.

Old Indian Trails
Expedition of 1907

Mary T. S. Schäffer

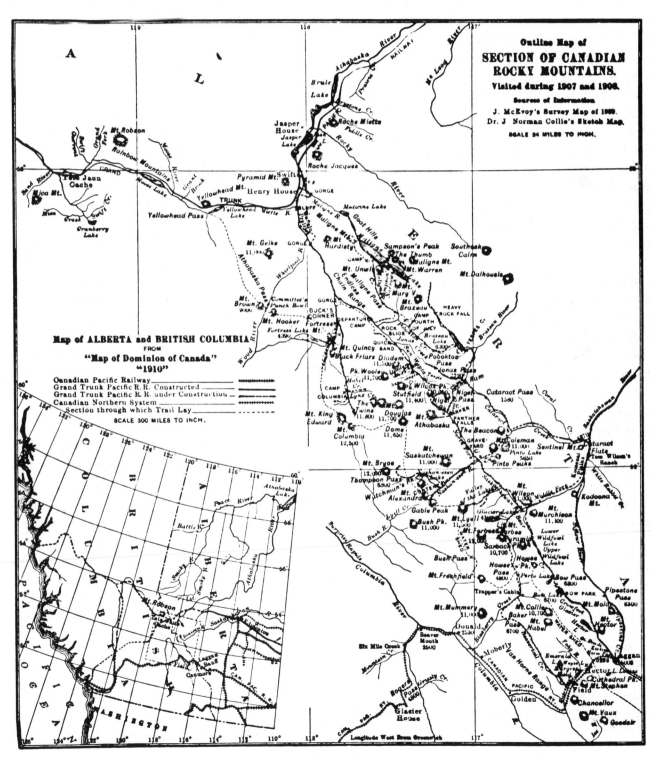

1: An Explanation

TWENTY years ago, ninety-nine per cent. of the tourists to the section of the Rockies of Canada mentioned in these pages, flitted across the country as bees across a flower-garden, and were gone.

There were comparatively few of them, and but a small modicum of enthusiasm distributed among them. Banff contained a hostlery which swallowed all who came and left few visible (so small was the number); Lake Louise boasted no hotel at all,—we slept in tents in '93, and from our door looked out upon that magnificent scene with chattering teeth and shivering bodies, and vowed never again to camp in the Canadian Rockies; Field, with her splendid drives and trails and Yoho Valley to-day, was an insignificant divisional point and eating station; Glacier, a tiny picturesque chalet cuddled close to the railroad track as though to shield her from the dark forests behind her, was full to the brim if so many as a dozen stopped off to view the one sight of those days,—the Great Glacier.* At that time no one dreamed of the fascinating caves† only seven miles away, hidden and unknown in an even more fascinating valley.

However, over an infinitesimally few those mountains had thrown a glamour and a spell so persistent and so strong, that with the first spring days, no matter where they be, warm breezes brought the call,—"Come back, come back to the blue hills of the Rockies!"

And we went; went year by year; watched the little chalets grow, watched the pushing of the trails into new points of interest, watched with veiled and envious eyes our secret haunts laid bare to all who came. And they did come, fast and furious! Steam heat and hot and cold water had done their work. The little tents on the shores of Lake Louise, with their balsam-bough beds and an atmosphere reeking with health and strength to those weary with the city's life, were

banished, and only found again by the determined few who had heard of the recently discovered Moraine Lake, Lakes O'Hara and McArthur, and Ptarmigan and Yoho Valleys. Point by point we fled to them all, each one of them a stronghold at civilisation's limits, each one of them a kindergarten of the at-first-despised camping life. In them we learned the secret of comfort, content, and peace on very little of the world's material goods, learned to value at its true worth the great un-lonely silence of the wilderness, and to revel in the emancipation from frills, furbelows, and small follies.

But the tide swept on. With jealous eyes we watched the silence slipping back, the tin cans and empty fruit-jars strew our sacred soil, the mark of the axe grow more obtrusive, even the trails cleared of the *débris* so hard to master, yet so precious from the fact it must be mastered to succeed.

Where next? Driven from our Eden, where should our tents rise again? We were growing lost and lonesome in the great tide which was sweeping across our playground, and we longed for wider views and new untrammelled ways. With willing ears we listened to the tales brought in by the hunters and trappers, those men of this land who are the true pioneers of the country in spite of the fact that they have written nothing and are but little known. With hearts not entirely on pelts, they had seen and now told us of valleys of great beauty, of high unknown peaks, of little-known rivers, of un-named lakes, lying to the north and north-west of the country we knew so well,—a fairyland, yet a land girt about with hardships, a land whose highway was a difficult trail or no trail at all. We fretted for the strength of man, for the way was long and hard, and only the tried and stalwart might venture where cold and heat, starvation and privation stalked ever at the explorer's heels. In meek despair we bowed our heads to the inevitable, to the cutting knowledge of the

* Illecillewaet Glacier
† Nakimu Caves

superiority of the endurance of man and the years slipped by.

From the States came Allen and Wilcox, (men of course), gathered their outfits together and left us sitting on the railroad track following them with hungry eyes as they plunged into the distant hills; to listen just as hungrily to the camp-fire tales on their return, of all the wonders of the more northern Rockies; came Stuttfield, Collie, Woolley, Outram (names so well known in the alpine world to-day), to tell again to our eager-listening ears of the vast, glorious, unexplored country beyond; came Fay, Thompson, and Coleman, —all men!

There are few women who do not know their privileges and how to use them, yet there are times when the horizon seems restricted, and we seemed to have reached that horizon, and the limit of all endurance,— to sit with folded hands and listen calmly to the stories of the hills we so longed to see, the hills which had lured and beckoned us for years before this long list of men had ever set foot in the country. Our cups splashed over. Then we looked into each other's eyes and said: "Why not? We can starve as well as they; the muskeg will be no softer for us than for them; the ground will be no harder to sleep upon; the waters no deeper to swim, nor the bath colder if we fall in,"—so—we planned a trip.

But instead of railing at our predecessors, we were to learn we had much for which to thank them. Reading the scanty literature which dealt with their various expeditions, we had absorbed one huge fundamental fact almost unconsciously, viz.,—that though this was a land of game,—of goat, sheep, bear, deer and caribou, one might pass through the country for days yet see no signs of wild life. Fish there are in plenty, yet for weeks, when the summer sun melts every thing meltable, and the rivers are clouded with silt from the glaciers, they will not rise to the most tempting bait, and the grouse disappear as though by magic.

Throughout the limited literature ran this simple ever-present fact,—a beautiful, but

inhospitable land, and the cause of many an unfinished or abandoned expedition, and a hasty retreat to the land of bread-and-butter.

Thanking our informants for their unconscious hint, we laid our plans both long and deep. Our initial experience of one night's camp on the shores of Lake Louise, when we had felt frozen to the bone, and had at the time promised ourselves never to do such a trick again, had been augmented by a flight of three days to Yoho Valley when it was n't Yoho Valley, only a lovely unknown bit of country, another chilly experience at Moraine Lake, a pause, then a week in the Ptarmigan Valley, and later a sortie of five weeks in the Saskatchewan country. In these trips we had gathered a few solid facts; surely with them we were more or less prepared for a whole summer in the country of which so little was known.

In spite of the protests of anxious relatives and friends, our plans were laid for a four-months' trip during the summer of 1907, and a vow made not to return till driven back by the snows.

The guide-in-chief[*] was our most important factor. To whom should we more naturally turn than to him who had watched over us in the days of our camp swaddling-clothes, who had calculated the amount of our first camp-fare, given us our first lessons in camp comforts, and in fact our very first lessons in sitting astride a horse and learning to jump a log without being shot over the head of our steed?

Three years' acquaintance had taught us his value, and as he did not turn us down, but kindly spurred us on in our undertaking, and cheerfully assumed the leadership, he made us feel we had worn a considerable amount of the tenderfoot from our compositions. Having always kept a strict account of the amount of food he had packed over the trails for us on our shorter expeditions, it became a mere matter of arithmetic for a longer one. If so many pounds of bacon lasted us seven weeks, how many pounds of bacon would last sixteen weeks?—and so through the entire gamut of

* William "Billy" Warren

—17—

the food supply,—flour, baking-powder, cocoa, coffee, tea, sugar, dried fruits, evaporated potatoes, beans, rice, etc., with a week's extra rations thrown in for emergency.

On him fell the entire responsibility of choosing and buying the best outfit of horses, saddlery, blankets, the hundred and one things needed and so apt to be forgotten, for in this land to which we were going there were no shops, only nice little opportunities for breaking and losing our few precious possessions.

It was his care also to choose the second guide to accompany us, not so easy a matter as it looks. This fourth member of our party must know how to cook a bannock that would not send one to bad dreams after a hard day's travel, to fry a piece of bacon exactly right, to boil the rice, and make bean soup, all at the camp-fire; it sounds simple, but try it. He must be equally skilful in adjusting the packs that there be no sore backs, he must have a fund of patience such as Job was never forced to call upon, and a stock of good nature that would stand any strain. The man, the horses, and the food, our Chief found them all, and here to him I give the credit of our success, claiming only for ourselves the cleverness of knowing a good thing when we saw it.

It *is* an "inhospitable land"; they who first tore the secrets from those hills have recorded it so; by their experiences we profited; the wise head at the helm steadied the ship and all was well.

And so in the east, the early spring days went by at a snail's pace, with a constant discussion as to the best air-bed, the proper tents and their size, the most enduring shoe, etc., with trials and tests of condensed foods, ending mostly in trials.

There are a few of these foods which are well worth having, and there are some of them, which we were profoundly thankful we had tried before carting across the continent. For instance, beware of the dried cabbage; no fresh air in existence will ever blow off sufficient of the odour to let it get safely to the mouth.

"Granulose" was a strongly recommended article to save carrying so much of that heavy and perishable, yet almost necessary, substance, sugar. The label on the neat small bottles read: "One half oz. granulose equal to one ton of sugar, price $1.00." Who would dream of passing such a bargain? Too good to be true, yet we did believe and were soon the proud possessors of "one ton" of condensed sweetness, as also of a stock of dried milk and dried eggs. Truth compels me to state that each of the three has its limitations, and to this day I wonder if that dried milk had ever seen a cow, or if any hen would acknowledge the motherhood of those dried eggs. To the inventor or discoverer of "granulose" I should like to whisper that I thought he had got slightly mixed in his arithmetic; if he had said his dollar's worth of "granulose" was only equal to thirty pounds of sugar he would have been nearer correct and we would not have had to eat so many puddings and cakes without sweetening.

The section of country which had so long been our dream, lies in the Canadian Rocky Mountain Range, directly north of that portion which is penetrated by the Canadian Pacific Railway. It is bounded by latitudes 51°, 30′, and 52° 30′; and longitudes 116° to 118°. Our chief aim was to penetrate to the head waters of the Saskatchewan and Athabaska rivers. To be quite truthful, it was but an aim, an excuse, for our real object was to delve into the heart of an untouched land, to tread where no human foot had trod before, to turn the unthumbed pages of an unread book, and to learn daily those secrets which dear Mother Nature is so willing to tell to those who seek. So the "Saskatchewan and Athabaska sources" were a little pat answer which we kept on hand for the invariable question, "Goodness! what ever takes you two women into that wild, unknown region?" It seemed strange at first to think we must announce some settled destination, that the very fact of its being a wilderness was not enough; but we could not be blind to the fact that nine-tenths of our loving relatives and friends thought us crazy, and the other tenth listened patiently as I ruminated aloud: "There is no voice, however famed, that can attune itself to the lonely corners of the heart, as the sigh of the wind through the pines when tired eyes are closing after a day on the trail. There is no chorus sweeter than the little birds in the early northern dawn; and what picture can stir every artistic nerve more than to gaze from some deep green valley to stony crags far above, and see a band of mountain-sheep, in rigid statuesque pose, watching every move of the unknown enemy below? Why must so many cling to the life of our great cities, declaring there only may the heart-hunger, the artistic longings, the love of the beautiful be satisfied, and thus train themselves to believe there is nothing beyond the little horizon they have built for themselves? Why must they settle so absolutely upon the fact, that the lover of the hills and the wilderness drops the dainty ways and habits with the conventional garments and becomes something of coarser mould? Can the free air sully, can the birds teach us words we should not hear, can it be possible to see in such a summer's outing, one sight as painful as the daily ones of poverty, degradation, and depravity of a great city?"

I was so strongly impressed with this very idea one day, as it came unwittingly from a dear friend who had no idea she was "letting the cat out of the bag," that I cannot resist speaking of it. She had taken the keenest interest in all our wanderings, had listened by the hour (yes, quite true) if we would but get upon our hobby, and showed a sincere pride in introducing us as her friends "the explorers" (the true explorer had better skip this part); broad-minded and sympathetic, even her thoughts were more or less tinged with the conventional colouring. Here is her introduction: "My friend, the little explorer, who lives among the Rocky Mountains and the Indians for months at a time, far, far in the wilderness. You would not expect it, would you? She does not look like it, does she? She ought to look some other way, should she not?" And then her listeners all bowed and smiled, and noted the cut of my garments, and said it really was wonderful. And I could have said: "Not half so wonderful as that you do not know the joys of moccasins after ordinary shoes, that there is a place where hat-pins are not the mode, and the lingerie waist a dream; that there are vast stretches where the air is so pure, body and soul are purified by it, the sights so restful that the weariest heart finds repose." Is it possible in such environments, for the character to coarsen, and the little womanlinesses to be laid aside? No, believe me, there are some secrets you will never learn, there are some joys you will never feel, there are heart thrills you can never experience, till, with your horse you leave the world, your recognised world, and plunge into the vast unknown. And all the thanks you will give us will be: "Why did you not tell us to go before? why have you been so tame with your descriptions? We never guessed what we should find." Alas! it takes what I have not, a skilled pen. Perhaps the subject is too great, and the picture too vast for one small steel pen and one human brain to depict,—at least it is a satisfaction to think the fault is not my own.

2: Trouble at the Start — Bow Valley

AND now with all necessary things gathered together, with trunks packed, not with frills and furbelows, but with blankets and "glucose," air-beds and evaporated milk, with "Abercrombie" shoes and dried spinach, we were off across the continent by the first of June, 1907. At Winnipeg we picked up some highly recommended tents, made of "Egyptian sail-cloth," exceedingly light weight and small bulk, though later we found they had their faults,—"but that is another story." Our trunks had been checked at Montreal to the little station of Laggan* on the Canadian Pacific Railway—our point of departure into the mountains, and in calm faith we dropped down the hill to Field, to get our breath and bearings, and wait for the bad weather to clear. This seemed likely to occur at any moment; for a fiercer winter than that of 1906 and '07 had not been known in the memory of the "oldest inhabitant"; the spring had been equally bad, and our reception was enough to cool even greater ardour than ours. We decided on June 20th as the latest day for the start; if the snows were not off the Bow Pass by that time, they should be, and even though it was so cold and chill, it was time by the calendar for the Saskatchewan to rise and on this point we meant to take no chances. Our entire outfit of horses and saddlery were for the time being in Banff, so we hied ourselves hither, primarily to investigate the "grub-pile,"[1] but in reality to behold the gathering of the new family. Why try to sketch our opinion? There were but two members on exhibition, one was "Buck," the sight of whom was enough to kill the most deep-seated case of horse-pride. Long and gaunt, with a hide of yellow tan, a mane and tail of black, dragged in from his free open life on the plains where he had never known a care, shod under the bitterest protest, he was a depressing-looking beast to us who had no idea where to look for the best points of a trail-horse. If we had

been guilty of speaking in an off-hand, non-chalant way of "our" horses we stopped right there, and engaged our minds with bacon and beans. The future, however, proved the homely and unpopular "Buck" to have been made of sterling stuff; strong and willing, he had but one fault, a pair of violently active heels. No one ever received greater respect behind his back than "Buck," and it soon became second nature to make a wide detour when passing him. His companions were not always as cautious as we, and I have never seen him forget a slight, or fail to punish it, not once but many times, by a resounding, sickening thud in the ribs of the offender when off his guard.

From now on I shall keep before me the worn, thumbed, much-jeered-at diary; its lead-pencil-smudged pages (in many places nearly obliterated) are dear to the eyes of its owner, and it is at least a record of the heart-beats day by day, with all the lights and shadows of the hills and valleys underlying the grimy, once white leaves. Alas! that my pigments are so crude and my brushes coarse, the scenes are so fair and the artist so unequal to her task!

As I have said previously, our plans were to leave civilisation on June 20th. Our troubles, however, began on the eighteenth, at the awful discovery that our most valuable trunk, containing bedding, clothing, and photographic material for the expedition, was not at Laggan, to which point it had been shipped the week before. It is here that I start the record.

June 20th. — The day has come but not as we had planned. Two days ago it was discovered that a precious trunk was lost, and the agent comfortingly told us: "It must be somewhere between Montreal and Vancouver, if it has not been shunted off to Seattle." This gave us at least a wide field for imagination, and a fit of the horrors at the same time, as we saw a long-planned trip dissolving into nothingness for the want of a few necessary

---

* Lake Louise station
[1] Local term for all food-stuffs.

Crowfoot Glacier

articles, while we could but gaze upon and admire the stony indifference of the four or five agents, to whom we had confided our troubles in all their harrowing details, yet remained so sublimely impassive. With determination born of despair, we hastened to Calgary and repurchased the few articles possible, though valuable photographic plates and a precious air-mattress were not to be replaced for love or money.

Incidentally we poured our woes into the ears of the baggage-master-in-chief at Calgary, not because we really expected sympathy, but more as a safety-valve to our pent-up despair. His actions astonished us quite as much as those of his subordinates.

In ten minutes reports were overhauled, and messages flying over the wires in every direction; the trunk had passed through Calgary and the baggage-master was confident it lay between there and its intended destination. In two hours that executive and energetic gentleman was aboard the west-bound train with us, and rigorously inspecting the baggage department of every little wayside station along the line to Laggan. At last our poor little tragedy had touched a railroad heart, and even were that trunk never found, we would have with our new and ill-assorted garments a comforting sense of sympathy from one human soul. Our new-found friend's kindness and energy were

Mary on the trail

rewarded. The trunk was calmly reposing at the Lake Louise chalet, where proprietor, baggageman, teamster, and station-agent had all vowed it was not, and at least there was one cause for thankfulness, that none of the searchers had fallen over it and broken a bone, as it was found in a most dangerously conspicuous place. At sight of it, all sorrow fled, and we could have hugged that dirty, travel-worn object with joy, whose every scar was by this time a point of beauty.

As for that baggage-master, he will live in our hearts as long as the memory of the trip remains. It is not time but circumstances which make us our friends; this total stranger had stood by us in our hour of need; through him the missing valuables had come to light, and were shortly distributed upon the backs of

the horses. The duffel-bags fell into line, sugar and bacon joined hands, and with a wave of good-bye and a cheery *au revoir* from our new friend, we set our faces to the north and the fire-swept hills of the Bow Valley. A brand new Waterbury watch said it was high noon. The low clouds, laden with sleet and snow, intimated that it was a ready far in the day, but there was emphatic reason for choosing a camp-ground far from the railroad track where the constant shifting of engines was liable to bring an untimely end to some of our family.

It seemed, as we wound slowly through the sparsely standing, burnt timber, that we had not left all calamity behind, but that it stalked beside us, hurling defiance in our faces with each gust of wind that swept angrily by, and reminded us of its power as the gaunt black trees crashed down about us. The new horses, accustomed to the open prairies, and nervous with the great packs they had never known before, erratically tore here and there in their endeavour to avoid the falling trees, and many times came very near to being struck. The fearful storms of the winter of 1906 and '07 had strewn the trail with timber, so that between jumping logs, chopping those we could not jump, and ploughing through the most disheartening muskeg, we at last, at nightfall, threw off the packs on a knoll with muskeg everywhere. Our first camp-fire was built in mud, we ate in mud, slept in mud, and our horses stalked around in mud, nibbling the few spears of grass which the late cold spring had permitted to sprout. The new air-mattresses came well into play, for we felt a comforting certainty that if we broke through the muskeg we would at least float. It did seem a rather dreary breaking-in for a whole summer's camping trip and, if it was to continue, somewhat of a trial to both spirit and flesh, but tired as we were, we crawled into our sleeping-bags saying, "It might have been worse!"

The next day was Friday. A superstitious person would have revelled in our woes. Clouds were hanging ominously low, a sickly sun tried hard to shine, gave it up in despair, and sank into oblivion. Beds were rolled up and tents folded, while hail struck contemptuously at us. Only too thankful to leave that marsh behind us, we rushed into worse troubles. Not a hundred yards from camp we plunged into the worst muskeg we had so far encountered. Our horses, as yet untrained, recognised no leader, and went down one by one; heavily laden, they were helpless in that fearful quagmire. Buck, who was loaded with about two hundred pounds of bacon and flour, was soon under water, pack and all, and was only saved from a watery grave by a quick application of a knife to the ropes, when down went the cargo and up came Buck. Both were quickly landed on more substantial soil, and the bacon had had its first bath, but never its last. I have been asked frequently the definition of "muskeg." The most lucid one I could think of would be, "get in a bad one, and you will see that there are no words adequate to its description." It is not a quicksand, it is not a marsh. In many instances, it looks like a lovely mountain stream flowing between banks rank with a rich growth of waving grasses; again, it is a damp-looking spot, but still overgrown with the same attractive, waving green. If not yet thoroughly acquainted with the signs, just watch your horse, he will begin to snuff the ground beneath him, and if there is any way around, it is well not to force him through that which his own judgment tells him to avoid.

The 21st was devoted to a distance of about seven miles, but it was seven miles of such going as one encounters only when spring unlocks the floods, and from that time on there was a most perceptible inclination on the part of the horses to watch and follow the leader, avoiding the side trips which led them to holes and consequent destruction.

Bow Park was our stopping-place for the night, a fine camp-ground for man and beast after the trials of the two previous days. For a number of years it has been a favourite resting-place for hunters and the few travellers who have been in that vicinity, and consequently porcupines are numerous. Poor little fellows! With not a hard thought in their hearts for a soul, gentle and almost tame, they are the bane of the camper's existence. Like other animals I could mention, they are fond of good living, but unlike some people, if good things are not to be had, they will fill up with what is on hand. The consequence is that bacon and saddlery, shoes and ropes, soap and tent-skirts are all grist for their insatiable little mills. Our sleep at Bow Park was broken by ominous rustlings of stiff quills dragging on the ground, gentle squeaks, then a sortie, a dull thud, and the listeners knew one more poor creature had come to his death because of an ungovernable appetite. Then we would turn over with the virtuous thought that we had made pillows of our shoes, that the cameras were under the bed, and other valuables hung from the ridge-pole, so that dozens of the enemy could do us no serious harm. My heart felt a little sad the next morning, there were so many inanimate bodies lying about who would never chew straps any more, and even a great corner out of a slab of valuable bacon failed to leave me with a hard thought for our amiable, neighbourly little enemy, the porcupine.

The day was Sunday; for the first time during the trip the sun rose warm and bright over the great crags hanging above us. Up and off beside the sparkling Bow River the foot-way improved, but the sun grew hotter and hotter, and we knew it meant but one thing—the snow-fields so long locked by the tardy winter would be pouring their torrents into the large river (the Saskatchewan) we must soon cross.

Having visited Hector Lake the year before, and knowing that its marshy shores would be well-nigh impassable at this time of year, we left it to its watery fastness, passed on, and with the brilliant sunshine bathing everything about us, came upon the Crow-foot Glacier, still gowned in her winter robes. Of peculiar formation, no one can ever fail to recognise her, her name fitting her perfectly.

Slipping from the horse for a photograph, then back again, the outfit was once more struggling through the high soft meadows, and in a half-hour emerged on the shores of Bow Lake. At its lower end the slush ice still floated, and the horses showed but small desire to step into the chilled waters. The bank, however, was an impossibility owing to muskeg, while the water's edge offered a hard, pebbly footing, and in spite of the cold, we skirted the lake for half a mile, when, turning sharply at right angles, we headed direct for Bow Pass.

Never have I seen the lake look more beautiful than on that fair morning in June. It was as blue as the sky could make it, the ice reflected the most vivid emerald green; in the distance a fine glacier swept to the lake - shore, whose every crevasse was a

Black-headed fleabane (*Erigeron melanocephalus*)

brilliant blue line; the bleak grey mountains towered above, at our feet the bright spring flowers bloomed in the green grass, and over all hung the deep blue sky. Around us hovered the peace which only the beauty and silence of the hills could portray.

From the summit of the Bow Pass (6800 feet high) we gazed to the north on as fair a picture as dreams could suggest. Winter was reluctantly loosening its hard grasp upon those open meadow-like slopes; the snow lilies (*Erythronium grandiflorum*), the pale pink spring beauties (*Claytonia lanceolata*), and the bright yellow violets (*Viola sempervirens*, were flirting with the butterflies and bees, pretending to be utterly oblivious to the mountains of snow all about them. We thought, as we wended our way over the crest of the pass, of lovely Peyto Lake which lay but a few hundred yards to our left, but with new fields to conquer, there was no time for a glimpse of the older friend.

Camping on the far side of the pass in a stretch of burnt timber, we shook ourselves into camp routine. Not so with our horses, they were to be cajoled with no such thought that their keepers had chosen the best there was in that section of the country for them; and if there is one thing a trail horse possesses, it is a clear recollection of the place he stopped in "last night." While our thoughts were on our supper, so were theirs, and they were "hiking" on the back trail, making for the luscious grasses of Bow Lake before any one had realised it. The consequences were that "M."* and I were left alone to kill time and get supper while the men "lit out" in search of the delinquents.

It was this evening that we had our first glimpse of mountain-goat. While waiting for the coffee-pot to boil, one of us picked up a very strong pair of binoculars, and stood gazing into the pocket which we knew held Peyto Lake, wondering what life there was in the hollow of those hills. The westering sun was drawing long purple shadows in sweeping lines into the valleys, a tiny chirp from the almost silent birds of the north, and we felt the coming slumber of night in the atmosphere. Suddenly a moving white spot far on the mountain opposite, then a second, then a third, caused the eye to steady and the hand to grow rigid. "A bunch of goat!" she gasped, and oh! what beauties they were! Strolling out on the impassable grass-grown cliffs after the heat of the day, with no fear in their movements, they were taking their own bacon and beans before the sun set in that sea of mountains. The coffee was forgotten, the bannock[1] burned, and by the time the men and the truants had returned we were still able to point out "our" goat through the evening haze, with far more pride than if we had shot them.

The trail down Bear Creek[†] is one of beauty from its very inception. We were up and off with the sunrise the next morning; it grew hotter and hotter, and in our minds we were watching the steady rise of the Saskatchewan River, still a day's journey off. There could be little hurry with such heavily loaded horses, so we camped that night at the lower end of the second Wild Fowl Lake.* Lying as it does under the shadow of Pyramid Peak,[†] the view was superb, while the music from the falling avalanches left no words for our thoughts. Just as the purple shadows fell, a silvery crescent stole into the deepening sky, and by its soft light we could still catch the outline of the avalanches as they fell with reverberating roar down the precipices opposite our tents. The camp-fire crackled, on the soft breeze came the distant tinkle of the horse-bells, a mosquito hummed, a night-hawk with his raucous cry swept past, the moon's rays filtered through the spruce boughs, the fire died down and the camp slept. And they ask if one grows lonely. Lonely? How can one, when all Nature sings the evening hymn?

A third day now added its heat to the other two, and the chief topic of conversation was the rising waters of the Saskatchewan. About noon we met a bunch of horses, fully sixty head, coming in from the Kootenai Plains where they had wintered. Tying up our own horses, we watched the procession headed by Tom Wilson, their owner, pass by. Then came the flower of the band, "Nibs," who was to leave his chums and follow the vicissitudes of his mistress for the next four months. Just an Indian-bred pony, with a coat that only one who loved him could say was beautiful, he proved himself a perfect trail-horse. The saddle was soon transferred from the reliable old Pinto, and Nibs was presented to his new rider.

From that day on introductions to all the horses followed fast and furious, and we found unique traits constantly cropping up among them. Living with them, trailing with them, watching over their interests, they soon ceased to be beasts of burden

* Mary "Mollie" Adams
[1] A bread made on the trail with flour, baking-powder, a little bacon-fat, and water.
† Mistaya River

* Upper Waterfowl Lake
† Mount Chephren

alone, and became our friends with characteristics almost as marked as though they were human. Some of them formerly timid from ill-usage, gradually forgot their faults in the daily kindness which was theirs at the hands of their new masters, and I shall never believe again that a horse lives with traits so bad, that he cannot be broken of them to a large extent by kindness. Certain it was that there were those in our band who at first were enough to try the patience of a saint, and in the end became perfect masters of their art.

Having caught Nibs, we waved a last "good-bye" to Tom who now started ahead with his huge band, he for Laggan and the tourists, we for the unknown north. Singing out, "Sorry for you going through the Bow muskegs with all those horses!"—he called back, "Sorry for you crossing the Saskatchewan!" and our hearts went flop as we realised the time for that crossing was almost with us. For Tom, who had both wintered and summered on the Saskatchewan several years, knew the power and the danger of those rapidly rising waters and we knew that he knew. By 3.30 in the afternoon we had crossed Bear Creek at its mouth. The water was boiling and plunging over the huge boulders and warned us that there was no time to lose. All got over that small stream safely which is not always the case, as the great force of the water is apt to cause a horse to stumble in so rough a river bed. One mile to the west of the entrance of Bear Creek into the Saskatchewan, there is one of the best fords on that river if you are bound for the north. On the ocean-like beach we took our stand, while "K.*," mounting the only horse of the bunch which we knew could take care of himself in the great river (Nibs of course), struck into the stream. The little fellow showed not the slightest hesitation as he took to the water but seemed rather proud than otherwise of showing off his ability to his new acquaintances.

Those were anxious moments as we saw "K." cross branch after branch of the great river. He slowly waded in, the water would creep higher and higher about the plucky pony's shoulders till horse and rider almost disappeared from view; they would then back out and try it farther up or down, then emerge to a bar and work over the next channel in the same way. At last after fifteen minutes, we saw him a distant speck in the brilliant setting sun on the north shore. He waved his hand, and we knew that our yet untried horses could be got over without much danger of being washed down-stream.

Yes, we got over without having to swim, but one never wants to take those large rivers which are fed by the great ice fields, other than seriously; the power of the water is that of the avalanche from the mountain-side, and it sweeps along throbbingly, intermittently, cruelly, and relentlessly. The horse, his head facing up stream a little to avoid the full blow of the onrushing waters, bends his whole body to the force; the rider, to help him in the balance, leans in an opposite direction; and as the water rises higher and higher, the feet have an inclination to fly up and the body to float out of the saddle. The temperature of all the rivers in that section of the country is about 42°, and as the water creeps to the waist-line one longs for the courage to turn back. As the deepest point is reached, all sensation of movement and advance ceases, every thought but that of self-preservation has gone bobbing down with the river which is flashing by, and it is then that you think of your guide's words of caution: "If your horse rolls over, get out of your saddle, cling to his mane, tail, or anything you can get hold of, but *don't let go of him altogether! He* may get out, you *never* will, alone." These are of course first sensations. Eventually when one has learned to trust his horse, becomes accustomed to knowing what to do, realises that caution and judgment mean safety, much of the danger is cancelled, but I should never advise a belittling of the possibilities for accidents in these mountain streams. It is the very contempt for danger which has caused so many of the accidents which are recorded.

* Sid Unwin

3: Trailing the North Fork

ON the night of June 25th, we camped at the junction of the North Fork and the main river under the shadow of that magnificent mass of crags, Mount Wilson. On a high point overlooking both streams our little white tents nestled among the spruces. Near at hand were old tepee-poles, bespeaking the sometime presence of the Indian hunter; across the river rose Mount Murchison, beyond her in the south could be seen our old friend Pyramid, to the south-west the Freshfield group; we were in a paradise of great hills. Just as darkness fell Chief returned from an inspection of the horses, with the information that the river had risen considerably, and that we could not return without swimming if we wished, and, though we would not if we could, there was just that much of contrariness in us, that we felt a qualm of loneliness as we realised that the door was closed for many a day to come. But there is always medicine for every woe, if only one knows where to look for it; this time it was a wave of mosquitoes which swept down upon us in the dusk. With all our forethought and caution we had forgotten the netting so necessary for that country! All thoughts of home and friends and other troubles were wiped out in the vain hope of inventing some way to rid ourselves of the small pests. Nothing seemed of any avail, and eventually, like hanging, we got used to them,—more or less.

The next few days we were to learn the art of self-control. We may have thought we already possessed it, but there is little in civilised life to prepare the nervous system for the shocks to be endured (with the best equanimity that can be mustered), on the trail behind untrained horses.

Though we had travelled the North Fork[*] before, it was not with an outfit of "green" horses. The river was turbid, angry and sullen. Swollen to the tops of the banks along the ragged edge of which the trail for miles seemed

to enjoy running, we stared momentarily into a watery grave, till weary of surmising on such wet troubles we gave it up and turned our thoughts to the crags of Mount Wilson around whose base we travelled for hours. Expatiating one day to a friend on the beauty of this mountain, he remarked: "I don't like Mount Wilson, I once travelled around its base for two days and it seemed as though I should never get away from it." Quite true, the proportions seemed almost limitless; and in its fastnesses the mountain-goat and sheep are able to elude the Indian hunter who is so merciless in his extermination.

So, though the way around Mount Wilson be long, it was yet interesting, for, when not too busy jumping logs or floundering through muskeg, we could gaze aloft thousands of feet and watch the game feeding on the brinks of precipices that even a Swiss guide would treat with respect.

Leaving the highways of Mount Wilson the trail descends, as I have said before, to the edge of the river where trouble in plenty was in store. Fox, a big, harmless-looking sorrel, with his full quota of two hundred pounds, in lumbering along with his fellow workers, by some unsurprising mistake, fell into the flood. From studying high jumps and deep holes before us, we turned around on hearing a sharp yell, our reveries rudely shattered by the picture of Fox. His face was the soul of serenity as he bobbed cheerfully about in the muddy flow with our two duffel-bags acting like a pair of life-preservers. As a drowning man is said to recall in a flash all his joys and sins, so through our minds ran an itemised list of the contents of those precious duffel-bags: clothing, glass plates, films, lenses, barometer, thermometer, compass, etc., and we one hundred miles from a telegraph pole! And then to behold that countenance of content! The water was cold and Fox was warm; his burdens had lightened the moment he struck the water which buoyed him, the bags, the hypo, and a bunch of dry blankets (dry

* North Fork of the North Saskatchewan

—27—

no longer) nicely. Sticks, stones, and yells finally brought him to shore but not to his senses, for the trail continued by the river, and the idea which had soaked into Fox's head by that tumble remained there, and whether the eyes of his masters were on him or not, he continued throughout the day to jump in at every available point. At first we mentally jumped too, but the day was warm, the process tiring, Fox firm in his determination, and, as we could not stop to examine our troubles, we cast all cares aside and rode ahead through brush and mire, emerging upon "Graveyard Camp" at five o'clock that afternoon. This welcome if gruesomely named camp lies at the junction of Nashan River (known on Stuttfield's and Collie's map as "West-Branch-of-the-North-Fork-of-the-Saskatchewan")* and the main North Fork, the name having suggested itself to us from the quantities of bear, sheep, goat and porcupine bones which strewed the ground.

From experience we had grown to naming our various camps, the easier to recall a location. With qualms and quivers we soon dug into the duffel-bags to find for once an advertisement which held good,—the duffel-bags had proven impervious to water after Fox's eminently thorough test, and our spirits flew up even though the rain, which soon settled in a steady downpour, soaked every article not previously tucked under cover. The music of its dripping on the tent walls at bed-time acted as a soporific, and we dropped calmly asleep with duffel-bags, barometers, rivers and stubborn horses blending in our dreams into one harmonious whole.

Rain seems to be a permanent institution at "Graveyard Camp." We had visited it first in 1906 when we made the discovery that horses could be taken over the pass east of that point to Pinto Lake, which is a beautiful sheet of water on Cataract Creek just east of Mount Coleman. It rained that trip. We have stopped there many times since and always in rain. This pass which may be called Pinto Pass†is not at all a difficult one on its western

* Alexandra River
† Sunset Pass

slope; on the east, however, are sheer cliffs of at least 1000 feet which looked at the time of our visit to cut off all possibilities of reaching the lake; but by keeping high on the shoulder of Mount Coleman we found an old game trail down which man and horse slid with what agility they could. The lake itself is famous among the Indians as a fishing ground—and no wonder. The outlet is deep and clear as crystal, and at the time of our visit in September, 1906, hundreds of speckled trout could be seen lazily swimming about or lying in the bottoms of the pools, all averaging fourteen inches in length. So heavy was our catch, that even our bacon-palled appetites refused to devour all we got, and we smoked them as did the Indians, in a dense smudge of sphagnum moss. To me the only way to eat the trout of those cold waters is to prepare them in this manner, as the meat is inclined to be soft and tasteless, even to palates grown uncritical on salt meats and bannock.

But we must go back to "Graveyard." With the cessation of rain, on June the 30th, the camp stirred early. It was Sunday; but only in our diaries. Out there in the hills all beautiful days are Sundays. There is a peace, a contentment, even a singing of the birds which is like no other day at home. Just as we left "Graveyard Camp," we passed the mouth of the enterprising little river Nashan which joins the main stream from the west, and decided to investigate it later. The previous cloudy days had reduced the volume of water in North Fork to such an extent that navigation of the river-bed was a much easier matter than the previous days, with the exception of miles of shingle-flats or coarse gravel, which make hard travel for horses. Every horse moved along in good order excepting Buck, who fairly sought trouble. Like many a human being he was entirely too inclined to "know it all" in those school-days of his, consequently he plunged in where wiser feet feared to tread. To cross a torrent he persisted in taking the narrowest part instead of following the leader, with the consequence that several times he and his bacon were

—28—

Mount Saskatchewan from the North Fork

submerged, which made him very cross and was certainly of no benefit to the bacon.

Camp-sites for the next twenty miles are comparatively scarce, for a site in this instance means horse-feed.

Scenery to the Wilcox Pass becomes finer as the mileage increases; the trail rises rapidly to higher levels, and glimpses from among the spruces show Mounts Saskatchewan, Athabaska, Wilson, Pyramid, and hundreds of minor peaks which no one so far has had time to name, much less to climb.

As the trail winds high among the notches of the hills, there comes to the ear a distant roar. As the trees part and the eye travels across the valley, a lovely little fall may be seen apparently bursting through the solid rock. Collie and Wilcox both mention this fall of the Saskatchewan, but give it no name.

As we later found a panther (or wild-cat)

had followed in our footsteps for a considerable distance along this special bit of trail, we named them the Panther Falls.

Camping at seven thousand feet, just south of the pass, we found an inexhaustible feast for the horses, who, after ten days' hard work, should have enjoyed their blessings.

Not so, however, for next morning in spite of hobbles, they were found four miles on the home-stretch. I am sorry to say my own intimate companion, Nibs, was the aggressor and instigator of the mischief, and on the band being brought back to camp, he was caught three times trying to sneak off again. As a final punishment the hobbles were clapped on his hind legs, and the poor little naughty buckskin, taking a few futile hops, gazed reproachfully at us and refused to move or eat for the rest of the day. It was a painful occasion all round but Nibs never forgot that lesson.

The morning of "Fourth of July" pounced down upon our high camp and our patriotic souls with a shriek of wind which pelted the tent walls with snow. It chilled the bacon and boiled beans till they were veritable lumps of candle-grease but failed to postpone a preliminary inspection of the pass with the geological hammer and the cameras. Alas for any photographs of the summit! The clouds swept down upon Mount Athabaska, the snow whipped and cut across our faces, and our fingers ached in the icy blast. Even Wilcox Peak at our very elbow disappeared. Not a ptarmigan was in sight, and the ordinarily plentiful mountain-sheep had certainly been more sensible than we—known enough to get in from the cold. A few small birds chirped sadly, and the frightened little rock rabbits, whistling notes of warning, whisked their tiny tails and scuttled to cover at our approach. It did n't seem a bad idea to copy, so closing the useless cameras, and each one leading his own horse, we plunged and slid down the snowy slopes to our home under the shelter of the spruces. As the sweeping wind bore the night down upon us we sent the old Fourth on its way to the past, not with fire-crackers and bombs, but with the snap and flame of the camp-fire, a salute worthy of a more hospitable Fourth than had been ours.

4: Through Unmapped Country

On Wilcox Pass

THE best trail over the Wilcox Pass is known but to a few. It was made first by Jim Simpson, a guide and hunter, who is eminently acquainted with every byway within a hundred and fifty miles of the railway. As it has been such a boon to us since we found it, he may not mind my passing its location on. Fully a mile before reaching what seems the most direct ascent, scan the hill-slopes on the right. A wide gravelly stream-bed will disclose itself; ascend it one hundred yards through scrub and brush, and faith will soon lead you to a steep but direct trail which cuts off many of the hardships suffered by laden packs in going any other way.

The Pass itself is one of the longest, spongiest, most tiresome passes I have ever travelled. Being 7800 feet high the winter snows lie late, while the August and September storms sweep it constantly. At its northern terminus we gazed out upon a new world to us and among the bewildering mass of peaks which Dr. Collie's party had explored for the first time in 1898, leaving such names as Woolley, Stuttfield, Douglas, Diadem, The Twins, and Alberta upon them. Those names bewildered us then, and I presume will continue to do so till the Government Survey reaches there, confers with the original explorers, and gives us a scientifically correct map.

At this point we sprang into a country new

to us, and which had been trodden by only a limited number before us. The hunter and timber-cruiser of course had gone that way, in the dim past the Indian, but all the real knowledge we could obtain for the next hundred miles was Dr. Collie's work on the Sun Wapta, Jean Habel's paper, "At the Western Sources of the Athabaska River" in *Appalachia*, 1902, and Dr. Coleman's article on his discovery of Fortress Lake in 1893.

This lake at present was our objective point. Over the Wilcox Pass we climbed, found an excellent trail down the other side and soon came into a fine little camp known to the initiated as "Sheep Camp," by a noisy, chattering mountain-stream. Here our trail dropped out of sight and failed to materialise in spite of much searching. A good-sized morning's work on the right side of that stream the next day inspired us to christen it "Tangle Creek." To proceed, we were compelled to get down to the Sun Wapta valley, whose wide white shingle flats we could see two thousand feet below us, and every one went valiantly at those slopes to get there. As the saddle horses (we having dismounted), had only their own necks to preserve, their task was a comparatively easy one, ours being to avoid their plunging efforts as we loaned them a little judgment in choosing their way over and around the precipices, also keeping one eye on the heavily laden packs as they slipped and slid down the steep grade entirely too close for comfort. When by some instinct Chief crossed the stream, landed on a good trail near the bottom, and we took count of noses with every one answering "present," with not so much as a pack shifted or a leg scratched, our faith in the new band went up to join our sentiments for the two men who made it a matter of "all in a day's march." Horse-tracks all over that steep hillside showed that we were not the first ones to attempt the descent of Tangle Creek on its right (or we might say its wrong side); and I think it was Bill Peyto, another well-known guide of this country, who first found that the easiest way down was a little détour on the left of the stream just

after passing Sheep Camp. Whoever he was I wish we had had his knowledge before the descent began rather than after; it would have saved a fierce scrimmage.

The trail down the Sun Wapta[1] (a tributary of the Athabaska about thirty miles long) is composed of shingle flats for nearly half its length, which of course is wearisome even to shod horses, and well-nigh intolerable to the poor fellow who has cast a shoe. As our outfit slowly wended its way down these flats on the second day, Chief's gaze suddenly rested on three white spots poised at the top of a clay bank, and in a stage whisper he muttered "goat." Fresh meat at last! Quickly consulting, "K." forged ahead on his pony with his rifle ready, and the rest of us dismounting, sat down in the open with a pair of binoculars to await results. Goat-meat did not sound tempting, but our mouths, accustomed to bacon for so long, watered for something fresh and we longed like cannibals for that kid. Alas! quick as he was, the mother and child of that family were quicker, and I shall always think that kid was out with his grandparents that day. For the old man was the only one visible to the hunter on his arrival, and with our wish for fresh meat in his mind, "K." shot him. "M." and I regarded his death instantly from a sentimental point of view, and a little later from a more practical standpoint, but at any rate he was not cut down in the bloom of his youth; for though "K." pounded his steaks to a jelly on the stones, and boiled and simmered his legs for hours, he failed to be "chewable" let alone digestible, and eventually his remains were cast into the Athabaska, and no one of that party ever again sighed for goat. Some time after, we tried the hind quarter of a yearling, and to our surprise found it as delicious as any civilised lamb.

Sheep we were to learn later was quite another matter, being really more tasteful than the domestic animal; but bear, porcupine, and *old* goat for the time being we relegated to Necessity's shelf.

[1] Sun Wapta—Stoney Indian for Whirlpool River. There being a tributary of the Athabaska, about one hundred miles north of the Sun Wapta, known as Whirlpool River, this fact has caused some confusion.

"K" (Sid Unwin) near

"The Endless Chain"

There are four points of interest on the Sun Wapta which any one going that way might well bear in mind. On the second day's journey down that delectable (?) river, there is one of the longest and meanest stretches of quicksand I have ever encountered, at least a mile of the horrible stuff over which the horses needed to "step lively" to avoid a painful exit from the world. On the third day we encountered a rock-slide on the river's left which seemed to raise an impassable barrier to all further progress, till, by plunging into the muskeg on our left, we came across the trail again around its western limitations. A short distance beyond the rock-slide and on the river's right begins a low, rocky ridge, which for length and unadulterated ugliness cannot be beaten. We trailed it for a day and a half and then named it "The Endless Chain"; well named too, for, on reaching the Athabaska shores, we found that it still stretched on in an unbroken line for miles down the river. As we neared the junction of the Sun Wapta and the main river we found that the former plunged through a fine canyon, which is elbowed in shape. Unfortunately the forest about it had been fire-swept, but it is still worth the walk through the scrub to see.

The hinted troubles of trail travel on the Sun Wapta grew into solid facts by July the 8th. Our way was strewn with very small burnt fallen pines, which cracked and crackled like match-sticks beneath our horses' feet, and though we found the trail, the one on the lead had plenty of cutting to do, and considering the burdened beasts and hundreds of varied specimens of flies, neither he nor any one else was indulging in unmitigated joys.

We boiled and we burned as the sun beat down upon us from an unclouded sky; and words or comments became useless as we leapt log after log, with all energy reserved to keep ears, eyes, and nostrils free from the swarms of gnats. Then all troubles ceased for the moment as we suddenly emerged from a forest of young pine and sighted for the first time the main Athabaska. Now, as we had been looking for that old river for three days, we naturally had some high ideas, and like all great anticipations the reality, for the time being, fell far short of the mark. To begin with, the valley at that point was arid, fire-swept, and generally nondescript as well as hot and fly-ridden; as for the river it was scarce the size of the Saskatchewan at the Kootenai Plains and just as muddy and turbid. It was distinctly disappointing.

5: On the Search of Fortress Lake

TO find Fortress Lake, now that we had at last really reached the shores of the Athabaska River, was our next aspiration. Riding down to the water's edge we struck the ghost of a trail, and just *hoped* it would go on and lead us to our destination. It was a very forlorn specimen on which to base any hopes, it never got much worse (there was scant chance), and it certainly never got any better.

Dr. Coleman discovered this lake in his search for the mythically high mountains Hooker and Brown in 1893; Walter D. Wilcox went that way in 1896, then Jean Habel in 1901. Like our predecessors we did not spend much time on public improvements and hurried on up the hot, unattractive, burnt valley as fast as the laden ponies could go over "down" timber and through thick pine growth, with an occasional stretch of muskeg to vary the monotony. Just as though the going was not already trouble enough, Dandy, a beautiful impulsive bay, looked for more. Gazing over a nine-foot bank, he saw the cool gurgling waters hurrying along below, and in the blow of an eye rolled and slid down into a narrow dangerous gorge where he went bobbing around like a cork. Not wishing to lose him or his cargo, the men went violently to work fishing him out. The bank was steep, his pack heavy, and with each effort to pull him up, the earth broke away and over he rolled. I looked over once just in time to see a great splash, and protruding from it four bay legs,—the biggest part of Dandy was out of sight. With a halter-rope in front and a club

behind, the flour, matches, baking-powder, and he were rescued for the time being.

Poor Dandy! You were really too much of a gentleman to ever be meant for the trail or a pack, and only by such bitter experiences were you ever to fit yourself for so menial a walk in life. We won't mention the condition of the flour on later investigation. Or I might mention it, too, by saying that the one good ducking put that flour into an impervious condition encasing it in a glue of its own, so that henceforth if it were only the flour that was swimming no one flinched. The sugar unfortunately had a fashion of shrinking with every fresh bath, while the tea and coffee swelled.

So while the horses were studying their lessons we were too. We could see in the near future unsweetened puddings and sugarless cakes, and in time the tea and coffee became so happily blended in flavour that only he who filled the pot knew which was in it.

Two days' travel up the valley brought us to the junction of a stream from the south and also to the first green timber and good horse-feed seen for many a day. According to Collie's map we should be within a short distance of Fortress Lake. Choosing a camp-site in the meadows to the river's right and opposite a towering rocky peak, we decided to look about before advancing farther with the horses.

My! I shall never forget the mosquitoes that night! How we rolled our heads in the hot blankets and in the midst of suffocation and heat, longed for the forgotten "bug-nets!" How we sopped our faces with citronella till we hated the name, and applied a highly advertised mosquito "dope" which was grey and greasy and, whose only virtue as a destroyer, seemed to be to catch the enemy by the wings and leave him kicking and struggling on the very spot which we wished to preserve from his ravages! But even the worst nights pass, and with the dawn we were up prepared to climb a fine mountain back of the camp ("Mount Quincy" —Coleman) to see if from some point of vantage we might locate that elusive lake. Amidst heat and mosquitoes and heavy brush we struggled to the rock bluffs, where one small party was tossed by another party up to a third party in such undignified, unceremonious fashion that party number one wished climbing had never been invented.

Just above timber-line the lake suddenly burst upon our view, a long, pale, blue-green ribbon tossed in dainty abandon among the fir-clad hills. To the right, across the valley, stood the towering black peak which frowned upon our little camp far below, and which we found later Dr. Coleman had named "For-tress," thus giving the name to the lake. The lake itself is estimated to be nine miles in length, and, at the extreme end, a fine peak

Fortress Lake

rises with snowy glaciers sweeping to the shore. It was a great sight, and well repaid us for the scramble up and the drenching we got returning to camp.

Knowing our lake was in such close proximity, the next day passed as only a woman in camp knows how to pass it. To study out how to do a large wash in a small tea-cup, to smooth out the rough-dry garments and avoid appearing as though one had personally passed through a wringer, these are chores which cause an off-day in camp to glide as swiftly by as the passing of the sun. I remember that night it rained and we had the luxury of supper served in our tent. Two gunny-sacks were spread on the soggy ground, the table laid with agate plates for four, then came piles of dried beef and ham frizzled together, after which rice-pudding with stewed currants and a rich fruit-cake were served. An appetite which is seldom met with at the most tempting banquet graced the feast.

Setting out on July 13th for the shores of Fortress Lake, only three miles from Fortress Camp, Pinky, a little white rat of a horse, was entrusted with our sleeping-bags. Not satisfied to follow the leader in navigable waters, he had picked out a way for himself and we suddenly saw him bobbing down stream, the bags shipping water with horrible regularity. Did he care? Not a bit! With yells and imprecations he was ordered to "get out of that!" but he only blinked his white eyelashes, till, seeing no one would follow him, and having struck bottom, he waded calmly ashore. As we emerged on the soft shores of the lake, Pinky strolled in last, placed his head by a tree so as to look tied up like the others, and plainly inferred by his actions, "Well I've brought those sleeping-bags, what was all the row about anyhow?" Poor Pinky! he was small, homely, and insignificant, he couldn't carry much but a pair of beds, but oh! the sense and thought inside that nondescript looking little head! Pinky was to shine as days went on.

The shores of Fortress Lake proved no place for a lengthy stay, being very soft and infested with mosquitoes. The surrounding forests were almost impenetrable. We had not taken sufficient requisites for making a raft, so that except for photography, we were better back at Fortress Camp.

This western tributary which we had followed, Coleman has called "Chaba," being the Stoney word for "Beaver." We explored it to its source, a matter of five or six miles, found any quantity of game tracks, glaciers, and a good-sized stream running into the Chaba from the south, about three miles from our camp. This stream tempted us, but summer outings in this country are only four months long at the outside, and as we had seen another and larger stream coming from the south-east,

we decided to explore it.

I do not know what we missed in the unexplored branch, but I do know the beauty we found in the one we chose to see. Returning to the junction of these two streams via the west shore of the river, two experiences are indelible in my mind. We were slowly trailing down the river-bank about ten o'clock in the morning switching mosquitoes as usual, watching Pinky, Buck, and Dandy, with now calloused eyes as at frequent intervals they carried the beds, the duffel-bags, or the bacon and flour into deep holes and out again, when suddenly miles down the valley we caught a glimpse of a tiny column of smoke. "A hunter! Who can it be? Why should he be so late getting his breakfast?" Of course no one could answer the questions. The uncertain column grew steadier, then heavier, and in an hour we knew it was no hunter but a forest-fire raging where we had camped but five days before. Whose fault had it been? Not ours, "for had we not carried many buckets of water to extinguish that particular fire? Strangers must be behind us." Not that one of us believed there was a stranger within a hundred miles of us, or doubted for an instant that we had been careless, but it was a comfort to talk that way and ease our minds of certain guilt.

As night settled down upon the valley, we all took a last, lingering, regretful look at the fire-demon eating his way up the mountainside opposite us and wondered "what villain had done the foul deed?"

With an uneasy conscience I for one felt pretty badly, and waking at numerous intervals, heard some sort of a creature scratching around the tent. The next morning "M." told me she had felt something soft and warm between her shoulders at daybreak and turning to investigate, a good-sized rat walked out and feeling he was *de trop* had, with great dignity, left the tent. She said his expression, as he glanced back over his shoulder at her, was one of the most intense annoyance, and clearly expressed the fact that "if she did not know enough to keep still he did not want to be there anyhow."

The fire was still raging on the other side of the river when the tin wash-basin tapped out "all aboard for boiled mush!" It was a frosty morning, a small fire had been built in front of our tent, and a stiff breeze was blowing down the river as we sat down to breakfast in the open. Just as I was conscientiously choking down a mouthful of awful boiled mush, my wandering eye landed on our recently reposeful domicile. There it was in flames and going up like newspaper! Of course every one jumped and rushed to save our home. How it was done I do not know, but in a trice the fire was out, and we four were standing there looking at each other and taking account of the damaged stock,—one wash-cloth half destroyed, a handsome silk neckerchief riddled with holes, sleeve of a sweater gone, handle of a tooth-brush snapped in the scramble, and worst of all, one half of the tent gone up in smoke. Moral,—no more "Egyptian cloth" or par-affine-dressed tents if they do weigh one-fourth that of an ordinary duck canvas! We went back to the boiled mush, reposing expectantly on the pack-mantle table; no tragedy would ever overtake that awful stuff.

Just as our belongings, scorched and other-wise, were being finally disposed of in the duffel-bags we heard an unfamiliar horse-bell, and out from the bush by the river stepped three men and five horses. "Timber-cruiser" was written all over them and timber-cruisers they were. They had originally come up the Athabaska from Edmonton on the south side of the river, reaching a point opposite our camp they were caught in a "jack-pot,"[1] and rather than chop or back their way out, they burnt their way through. Then seeing fresh cuttings on the north side, they concluded surveyors had just gone through, that the north side was the correct route, and so built a raft and crossed over, a flattering tribute to our men's labour. If their disappointment was keen on finding the surveyors were only four picnickers, our sensations were decid-edly joyful at knowing that the fire burning so hideously on the mountain opposite was not to be laid to our door after all.

[1] Jack-pot = fallen timber, muskeg, anything representing trouble on the trail.

Sid Unwin and the scorched tent

—37—

6: To the Base of Mount Columbia

AND now for that unknown branch of the Athabaska we had passed on our way to Fortress Lake. It was decidedly alluring. From "Burnt Tent Camp" we had looked through the folds of hills to a snow-white peak absolutely pyramidal in form, and that it enticed our wandering footsteps no one denied. Mounting our steeds and crossing the river with a certain amount of soakage, we soon struck an apology for a trail. Doubtless Jean Habel, the German climber, had been the last white man to go that way (as he is also the first recorded), for we very soon concluded that the great white pyramid was Mount Columbia, whose northern slopes Habel had visited in 1901.

As Chief and "K." wished to explore ahead a little before going in with the whole outfit, the other two of us had one of our rare days in camp. These days always began with admonitions from the departing ones "not to meddle in the kitchen department, or to waste the laundry soap," and always ended with our flying at both the minute our guardians were out of sight. I must confess, however, one other idea always leapt ahead of a good morning's wash or baking during these temporary absences of our caretakers, and that was *bears*.

How often people shake their heads, and speak of our wanderings in the hills as "brave and courageous." How little they know about it. A bear, and that a grizzly, is the only fear I have and as I've never met one I'm not quite sure of my ground even with him. Brown bears and black bears we have seen hurrying away from our advancing forces, but hunters have told me a grizzly courts a stand-up fight and fears no one; also that he fails in one accomplishment—*he cannot climb a tree. Neither can I.* However we do much under stress of circumstances; and the first idea that pops into my head on seeing the backs of the men disappear in the distance, is to look for a tree I might climb in case Mr. Grizzly should materalise. Like the burglar under the bed,

I've been looking for him for many years and so far he has never come.

But with our men gone to explore the Columbia Valley (or West Branch of the Athabaska), a rather thin and wispy tree picked out to escape from the imaginary bear, my own mind settled down to the problem of making a whole tent out of a half-burnt one, while "M." took up the homely duties of baking and washing. All day long we pieced and patched, occasionally hoisting the tent to the ridge-pole for a fitting, and the result was something wonderful. At the end of the day as the long cool shadows fell across our home and valley, we heard the distant call of the home-comers. A fine fruit-cake, a beautiful bannock, and a very peculiarly shaped but rain-proof tent awaited their arrival. There was a polite grin, and one ingrate remarked as his eye lit on the restored tent, "It looks just like a chicken-coop," while the other suggested "a resemblance to a snow-plough or a bat." Perhaps it did. To me, with fingers stiff and sore from using a darning needle, coarse black patent thread, and a pair of nail scissors all day, it was grace and beauty personified; and with the passing of the next thunder-storm the grudging "Oh it's not so bad" was salve to my bruised fingers and tired back.

On July 28th with tents whole once more, refreshed horses, and five miles of new ground explored the previous day by the men, we were up and off early in chirpy mood bound for the new valley.

It was a wild stream this West Branch, and owing to the previous hot days it was a little higher perhaps than at our first crossing of it. Still, by following the leader absolutely, there was no reason to expect trouble. But in those early days of the new band there was never any accounting for the movement of some one of them or the other. This day it was Buck. The river bottom was bouldery and rough, four or five horses had gone over carefully, scarcely wetting the cinchas; and

Mary in camp

Mount Columbia from the north

then that yellow, aggravating Buck and his bacon came in. I can see his face yet as it expressed the words, "Stupids, I'll show you a better way"; and sallied independently into the stream among the roughest bunch of rocks he could have picked upon, and the current promptly knocked him over. Struggling up, he struck out for land and, in his nervous haste, got his left foot caught in the halter-shank. Under the circumstances four legs were few enough but three were just about useless. Down he went! Chief, with his drawn knife, tried to push up to him on Pinto, but this writhing, tumbling thing in the water was an unknown object to Pinto, and sometimes when Pinto would n't, he did n't, and this was one of the sometimes. Once more Buck pulled his bacon and himself to the air, but his nerve was going fast and I saw him flop weakly over, then three unresisting yellow legs stood up stiff and still, and every one thought that Buck was "all in." Just as we had concluded that his hour had come and probably passed, a feeble wriggle of the legs brought him once more to the surface with all fight gone, and he stood gasping for breath, ears laid back flat, and the water pouring from him. This time Pinto recognised his friend. Chief reached out, cut the halter-shank, and Buck dragged his weary way to the shore with his load. It surely seemed as though we should stop then and there and give him "first aid to the injured," but he was forced to step into line, his ears gradually came back to their normal poise, and in an hour he was strutting along as briskly and independently as usual. However, he had learned something, and from that day forward Buck always took cognisance of the route laid out by the leader and was mighty particular how he followed.

The unknown (to us) branch of the Athabaska proved to be about thirty-five miles long. The first two days' march were decidedly bad with fallen timber and lots of muskeg. Habel's trail and an occasional camp of his were easily recognised, whilst the numerous caribou tracks were reason enough for so many tepee-poles along the whole valley.

There were also several trees with Cree writing on them, indicating that the Crees from around Edmonton, and not our friends the Stoneys from the south, were the hunters of that valley.

The day of the 31st of July dawned clear, hot, and beautiful. Chief and "K." explored ahead as usual in the new country, in preference to driving the horses from good feed to an uncertain quantity. Our tents were pitched on an island, a very cosey one at that, and "M." and I prepared to fill in a lazy day. We boiled beans, killed bull-dog flies, drove the horses out of the tents where no other grass than that seemed to suit them, and visited an old camp of Habel's. There stood the record of his visit carved on the stump of a felled tree, "1901 Habel, Campbell, Barker, Ballard." Only six summers had gone by, yet his trail was fallen in, the boughs of his bed were curled and warped, the fire-place grown over with moss, and Habel himself, probably the first explorer in this valley, had been sleeping the long sleep for five years. As we went back to our little home of cosey tents and cheery camp-fire, and horses wandering comfortably about, we wondered—wondered—where five years' time would find us, and who would follow in our footsteps. To shake off the sadness, and to give the trail-breakers a welcome, a bright idea popped into my head, "They shall have a boiled pudding." I made the pudding and we all tasted it and it was a good pudding, that is if it had been intended for a cannon-ball and not for an object of diet. It probably lies there to-day; our camp-site may fade, our trip be forgotten, but that pudding ought to be there when the next explorers go through.

Our third and last day's drive to the base of Mount Columbia will last while memory lingers in those hills. No breath of fire had ever scorched those last miles of green, green slopes. The soft ground disappeared, the river was fordable at any point, the wide shingle-flats allowed us to wander anywhere, and caribou tracks were there in thousands. Waterfalls springing from the very summits of unnamed peaks fell thousands of feet; the names of Woolley, Stuttfield, Alberta, and

Diadem danced before our eyes as mountain after mountain came into view, but all that we knew was—there lay Columbia before us.

No feed for several miles was in sight to tempt us to linger, so we hurried forward over the shingle-flats till under the shadow of the mountain. There we halted. The sight was a fine one; snow-clad and glacier-draped, she was a beautiful example of exquisite symmetry. Outram, who is the only one to have ever reached her sharp and snowy summit, gives her an altitude of 12,500 feet. Having ascended from the southern side he had ample opportunity to gain a general knowledge of the ice-fields adjacent to this splendid mountain. He says:

"But the crowning feature of the panorama was the survey of the immense area of the Columbia ice-field, possibly the largest known outside the Arctic regions and their fringe. It covers about two hundred square miles, being upwards of thirty miles in length from the head of the *névé* to the tongue of the Saskatchewan glacier, protrudes its glacier ramifications to every point of the compass, and occupies the geographical centre of the water system of one quarter of the continent of North America."

From our point of vantage, the mountain swept up in an almost unbroken plane for about 8000 feet. On the eastern slope a fine glacier clung, descending almost to the valley, and from the western shoulder, trending almost due north, arose a fine rocky formation which we designated "Edward VII." This mountain, with marked horizontal strata and whose true summit lies much to the west of its centre, may, however, be the mountain which Dr. Collie saw through the haze and smoke from the summit of Mount Athabaska in 1898 and called "Alberta."

Coming from the west and sweeping around the northern base of this mountain to join the stream from Columbia, was a good-sized body of water which we explored two days later. At the present moment, however, our minds were compelled to turn to the practical affairs of life. Here at the base of Mount Columbia we longed to camp, but excepting scenery and shingle-flats there was nothing upon which to feed the

very hungry horses, so we reluctantly (and oh, how reluctantly!) crept back into the saddles and slowly retraced our way down that fair valley looking right and left for grass. Five miles back on our tracks and on the river's left, we came across two small islands with a limited supply of poor feed upon them. Indians had been there during the hunting season; bones of sheep and caribou littered the ground, racks for drying and smoking meat stood around, and tepee-poles were pitched in clusters where the squaws must have placed them several years before.

The whole valley is a bad one for horses, the grass being limited in both quality and quantity; but for that important fact it was the first ideal home we had struck since we crossed the Wilcox Pass.

Our tents were pitched on the softest and greenest of moss carpets, beneath spruces which kept off the beating rays of the noonday sun, and sheltered us at night from the chill winds which swept from the Columbia ice-fields. After getting nicely settled I found a little visitor on "M's" bed, a fat comfortable-looking toad. Not particularly desiring the company of toads, yet not wishing to hurt his sociable feelings, I hopped him gently outside; in half an hour there he was perched on my own bed, and looking up with intense defiance at me. Again I hopped him out. In an hour's time I saw his small phiz leering at me from a spot of refuge which he had discovered in the folds of my blankets. The time seemed ripe to deal firmly with that toad if I was n't going to have him for a bedfellow, so gathering the ugly little intruder up gently, I deposited him quite fifty yards from either tent, warning him off the premises on pain of absolute extinction. Then we forgot him. When the stars had come forth in the gloaming (it never seems night on the northern trail), and the owls were hooting in distant tree-tops, and the wind sweeping down the valley from the great ice-fields, each said good-night and turned into his and her blankets. A beautiful silence fell like a cloak about the camp, so beautiful I only whispered, "Where do you suppose that toad is?" Before I could get a surmising reply, there was a curdling howl from the "chicken-coop," and a voice muttered, "He's squashed flat!" I had my answer.

Except for the delightful trailing at the upper end of the valley, as described, the way is very poor indeed. It is stony and rough in places and the crossing of the numerous mountain streams ugly. Even if only two or three yards wide, they proved in many instances very deep and soft with clay-like banks which were treacherous in the extreme. Fortunately a couple of cold nights had brought the river down a foot or more, and several bad holes were thus circumnavigated on our return trip.

What ailed the horses the morning we left "Columbia Camp" I do not know. A spirit of meanness or rivalry seemed to have entered their heads. Bugler, "M's" pony, announced in emphatic actions that he was going to be up next to the leader; Brownie as good as told him that he wanted that place and cut in by slipping around the whole bunch. Bugler's rider, wishing to see how the game would go, did not interfere, and Bugler gave Brownie a nip on the rump which sent him flying to the rear. Then Dandy took a hand, only to get the same warning to keep off the premises. Little blinky-eyed Pinky then tried it, and was so enraged at the treatment he received, that he retired to the rear with his sleeping-bags and was not seen nearer than half a mile during the rest of the day's march. That was not an uncommon affair with Pinky however. He was very easily insulted, and, possessing a naturally exclusive disposition, we had grown quite accustomed to his wandering alone far behind. But Buck evidently began to think Bugler was having things entirely too much his own way, and up he sauntered in such a meaningless, non-committal fashion, that even the amused riders did not take in the significance of his act. Just as he slipped between Chief's horse and Bugler, out flew the Sorrel's white teeth, and Buck caught it as had the others. But this time it was no shy Dandy or thin-skinned Pinky or humble Brownie, it was

just Buck. In the glare of the noonday sun I caught a glimpse of two steel shoes, a dull thud was heard, Bugler's ribs and those steel heels had come suddenly in contact. It was a surprised and humbled Bugler who promptly edged out of the fray, and for days to follow he would drop politely back when the ever-remembering Buck sauntered up with his ears laid flat.

Another exhibition of horse sense took place in that valley of abominable holes. The spot was a mountain-stream between two sharp hills. The crystal water poured down into a hole criss-crossed with fallen timber. The hole itself was bad enough to cross, but the timber made it a veritable trap, and we all wished we were beyond it even before we reached it. The saddle-horses and two or three packs had gone through fairly well and had climbed the sharp hillside beyond when a call came from "K." that assistance was needed. We did not turn back with Chief, it being quite enough for us to listen to the words of encouragement and shouting which came up from the ravine below.

One pack after another slowly crawled up the hill into view, all but Brownie, and then we knew who was in trouble. From our high point, however, we commanded a view of the trail one hundred yards back of the hole and this was what we saw. Pinky was running light that day and as usual was far in the rear. As he rounded the bend he spied the trouble just ahead, paused, studied the situation out, turned, and went deliberately back to the bank of the main river. There again he stopped, looked first at the angry waters, and then at the hole again. Having settled matters to his own satisfaction he stepped to the brink, plunged into the river, was shot down stream fifty yards, and landed nicely on the only bit of gravel to be found within a half mile. Shaking his little whitey-brown hide and blinking his white lashes over his wee ratty eyes he sauntered up to his waiting friends, ignoring completely our giggles of amusement at the neat way in which he had got around that hole. In a few minutes Brownie came up weary and spent, with a saturated solution of groceries on his back. We asked no questions, we just knew from every one's attitude and silence that Brownie had been saved only in the nick of time, and we were simply thankful the old fellow was there at all.

Trailing is great fun, especially in untried by-ways, but the small hairbreadth escapes and the perils which come upon our four-footed friends without warning are sometimes a little trying to bear.

7: Back on the Old Familiar Trail

ABOUT noon on August the 8th, having said a long farewell to the main Athabaska, her tributaries, the beautiful mountains at their sources, and dug a hole deep in our memories wherein we deposited all small trail woes, we turned the corner and made for old "Match-stick Camp" on the Sun Wapta. We were soon traversing the burnt section so recently made by the timber-cruisers. The ground was still hot from the fire, and so were our hearts as we looked on that four square miles of ruthlessly, carelessly, uselessly destroyed timber. It was with sincere thankfulness that we turned into the above-named camp and found everything as green and fresh as the day we left it, a sure guaranty that the fire *did* belong to those "cruisers" and not to a stray brand from our own fire-place. I can imagine no more haunting memory of the trail than to feel that I or my companions might be responsible for any of the many forest fires which have from time to time disfigured that glorious mountain country of which I write.

Back by the Endless Chain, around the great rock-slide, and gingerly over the quicksand we made our way up the valley of the Sun Wapta to a well marked creek called by Dr. Collie "Diadem." Our march of recession was marked by feasts of strawberries and cream, strawberry shortcake and strawberry pie; every open spot was a strawberry patch. Honey and maple-syrup were getting low in the larder, but who cared while these delicious berries lasted? Whether it be environment or appetite I know not, but nothing from a civilised garden ever tasted half so delicious as those crimson bits of sweetness after a long day's march.

Before reaching Diadem Creek, Pinky once more illustrated his superiority of mind over the small amount of flesh vouchsafed him. About half way up the valley on the river's left is a stretch of muskeg as mean as one is ever liable to encounter, mean just because no one suspects it is muskeg until his horse is completely entrapped in it. We had been ambling along quietly for hours, when suddenly the three lead saddle-horses were floundering and plunging through the bad spot before we knew enough to get off; Roanie who was at our heels had sailed in with his pack and was plunging, kicking, and rushing through the death-trap before any one could ward him off. Chief hurried up, cut off the advance of the rest of the outfit in the nick of time, then led them by twos and threes up and around the mountainside. Pinky coming up last, sauntering along with head meditatively bent, reached the brink of the trouble after all the other horses had been personally conducted over the hill. He stopped and inspected that muskeg, looked up the mountain, turned, and strolled leisurely in the direction the men had just taken the other horses. He never followed in the footsteps of his companions however. Nonchalantly walking in among his waiting friends on the far side of the mess, that stupid, witless-looking Pinky had not one splash of mud above his hoofs while the others were grimy to the cinchas. Pinky was a born trailer. Oh, we laughed of course at that tiny bunch of bones taken along as an extra in case of trouble, but he had every one's respect.

August the 12th found us at Diadem Creek, which heads from a mountain of the same name. Here Dr. Collie mentions camping and climbing to the various high points in that vicinity, and it was here that "K." had killed the grandfather goat whose meat proved so untoothsome. But one cannot camp with twelve horses without grass; search as we would none was found, nothing but epilobium and drias no matter which way we turned. So we were compelled to go about five miles up stream to our original first camp on the Sun Wapta, where we trusted the small amount of slough grass had taken on a fresh growth in our absence.

Feed on the Sun Wapta is so scarce for about fourteen miles in this part of the country, that this small patch is easily overlooked by a person visiting here for the first time. It lies on the river's left about three miles from the mouth of the stream which plunges direct from the Wilcox Pass. Just beyond this camp-ground a large stream enters the main river, heading from the cluster of mountains of which Mounts Woolley and Stuttfield are part, and this stream we determined to explore.

The following day being Monday and no serious climbing anticipated (this is only a story of the valleys), washing was in order. For two hours, basins, soap, and clothes held sway, and I 've often wondered what a real "wash-lady" would say to a week's wash being accomplished in a collapsible rubber hand basin (which was always collapsing), with hot water which sometimes smelled of tea or showed signs of being heated in the mush-pot, with no boiling or bluing and not a flat-iron to finish the job. The ease and comfort of such an existence has taught me that there is a lot of unnecessary fret and worry in civilised life. A handkerchief which has gone through the motions, then hung in the fresh air and golden sunshine, is far sweeter than any laundry could ever turn out. The Indian has taught us a whole lot about "the simple life," though according to his ideas I have not quite graduated, for to the naked eye he appears to use no water at all, but our little band still clings to a few traditions of our ancestors.

That day I even tried washing our dwindling supply of rice. It had been in and out of the rivers so much for the past few weeks that it was passed upon by the family as decidedly "musty." With a handful of rice, the same amount of clean river sand, I rubbed the two together, then rinsed off the latter and spread the rice in the sun to dry. As a theory it was splendid. The little grey dabs of mould disappeared, leaving the travel-stained rice snowy white, but the resultant pudding, even with a liberal supply of raisins, retained a flavour which could be ignored only by one in a starving condition. We were not starving, and one of us hated the stuff at its best, so it was consigned to the little chipmunks.

With laundry spread out to dry, a luncheon in our pockets, we all started out to investigate Sang-Sangen[1] Creek just back of the camp. No sooner had we entered its precincts than we found ourselves in a magnificent amphitheatre not over a mile long. At its far end descended a splendid glacier, on the left stood a fine mountain, and to our right rose a peak about nine thousand feet high. This we climbed and stood in the midst of Collie s and Stuttfield's mountains. Far away to the south we could see Mount Wilson, much nearer were Mounts Athabaska and Saskatchewan, but the peaks frowning almost over our heads were a bewildering gathering of giants which were straightened out only by Dr. Collie some time later.

Our return via Tangle Creek to Wilcox Pass was made with far more elegance than our descent of that stream. There is a good trail on the creek's left which carries one almost to "Sheep Camp," and from there you are practically out of the woods.

Much game is supposed to exist on the pass, but in our various traversings of it we have never come across but one sign of wild life. Travelling quietly over it on the fifteenth day of August, "K.," who was leading, suddenly pointed to a pair of ears just visible behind a rock two hundred yards ahead of us. Of course the binoculars were in the duffel-bag, and it took some moments to see that it was a fox. His coat was almost black, with splashes of deep mahogany brown, a most peculiar and handsome effect. Above him swooped and hovered a hawk. Warning us to stand quietly, "K." slipped forward with his rifle and then began a game of "hide-and-seek" with the great rock boulders as a playground. For half an hour the two men followed the fox here and there, at times recognising his whereabouts only by the presence of the hawk, which followed his every movement, giving the game away terribly. But the wily old fellow was evidently quite at home, the hunters with a broken front sight on the rifle were not, and he eventually made good his escape. The hawk, finding "nothing more doing," rose and soared away into the

[1] Stoney language for rice.

heavens, and the rest of us hurried on down the slope to "Jim's" camp, where the sensible horses had been slowly making their way for some time. Two months going to school was turning out a nice working bunch.

Hoping to get a different view of the mountains seen from Sang-Sangen Creek, the following day we climbed Wilcox Peak (10,050 feet). With that contrariness of inanimate things which followed every climb we made during the season of 1907, the weather thickened in proportion to the ascent. Our camp was at 7500 feet, very little below timber line, so that there was not much to boast of in the mountaineering line when we reached the highest of the three or four peaks, but it seemed a weary grind to us who loved not climbing.

Just as we seemed within a few yards of our goal, when "K." was skipping along like a goat, and I laboriously trudging and grumbling behind, trying to keep him even in sight, I saw him disappear behind a wall of rock. Dodging around it I found Wilcox Peak on that side had been cut down as clean as a whistle, a sheer wall of two thousand feet at least stared me in the face, the rock wall loomed above, a two-foot ledge of rock jutted from its side showing "K's" route to success, while "K's" back disappearing behind another rock showed his indifference to such things as ledges and two-thousand-foot drops. It was too much for my stock of alpine courage and I yelled for help. He called back encouragingly, and comfortingly, "Oh, that's safe enough, hold up your head, don't look down!" So I meekly stared aloft, and followed, too scared to disobey. A few minutes later the last summit was reached, a cairn was found, and in it a small bottle whose enclosed paper recorded the above altitude. Our disappointment was keen enough when we looked off to the group of desired peaks and found them too enveloped in mist for photography to be of the slightest use, and so, like the King of France, "we climbed down again."

About dawn the next morning I opened one sleepy eye, saw six inches of snow on the ground with plenty more following, and knew there would be no hurry to get to Camp Parker, five miles below, so turned for another nap. In my half dreams I heard a distant shout, and thinking it was one of the men calling for a helping hand to bring in the horses, paid no further attention. Imagine my surprise, on hearing a clearing of the throat at our very tent-door, to waken fully and behold a strange, full-bearded, spectacled, and most respectably clad *man*. Nine weeks' trailing through the worst kind of brush and scrub had reduced our men to actual rags (not to mention what our own outward appearance might be), and I confess to an overwhelming dazzlement at the sight of the gentleman's neat black rain-coat. Bowing as though in a drawing-room and doffing his spotless hat, he said, "I hope I don't intrude?" Not wishing to be outdone in politeness even under such limited circumstances, I struggled up as far as the confines of the sleeping-bag would permit, ducked as gracefully as possible, and murmured "Certainly not." He was a truly remarkable man, for being a hundred and twenty-five miles from a railroad, two women were probably the very last objects he expected to find in that tent in a snow-storm, and yet there was not the twitch of a muscle nor a quiver of the voice as he said, "Are there any men in this camp?" I pointed to the "chicken-coop," twenty yards away, and the next half hour "M." and I spent in sizing up the stranger. On his departure, Chief came over to make the fire, reported that this other outfit was camped two miles down the valley, that the man had started out in search of the trail across the Wilcox Pass, saw our horses feeding in the meadows below, and eventually found our camp. With the necessary information obtained as to his route, he had departed, leaving no clue of himself or companions other than that he had "been to Fortress Lake in '93." Courtesy of the trail forbade too much questioning, so we labelled them "timber-cruisers." Perhaps. Then "1893" and its significance suddenly popped into somebody's head, "Why, that was the year Dr. Coleman discovered Fortress Lake." Well, inwardly I decided that trail etiquette might go to the winds as far as I was concerned if we met in the valley below and I certainly intended to see that we did meet. Curiosity should take precedence of politeness. In a pelting, wet snow we got off by nine o'clock, straining our eyes to catch a first glimpse of the strangers. Sure enough, in fifteen minutes through the thick flakes we saw them coming towards us, four men and nine horses. Pausing to bow to our morning visitor, I casually asked him if in '93 he could have possibly met Dr. Coleman around Fortress Lake. "Well," he replied, "I happen to be L. Q. Coleman, and that is my brother, the Doctor, over there." So here were we literally falling over the man whose maps and notes we had been unable to obtain before leaving home, whose trails and camps were all we had to read in the long days on the Athabaska, whose name had been on our lips daily for weeks; it was just a little stranger than fiction! As our new-found acquaintances pitched camp very near the meeting-place, we made an excuse for visiting them a little later, and deluged the Doctor with questions till he must have been glad to have seen our backs when we said "Good-bye" and returned to our temporary home at the junction of the North Fork and Nigel Creek.

Now that the Fortress Lake region had been investigated, not to our complete satisfaction but with a certain amount of curiosity satisfied, our thoughts and feet turned to the "West-Branch-of-the-North-Fork," or as we have chosen to call it "for short," Nashan River. The primary object of this visit was that from its head-waters we might climb sufficiently high to obtain a view of the Columbia ice-fields, Outram's description of which I have quoted, and to whom we were indebted for our curiosity.

The trip back to Graveyard Camp was without event, unless good weather and low water be recorded, with the exception of a small incident which may be a finger-board of warning to those who have not yet been over the ground. About four miles north of Graveyard Camp the river runs through a narrow

A. P. Coleman

rock-gorge utterly impassable for horses and compels the trailer to seek a way up the right bank of the river where a good trail leads over quite a high shoulder. As the men were busy pushing the horses along, "M." and I to aid the horses started ahead for the bank, which we took for the one we had descended a few weeks before, first crossing a narrow branch of the river. It was as harmless a looking bank as one could well imagine. "M." struck up first on what appeared a hard white clay bank, when to our surprise in went Bugler up to the cinchas. She stepped quickly from him and herself was instantly engulfed to the knees in a white sticky mire, while Bugler plunged and kicked and finally extricated himself, reaching the more solid ground above. Seeing that the packs were gaining on us rapidly,

I left "M." floundering in the mud and with Nibs tried a more promising-looking part of the bank about twenty yards north of "M's" Waterloo.

Our judgment proved as poor as "M's," and down we sank into that nasty white clay. As poor Nibs floundered about, his feet became entangled in the roots of a tree and my head was soon in violent contact with the branches of the same. To save both the head and the horse I was forced to beat a hasty retreat by sliding off over his tail when I landed in the cold river up to the knees.

No harm, however, was done save that those implicated looked as though they had been whitewashed, and the grown-wise trailers, who had been solemnly taking in the situation from more solid ground, kept away from the trouble of their own accord. With cool deliberation they turned, walked up the river about one hundred yards and hit the true trail.

Knowing on our first visit to this spot in the spring, that we would be back there later in the summer, our men had lightened the work of the pack animals by caching several hundred pounds of food in a hunter's shack eighteen miles to the south of us. Taking account of stock that night, the larder disclosed one grouse, one-half pound of bacon that had seen better days, flour for three days, a little salt and a small quantity of mouldy tea, a pretty neat calculation for a month's absence from the "grub-pile" in strange country.

The following morning the men were up at dawn and off down the valley for the cached food, leaving us mistresses of the situation for twenty-four hours. It was a rather uncanny sensation of loneliness which swept down our spines as we saw our preservers disappearing in the distance, leaving us with only our two saddle ponies, the wide shingle-flats, and the frowning hills as protectors. Casting my eye around for the usual tree which was to be our haven in case of the untimely arrival of the ever-expected grizzly, we tidied our tents, saddled up our ponies, gathered together the cameras, and went off on a photographic

tour. Laundry and cooking for once had to be abandoned. There was no soap to wash with, and nothing to cook, so our ordinary amusements for the nonce, had to be abandoned. I think we both felt like youngsters playing "hookey,"—a strange sense of unaccustomed freedom possessing us. Alone! Really alone! Except for our two departed friends, not another human being within a hundred miles of us. With wistful eyes the ponies gazed down the long valley in the direction of their departed friends; freedom such as this had no attractions for them.

A mile across the flats we forced our unwilling steeds, set up the tripod, and proceeded to get a view of Pinto Peak and far-away Mount Wilson. Suddenly we noticed the horses pricking up their ears and Nibs began to whinny. Looking in the same direction, we saw coming down the river an outfit of about ten horses. Where was all the loneliness we had boasted of now? Who could this be invading our Eden? Leaving "M." to guard the cameras and mounting Nibs, who evidently thought it was his missing companions, I galloped out across the flats to see who the intruders were. It was "Jim" for whom we had been looking all summer, and with him a charming little English lady*who was out on an entomological expedition.

It was a comical meeting there of the two of us, one from the civilisation of London, one from Philadelphia. Shorn of every rag of vanity, the aristocratic little English lady rode out to meet me on her calico pony, clad in an old weather-beaten black gown, over her shoulder a "bug-net," yet every inch a lady, from her storm-swept old Panama hat to her scarred and battered hob-nailed shoes. As she gave me the bow I should have received from her in a drawing-room, I could but fancy the small figure she was saluting, as with no hat, clad in a boy's dark blue shirt, a scarlet kerchief at the neck, an old Indian beaded coat on, there was little of Philadelphia left clinging to my shoulders.

*   Mary de la Beach-Nichol

Jim Simpson

Encouraged by a hearty invitation, the party decided to camp near us for a couple of days, and the alacrity with which we accepted their invitation to supper that night was a positive disgrace, but we were so tired of mouldy tea, etc., and butter and jam would be such a delicious change that we quite forgot our manners. Then it was such a treat to hear what some one besides ourselves had been doing, even though it was not from the outside world, and we talked far into the night around the camp-fire.

The next day our guides returned with the food. Then there was an invitation to "our house," another chat around the blazing logs, a lingering good-bye when they left us the following morning with letters for *home*,— then we returned to our usual life.

8: Nashan Valley, Thompson Pass, The Icefields of Mount Columbia

AS this chronicle now leads us up Nashan River, I might here give our apparently high-handed reason for changing the well-known or rather lengthy name of this river, printed on the present maps of that region as "West-Branch-of-the-North-Fork-of-the-Saskatchewan," to "Nashan," or, in full, Nashan-esen (Wolverine-go-quick). It is the Stoney-Indian name for our friend Jim Simpson, given him by his Indian admirers out of compliment to his speed in walking on snow-shoes or off. Jim's axe in this country has done more to make the old trails passable for future comers than any others, and this little tribute to his labours seems small enough,—to name a beautiful valley and river for one who has helped to make a hard road easier.

As week after week we had cast aside the barriers and entered those valleys of the north of which there is little or no description, each one had seemed fairer than the last. Thompson*came this way in 1900 looking for a practical pass across the Continental Divide, expecting to meet Stuttfield and Collie who were coming up the Bush River. They did not reach the low divide which he found, by several miles however, owing to the terrible conditions underfoot, but later named it the Thompson Pass. Outram entered the valley in 1902 bound for the Columbia icefields, but no one so far had taken horses down the western slope, though it looked, in our bird's-eye view of it, perfectly feasible.

There had evidently been a favourite Indian hunting-ground at the gateway of this river. Crossing the wide flats and bearing to our right, a well marked trail led to a twenty-foot embankment on which stood several sets of tepee-poles, and bones were strewn about in every direction. For four miles the trail meandered on the hillside to the river's left, owing to soft

ground in the valley below, and very beautiful it looked as we gazed down upon the tall marsh grasses fringing the clear pools and waving with the sweeping winds. It was nearing the end of August, and even then autumn was stealing in with yellows and deep red browns to mingle with the deep greens.

As the familiar mountains in the east disappeared behind us, we steadily crept towards those we had not seen before. Out from the folds of hills before us, rose beautiful Mount Lyell on our right, and as the tribulations underfoot increased, the view before us grew more splendid, for Mount Alexandra and Gable Peak bore steadily down upon us, with frozen rivers hanging from summit to base.

The last six miles to the foot of these two mountains was a trial to spirit and flesh (barring the scenery); the fine pebbly flats grew to boulders, and then to regular rocks. The warm day had brought down torrents of water, and our advance became a chase back and forth over exposed bars, till several times I wondered if we might not see either a passenger or a pack bowled over. Occasionally we tried the shore, only to give up the fight in the scrub and again take to the stones. It was in one of these detours that Pinky failed in his usually good judgment. As was customary, he came strolling leisurely along well behind; we were fighting our way through dense brush at the moment and turned to our right to avoid an embankment on the river. Twenty yards from this high bank the brush became so thick that the leader took to a deep arm of the river and we all plunged in to follow him to a long bar out in mid-stream. With packs splashed, and ourselves soaked to the waists, we crawled out and instantly caught a glimpse of Pinky's white hide silhouetted against the dark forest just above the high bank; with calm and meditative mien he was watching the last of the pack train worrying its way through

* Charles S. Thompson, member of the Appalachian Mountain Club

—51—

the thick brush, plunging into the deep water, and dragging the soaked packs out on the other side. We paused to see what he intended to do with the situation. He craned his neck in the direction his companions had just gone, then looked over the bank, and decided to take a short cut. In he plunged, the waters met above him, and nothing but agitated ripples were left of him. It was probably seconds but it seemed minutes before the surprised Pinky rose to the surface. With ears flattened back and mane plastered to his neck, he emerged with a disgusted expression and joined us on the bar from where we had been watching him. The whole performance was so comical that we all burst out laughing. Shaking himself, and with one withering glance that took us all in, he passed us by and haughtily strutted ahead, every movement of his body showing indignation at our thoughtless behaviour and for the rest of the march, perhaps two miles, he kept far ahead of even the leader, never deigning again to notice the rabble which by this time would have been glad to apologise.

There may be those who read these pages who will think that I have infused too much human personality into our four-footed companions of the trail. I, too, might have thought so once, but that time has gone by. A daily acquaintance with them had bred friendship, affection, and understanding. On the trail we lived with them and talked to them till they and we understood each other's movements thoroughly; their characters were as individual as our own. They knew the master who exacted obedience, and with the kindness, firmness, and care which was their portion in that outfit, we have frequently started out on a long trip with apparently stupid, untrained horses, to return with a wise thinking bunch which only needed a hand to place the saddle and pack for them, for the rest they were the masters of the situation.

But I have left Pinky trailing up Nashan Valley all too long, while myself riding a different hobby-horse. To work. Gable Peak and Mount Alexandra whose separate glaciers formed a splendid whole at the forefoot, seemed slowly creeping down upon us, rather than we upon them. Within a few yards of a narrow gorge, through which burst the waters from these glaciers, we found a level spot on which we pitched the two tents, and a hundred yards away a poor apology for horse-feed, all we had seen for the last four miles. The level spot was a ragged edge of the gravel flats, so once more we were thankful to be the possessors of air-beds. Just as we were dismounting some one said: "There's a lynx!" Sure enough there was the tawny gentleman slowly ambling by on the other side of the river and looking across at us as though it was an everyday occurrence for him to meet an outfit in his afternoon strolls. With cameras set, two of us dropped all else and hurried toward him as fast as the rough boulders permitted in hopes of catching his portrait. But the distance and impediments were too many, and still unhurried, we saw our quarry spring into the river, swim calmly across, and trot away in the dusk of the forest with quite an unruffled countenance.

With home set up and lunch devoured, and with the impression that houses built on rocks were a pretty safe investment, we strolled towards the gorge whose proximity forced necessary conversation to be carried on by yelling. Here enormous boulders formed a short, deep, picturesque canyon and beyond stretched a magnificent rock-strewn amphitheatre through which flowed the stream from the massive ice-tongue. With only a stretch of imagination I could have put out my hand and stroked fair Alexandra's face, and patted the rough crags of Gable which loomed above the four atoms of humanity who peered aloft at their greatness, from that great silent theatre whose players had been turned to snow and ice.

Reaching home we were surprised to find that the river, which had been twenty yards from our front door when we left it, was a scant two feet away, and we began to think of spending the night in uncomfortable quarters on the steep hillside. Deferring shifting camp till supper was despatched, we returned to our tent after that meal to see that the channel had moved back ten feet again. This permitted the usual camp-fire and all was serene.

Opening one eye the next morning at 5.30, I saw the clouds were drifting very low, but if raining, the roar of the gorge drowned all sound of it, and the most interesting item at the moment was that the river had again crept to the door of the tent and washed away every semblance of the great fire we had had the night before. Still 5.30 is no time for fretting about being drowned or washed out, and I nodded off again not to wake until the chop of the axe told me it was seven o'clock. Then the river had crept yards away from us again, but had left a healthy little stream behind the tent which had washed away the kitchen fire and scattered the chopped wood all over the country. With a river that never knew its own mind five minutes at a time, thus preventing us from knowing ours, we were glad to leave that otherwise beautiful elbow and start up the main stream heading from the Thompson Pass.

From the junction of the two streams to the head of the valley it was about fifteen miles, but not a really good feeding-ground the entire distance. The way was beautiful through gorgeous green forests with Mount Lyell behind and Mount Columbia beckoning us on.

With tired hungry horses we camped where a few spears of grass through the open forest were only a tantalising aggravation, and the rest of the day was taken to search for the best way to get to the Thompson Pass. It was certainly a ghastly camp; the rain fell in torrents, the horses persisted in losing themselves in the thick timber and then crying for each other. "M." and I dried the saddle-blankets and cooked the meals with the rain trickling down our backs and were mighty glad when the men returned with the announcement that they had found a way and we could be off next morning.

The ascent of the pass was full of those minor incidents which accompany the breaking of a new trail with horses, the steep, heavily wooded hill-slopes being interspersed with horizontally placed rock ridges, which were a trial to the flesh.

Nibs and myself had been busily getting acquainted for several weeks now, but I was still to learn a good deal more of his character. As he was quite a superior little chap, his saddle had been bought in the east, the cinchas of hair being my special pride.

Climbing up one narrow rock-ledge after another we were making progress foot by foot, pausing while a tree was felled, creeping a little farther, and pausing again. Suddenly after a short bit of stiff travelling, Nibs turned his head and gazed at me from one soft brown eye. It was such a suggestive look that I patted him on the neck, said: "All's well, my pet," and shoved ahead. In a few moments a worse-than-usual obstruction met us, a rock-ledge three feet high, a huge log resting across it, and a precipice beside it. To give us each a better chance, I slid from his back and to my surprise the saddle slipped too. Sharply from the rear came the order: "Move on, you are holding back the packs!" If there is one camp trait I do admire it is obedience, so the impulse was to obey promptly. Instead of quickly releasing the back cincha and throwing the saddle clear as I should have done, I straightened the saddle, climbed the rock, and told Nibs to jump. He did, with the inevitable result that the saddle flew back on his rump. In a flash I could see the consequences,—a frightened plunging horse, and a silly rider tossed over a precipice that was a hundred and fifty miles from a doctor. Doing the only thing left to do, I seized his bit and spoke to him. He became quiet instantly, then slowly turned his head to see what made the rumpus behind him, turned gently back, popped his soft little nose into my buckskin coat, and trembled with the fright of what he did not understand.

Wise little Nibs! I loved him before, after that,—well who wouldn't? Chief peering down from above, called: "Well, I'd like to see any other horse in this outfit do that; you're pretty lucky!"

Never again did I fail to examine matters

if Nibs paused and told me something was wrong, and never again will I be guilty of buying eastern saddlery for western use.

The second hairbreadth escape I found later recorded in "M's" diary. She saw it, I did not, though it was my hair that was involved. I copy it as she left it. "A little farther up we were waiting on another ledge for 'Chief' to cut down a tree which blocked the way, the tree fell a little nearer the horses than he meant it to and frightened Pinto. Pinto jumped back, hit M., knocked her sprawling (her hairpins flew in every direction), and stepped on her foot. Very painful for the moment, but no serious damage as I was afraid when I saw her roll over on her back with her yellow slicker arms waving in the air, Pinto doing fancy steps over her."

After these two small incidents interspersed with plenty of scrambling and tussling, at six thousand feet we came to a lovely ultramarine lake about a half mile in length. From its left rose a picturesque peak, and at its head stretched a fine rock wall from mountain-side to mountain-side, with spruces nestled in the ledges.

Making our way round to the right of the lake the horses were soon up to their necks in alpine flowers. Columbines nodded their yellow heads from stalks three feet tall, while deep blue larkspurs, snowy valerian, flaming castilleia, and golden arnicas hailed our coming with flying colours.

With tents pitched in our ready-made garden, the exquisite lake lying before us and reflecting the rocky peak, there seemed little else for which to wish. As the night swept down upon us bringing with it the icy wind from the surrounding glaciers, a great camp-fire cast gleaming flashes across the blackening waters and drove from our home the biting breath of the frost.

Was it the cold sifting through the blankets the next morning, or was it the beauty of the place that woke me, or was it only the incessant tap of Pinto's bell at the first gleam of dawn? It matters not, they were all there;

Lake Nashan lay stretched before us dark and still, and far above her towered the mountains tipped with the first rays of daylight.

The rest of the camp was asleep; I was all alone; all was so peaceful, it seemed more like a wonderful dream than reality, and I dared not mar it with a sound. Creeping gently down among the blankets, I tried to catch a fugitive nap, but the picture outside kept enticing me, so that at six, at the risk of snapping a twig and thus rousing those who needed sleep far more than scenery, I slipped from the comforts of bed and watched the coming of the day. The trees, the bushes, and the hardy little alpine flowers were all festooned with millions of frost needles, and as the sun's rays touched them, I saw their beauty die. Two ducks from the near-by marsh grasses craned their necks toward the stranger, swam cautiously out, and silently paddled by, peering at me with bright, unafraid eyes; the amphitheatre of snowy summits was tipped with a rosy flush and the aquamarine tints of the lake were richer and deeper than the night before.

There was no more going back to that bed. I was too afraid of missing some of the play. So gathering together some frosty sticks and a little paper from our precious horde, a bright fire was soon sending a straight column of smoke into the still air, a glow of warmth into an over-enthusiastic body. Then the little tea-kettle and I sat there and sighed as we watched the old sun start on his daily round.

Breakfast an hour later tasted especially good, even the water-soaked coffee improving in flavour, and by ten o'clock we were ready for a tour of Thompson's Pass and any comfortable-looking peak whereby we might have a glimpse of the Columbia ice-fields from the south side.

The ascent to the pass is short and sharp, being over and around a series of rock-ledges similar to those up which we had dragged the horses the day before. At the last ledge we paused and looked back on my morning dream now bathed in the noon sunshine. The lake,* green as an emerald, lay like a forgotten gem at

* Cinema Lake

—54—

Watchman's Peak from Thompson Pass

the foot of the rugged rock masses, our tents like butterflies nestled among the flowers; Watchman's Peak (Outram) guarded his charges silently; across his shoulder Mount Alexandra's snowy slope glistened, and in the north-east Mount Saskatchewan stood out boldly among the lesser mountains.

Over the park-like hills all carpeted with trollius, snow lilies, and heather we made our way, till reaching the highest point of the pass, we stood at 6800 feet and looked toward the west. . A richly timbered valley spread before us, from which flowed a small stream and joined the main river coming from a valley at right angles to the one down which we looked.

I do not recollect seeing a sign of sheep or goat throughout this short but beautiful climb, but the turning of the sod by bears in search of rodents, which form for them such a delicious meal, was remarkable. It was for all the world as though a lot of pigs had been

turned loose in an orchard. In many places I felt that my arch enemy of the hills (the grizzly) was just around the corner, so kept close to Chief's heels with a sub-conscious sentiment that he might be chewed up first, for there was no tree to climb that would do me much good.

The Bush Valley from this point looked so free from trouble and care, it was very hard to realise that it was the cause of so much annoyance to Dr. Collie and his party in 1900.

Turning our eyes from the valley to Mount Bryce on our right, two pairs of enquiring eyes gauged his slopes for a possible short ascent. Possibly from no other point is this mountain so impressive as from the Thompson Pass. It looked very compact with its snowy ridges standing forth boldly in the sun, and a fine glacier-tongue sweeping down to the level of the pass. A rocky spur of the mountain still farther round to the north held out the hope for which we were looking, so with camera, tripod, and a cake of chocolate we started up its shaley, shifting, sliding slope.

After a hard grind with "two-feet-up, slip-back one," we stood at the height of our ambition and looked into another world. Thirty miles to the north lay Mount Columbia, but far less impressive than the view we had had of it from the Athabaska side. Between us and its pure white summit lay that frozen, snow-packed, silent sea of which we had read in Outram's book. From this point we could easily imagine the course he took from his camp in the valley south of our position, for his long tramp over the ice-fields to the mountain-top. The Twins to the right of Columbia, (one a rocky, the other a snow-covered peak) were also very interesting, and looking to the west and across the Selkirk Range, there seemed mountains enough left to last an ambitious climber for a century.

But it was three o'clock. The winds were biting cold, fingers were growing numb as they manipulated the camera, and though all so rare a sight, won only by a tough scrimmage, we were glad to duck under the ridges and slip and slide down the scree to the grassy meadows of the pass.

Reaching the precipitous rock ridges once more and looking over, the picture indeed was fine. The faint tinkle of the horsebell was heard almost beneath us, the lake looked like glass, and in the evening shadows was more emerald than ever; "M.," doing a bit of forgotten laundry, was sending out great ringlets across the water in her energy, and a blue column of smoke ascending from the camp-fire must surely smell of fried grouse and bacon if only our noses had been long enough to sniff it.

A long "Yoho" from us, a faint reply, and quickly dropping down a thousand feet, we were soon home by the fire to a nice supper of grouse, bacon, apple-sauce, and beans. Doesn't it sound good, and don't you envy us such a feast, when the ceiling of our banquet-hall was the blue sky of the Rockies, the walls the brave old hills themselves, and the orchestra a hermit-thrush singing his vesper notes? To be sure our table had no legs, and the cloth was an old pack-mantle which had seen much service, but health was good, hearts were light, and no ripple of worry from the outside world could touch us.

The three days at Lake Nashan were an oasis in the desert of rain which had been our portion all summer. Domestic duties on the last day were conducted with hot water, soap, darning needles, and stray buttons, and ended with a rosy sunset and brilliant stars,—a sure portent of storm. Consequently it was a great surprise when Pinto wakened me at five o'clock next morning (by chewing our front-door mat), to find the air as keen as Christmas, the frost covering everything, and the lake with not a ripple on it. Photography waits for no one, so I bounded forth with camera and tripod, raced hither and yon in the frosty air, and returned breathless, successful, and half frozen to be asked if I had lost my senses. No, it was only a case of intoxication where the cold and beauty had gone to the brain.

With the usual desire to get under way as early as possible, every one was "stepping lively" after breakfast, and I frantically trying to load plate-holders in the back of the tent, when there came such a crash and clatter it sounded as though the whole bunch of horses, was rushing down upon me. Fearing to light-strike the plates, I remained rooted to the spot, till informed that order was restored. "K's" riding pony, a pale, yellow, ænemic, nervous thing, not over-blessed with sense, had been tied to the fire-place. For some unknown reason he took fright, uprooted the same, and went smashing through the camp dragging the whole thing with him. Such movements were only momentarily disconcerting however, Whitey's actions were quite frowned upon by the rest of the family, and order was quickly restored.

It was hard to go from that beautiful place, to leave the little lake to the butterflies, the gophers, the ducks, the bears, and the flowers. But neither our coming nor going left one ripple on her placid face; born to loneliness she would not miss us. The day remained fair and quiet. Mount Bryce's hoary head shimmered in the sunlight as we dropped over the hill into the timber, and in an hour Mount Lyell, who had persistently remained hidden on our way up, stood forth boldly in the elbow of the valley toward which we were travelling.

Finding a good trail on our left, we were not compelled to stick to the river and again visit the base of Mount Alexandra; but preceded by a friendly-looking lynx which trotted ahead of us for some time on the trail, we emerged on Camp Content, an old camp-ground of Jim's.

Our march of recession down the Nashan was made in pomp and splendour. The day was very warm, and great thunder-clouds rolled across the sky where no clouds had been for three whole days. Alexandra, Lyell, and Gable Peaks looked uncommonly fine decked in their fresh gowns of snow. We wished it were possible to sit facing the horses' tails, to take in all we were leaving behind; not that the horses would mind, but

Horses at Nashan Lake

though the cold nights were shrinking the river very materially, there were many fords left where we were forced to tuck up our toes to avoid a wetting. Then down came the rain, out came the slickers, and we entered Graveyard Camp to the accompaniment of a deluge, pitched our tents among the bones, and gathered sodden sticks for the necessary fire. But it's never home at Graveyard unless it does pour, so no one minded.

9: Off to the Brazeau Country

AFTER a day's rest, our films developed, all food, save that needed for our trip into the Brazeau country, cached safely, we started off again to a new corner of the globe. Two days in camp seemed about all any of us could endure with equanimity; the spirit of the gypsy haunts those valleys and enters the breasts of those who pass the portals, we were now gypsies heart and soul.

We had two objective points in view: to find Brazeau Lake discovered and named by Dr. Coleman in 1892, and then search for a lake said by the Stoney Indians to lie north of the Brazeau and called by them Chaba Imne or Beaver Lake.   Not that the Indians had told us anything of this lake (they are too afraid of the white man trespassing upon their hunting-grounds), but they had mentioned its existence to our friend Jim and he had passed the information on for what it was worth.   Our way was via Camp Parker which lies at the junction of the North Fork and Nigel Creek. Parker, besides being beautifully located, is a very popular camp, as horse-feed is to be had there in unlimited quantities.   But alas for the soullessness of the average camper! When he has drained the last drop from the condensed milk-can, has finished the maple syrup, or cleaned up the honey-jar, he drops the useless vessel on the spot, and Camp Parker has consequently developed into a rubbish heap.   But from long experience I realise that it is useless to ask the rubbish-maker to place a stone in his empty cans and toss them in the river or into a hole, and the other average camper will go on to the end of time tripping over the objectionable stuff.

So, though it was September the 8th and the

best part of the summer gone, we started again for valleys new to us. As we left Camp Parker we found the trail to Nigel Pass led us via the creek of the same name, first through a park-like forest, then over high grass-covered slopes, and finally surmounting the last alpine-flow-ered ridge we turned for a long look back. Mount Saskatchewan stood out above all other peaks and was easily recognised by its marked horizontal stratifications, but Nigel Peak had lost some of its fine symmetry from the different point of view.

At the summit of the pass, the well-marked trail we had followed, died away on the bare rocks but was quickly taken up on turning to the right, crossing the ridge, dropping into a short gully, and climbing a few yards to the stony slopes of the mountain facing us.

The descent from the pass was steep, rug-ged, beautiful but quite unphotographable. A pretty little twin fall greeted us at the foot of the shaley hillside and formed the beginning of the main branch of the Brazeau. This branch, till its junction with the waters from Brazeau Lake, runs through a fine open valley about thirty miles long, and the trail was undoubtedly of Indian manufacture.

About fifteen miles down the valley, seeing better feed on the other side, we crossed the river and found a much more travelled trail than the one we had been following. With saddles and packs tossed off, the horses all hobbled, and minds turned to camp arrange-ments, we looked up to find that every last horse but Pinky had ignored all the surround-ing good feed and betaken himself across the river to mere pickings on the other side, —such is the contrariness of a trail horse! Pinky had meditated a moment too long and for obvious reasons was nabbed and picketed.

"Going" on the Brazeau for two days and not a lake in sight was getting a little trying and

Crossing Nigel Pass

monotonous, so after a hurried lunch, in spite of awful antipathy to climbing, I decided to join forces with "K." and see if by chance that lake could be located. A stony ridge on the opposite side of the river looked as though from its summit one might peer into two or three valleys which apparently converged several miles east of us, and it seemed as though Brazeau Lake might lie in one of them. The two of us mounting the disgusted Pinky sallied across the torrential stream, the rear passenger expecting at any moment to slip into a watery grave; then tethering our steed for the return trip, we struck off up the scrubby hill. At about 7000 feet, on emerging from the thick timbers, we looked below and had our first glimpse of the lake. Unlike most of the lakes in those mountains it seemed utterly devoid of colour and quite uninteresting from that altitude; very long and narrow, it was fed from large glaciers at its northern end, and from these rose a fine snowy peak. When a few months later we obtained Coleman's report on his visit to this section, a paper which would have been of inestimable value to us at the time, we found he had called this peak "Mount Brazeau," had made an unsuccessful attempt to climb it, and considered it a mountain over 11,000 feet high. Just at dusk, weary but successful, we stumbled upon Pinky at the river's edge, mounted him, and ferried over, where emerging into the light of the camp-fire, the sizzling bacon and a big fruit-cake looked wonderfully good to appetites sharpened on the scree of the mountain-top.

It was September the 9th when we crossed the high shoulder of a mountain, dropped down to the main stream, forded it, continued up the river's left bank for a mile, and came upon one of the most beautiful camp-grounds I ever saw. Crossing an open meadow of rich tall grass in which flowers blue, red, and yellow grew, we entered a little theatre whose walls were of spruces. The stage had at one time been set for an Indian hunting-party. There stood the tepee-poles as the actors had used them last,—five lodges. But the grass waved there untrod, moss covered the long-deserted fire-places, and probably many of

those who had last played their part there had gone to the Great Theatre of all. Goat and sheep bones, bleached by many summers' suns, lay strewn about, a little circle of symmetrical pebbles (a favourite plaything of the forest child) told of the sometime presence of children, and a crudely fashioned horse lay on a crumbling log. It was all such a pathetic story, such a bit of the savage life before the days of reservations, when whole families took to the trail for the fall hunt, the bucks to bring down the game, the squaws to skin the animals and smoke the meat; the children to play at the life which for their elders held such little joy. Yes, a deserted stage, the actors gone and for many of them "lights out."

As the day was still young we regretfully left the beautiful spot and again took up the old well-beaten trail we had followed all morning. The outlet of the lake was reached after half a mile, along which distance ancient blazes on the trees pointed to many a line of traps; what a wonderful large and small game country it must have been! We had had an uncommonly wet summer, one cold cheerless day following another, so that the traverse of that lovely six-mile lake in the brilliant sunshine, in spite of stones and fallen timber, was a perfect treat.

A none too satisfactory camp was made at the upper end of the lake where I cannot recollect our horses having much to eat, but they would have to remember, as many times before, a few of the good meals in the past and trust to better days to come.

With the day gone, the stars came forth one by one till the heavens were brilliant, but as the last pine-root fell into glowing coals, and we counted how many blankets we could stand on so balmy a night, there struck upon our ears a mutter of distant thunder. With the gentle pat-pat of the first drops of the coming storm (the sweetest, laziest music of the trail) we dropped asleep. Somewhere toward midnight I waked as a blinding flash of lightning lit up for an instant the tent-walls. The game was on. It seemed as though the giants of the mountains were playing pitch and toss with a

Brazeau Lake

mighty ball, which, as it bounded from crag to crag with roll and rumble and roar, made the four listeners feel their insignificance with the great battle raging above them. The rain came down in torrents; the giants tossing their ball miles away, took up another, tossed it on, and I gladly ducked under the waterproof covers leaving the old fellows to fight it out.

About 5.30 the next morning I roused to the fact that the tent-wall was within an inch of my nose, and something very heavy resting on the bed. Wriggling gently round I saw "M." calmly viewing the situation from her corner of the tent. The ridge-pole had sagged so completely that there was just about a half-inch left till it would drop from the cross poles in front. If there were pounds of snow on my side poor "M." was pinned down by three times that amount. She had n't budged, she dared not, and the snow was still falling thick and fast. Not possessing her calm and unexcitable disposition, I yelled for the life-guard, pulled myself out of my bag, bounded from beneath the danger, and fled to the open, meeting the rescue-party on the way. They, wakened from a sound sleep, looked as though they thought it a case of mountain-lions or bears. The great weight of snow was quickly beaten off, a prop for the ridge-pole placed inside, everybody wished he had had a camera for the other body, and as there was no thought of trailing for that day through a foot of freshly fallen snow in strange country, all retired again to enjoy the uncommon luxury later of a nine o'clock breakfast, for, on the days of march, breakfast was usually at the festive, sometimes chilly, hour of six; and like many another tonic, the dose was often hard to swallow, but the results were fine if the days were hot or wet, and the long lazy afternoons a splendid reward for the bitter pill.

For two days we lay impatiently in camp watching that persistent and aggravating snow, fearful lest the Indian trail to and over the pass to the mysterious lake be cut off for that year. With the first clearing weather, the horses were brought in with frozen hobbles, with icicle-bedecked tails, and camp moved nine miles up the valley over a well-defined trail. Our hopes mounted with the sun, for surely that trail led to something. Apparently it did,—to a great rock wall where the boulders as high as tenement houses lay piled up for five hundred feet, utterly choking off all advance. We gazed at it and at each other hopelessly, smiled grimly, and set up our homes on the gravel-flats.

No one was willing, however, to think the Indians had ever stopped there, and in the afternoon an exploring party ventured forth afoot, climbed around the objectionable stone-pile, and looked down upon a high fair valley of grass and dead flowers, and most welcome of all,—the lost trail. Descending to this valley, we started back on the well-beaten way, and found as fine a bit of trail as we had so far met. Over and around these great rocks we took it up foot by foot, and tumbled into camp, jubilant, as sure of a pass and the new lake now as though we had actually seen it.

The crowning day of our expectations arrived with clouds settling around us like a night-cap. But just as the outfit was in order for the last ascent, the cap lifted, and our spirits and the horses mounted together the devious, winding, hidden way in the giant stone-pile. Beyond stretched the open meadow, then stiff forest-clad slopes. Timber-line was reached and passed, grassy slopes succeeded, hope held, and still we climbed. And then the grass failed us and dwarf willows took its place. Here and there a bit of alpine goldenrod still held its head bravely against the frost, and frozen little for-get-me-nots drooped theirs; to right and to left of us, rocks ever rocks, and on the mountain-sides ahead, miles of glaciers closing in about us. The higher peaks of this unknown coun-

try were shut away from our eager eyes by the low, tantalising clouds from which came flurries of snow, and the icy winds shrieked about us.

On we stumbled through the deepening snow, sometimes on, sometimes off our horses (it was so perishingly cold!), till we could have been at little less than 8500 feet, and still no gateway opened in those limitless walls to let us through and down into some warm valley with an unnamed lake hidden away in it.

Beyond all sign of verdure a halt was called, and a tour of inspection made. It was certainly a dreary scene. Only the rocky niches could hold the powdery snow against the hurricane, leaving the black forbidding cliffs to stand in bold outline against the wintry sky. From out the clouds to our left and before us, fell glacier after glacier forming a semicircular frontage of quite two miles. In a rock-bound valley below us was the only bit of colour in the whole scene, two cold steel-blue alpine lakes. A dreary, weary, hopeless waste, and not a gleam of sunshine to lighten our lagging steps!

While in bitterness of spirit "M." and I took in the woe-begone condition, and stamped our feet and chafed our chilled fingers, Chief and "K.," on foot, were climbing the final knoll to look into the last beyond. Our reveries were suddenly broken by a sharp yell and violent gesticulations toward the great black mountain opposite us. We had not the faintest idea what to look at, and saw only a perpendicular wall a thousand feet high whose side face seemed covered with sheet ice. In a few moments the men joined us. On the last rise they had surprised (and been surprised by) a band of mountain-sheep. The beautiful creatures had probably never seen a human being before, or if so, only their arch enemy the Indian hunter; both parties had stood paralysed for a second, when the sheep, on the alert, had turned and fled up the precipitous icy rock-face faster than our eyes could follow them. It was easier to note their progress by the falling stones which their little feet loosened, than to follow their quickly moving bodies against the dark rocks. Even the most skilled mountain-climber would scarce have attempted the difficult route over which they bounded as though crossing a meadow of upland grass. Reaching the high and inaccessible crags they paused, and gazed upon us far below; then a magnificent ram appeared to take the lead. The others disappeared, but the massive head of the leader with his great horns stood motionless against the grey sky, his attitude alert, his body immovable. Only as we moved back and down the valley could we see that he shifted his position sufficiently to keep us in view.

Such a picture! The dreary wastes of naked rock, the cold glistening glaciers all about us, the early snows in the unexposed niches, the dying alpine flowers at our feet, then far aloft clinging to the great black crags outlined against an angry sky, that emblem of the vanishing wilderness, the Rocky Mountain sheep!

It was intensely interesting to watch them, but the day was growing late, the men reported that beyond the knoll it was utterly impossible to drag a horse, and we had far to return. Cold and discouraged, with mouths watering for those mutton-chops so completely out of reach, we consoled ourselves with the real beauty of the statuesque creatures looking down upon us, and as we could not get them, waved them a generous "good-bye" and meekly descended all those hills of weariness we had been six to eight hours climbing.

There was just one solution for that well-defined trail which had so insidiously led us on, *i.e.*, so numerous were the signs of wild life that many an Indian must have led his horse to those far cliffs to bring down the trophies of the chase; and yet—well, I'd like to take the Stoney Indian up there who was responsible for such a trudge, and see if we really might have pushed through after all.

That night the disappointed explorers camped above the big rock-pile with the thermometer standing at 20° and a fine snow sifting down. The next day that instrument refusing to emerge from the twenties, we dawdled in camp, shampooed with snow-water, and anxiously scanned the sky as well as the receding bacon, counted how few of the fall weeks remained, and the distance yet from a railroad track.

10: Jonas Pass and a Pair of Snow-Blind Eyes

SNOW-STORM after snow-storm swept across our trail as we retraced our disappointed steps down Brazeau Lake and up the south side of the stream flowing from Nigel Pass. But discouraging as the conditions were, the nearness of Jonas Pass and its reputed grandeur tempted us to stop a couple of days to take a look at it. Camp was pitched opposite Cataract Pass (our homeward route), and the next morning, taking all the horses and enough of our diminished stores to last three days, we plodded up a very steep hill by a well-marked trail, soon struck snow, and stuck to it. At the summit, the sun broke forth brilliantly, and the horses plunging and stumbling to their cinchas in snow, we made a slow and weary march across and down the north slope of this glowingly described pass. Tracks of birds, foxes, rabbits, and other small animals entertained us to some extent, but refused to take my mind completely from a pair of dark glasses reposing forty miles away in our cache at the North Fork.

The scenery for which we were enduring so much discomfort failed to prove very exciting, and not till we caught sight of a fine black bear a quarter of a mile ahead of us, very busily engaged pawing for berries beneath the snow, did any of us rouse from the lethargy which had settled upon us all.

"K." was out of the saddle removing his rifle almost before any one could remonstrate with him; then he suddenly remembered an accident of a few days before, when the front sight of said rifle had come in violent contact with some harder substance and removed it bodily from its point of usefulness. He was a good shot, however, and could not bear to let one of the finest pelts of the summer go, for the mere absence of a front sight. While the rest of us held the horses back, "K." slipped quietly forward and the next moment was out of sight.

The bear still pawed in the snow for his berries. We waited. Then came a loud report. The bear raised his head and looked about. Was he hit? A second report followed; the listening bear shook himself savagely and started across the valley in the direction "K." had gone. The next few moments to the watchers were uncomfortable in the extreme and we waited for the third shot. Nothing came. When sufficient time had elapsed for "K." to have skinned the bear or the bear to have made a meal of him, we moved up. It looked very strange, there was the point in the snow where "K." had knelt to fire at the bear, there beside his footprints were those of a bleeding bear, the blood-spots trailing off uphill, then we saw "K." had followed him, and silence still reigned about. It was very cold, the snow was at least a foot deep, and we were all tired, but where was "K."?

Chief built a fire and again we waited, the horses stood about and occasionally doubled up and tried to lie down with their heavy packs. Waiting at last seemed useless, and we started ahead to look for some very necessary feed. One hundred yards from this resting point we took up "K's" trail; he was following the bloody tracks of the wounded bear which was travelling down the valley, and we with the hungry horses followed on behind.

Gradually the snow disappeared, the sun was setting, a chill wind swept up the valley, no feed was to be found to right or to left, nor did "K." materialise. We finally made camp on the only open spot that was not covered with trees, and *it* was covered with stones. Just as the last tired horse was unpacked "K." walked into camp, a weary and disgusted hunter. His second shot had hit the bear, the next three cartridges had missed fire, he had followed the wounded animal for miles in the snow and at last lost it on a rock slide. We were very glad to get "K." back safe and sound, the pelt amounting to very little to us, who had been stretched so long on the rack of suspense.

That one night on the far side of Jonas Pass finished the region for every one of our

Descending from Cataract Pass

party. The poor horses, weary with the long drag of nine miles up the pass and five down on the other side, with nothing but heather on which to make a meal, were in forlorn condition. As for us, anchored on a stone-pile and held there by the same, we were in momentary fear of being uprooted and blown back up the pass by the high wind which had now become a hurricane. The smoke, from the very small fire which we dared have in that blast, swept into our tent and eyes, so that by 7:30, after a supper which tasted like chilled candle-grease, I crept to bed with painfully sore eyes, and wished I was back on the Brazeau.

Not a lingering look was dropped behind as we left that miserable camp the next morning and hurried back across the blinding wastes of snow. The hungry horses trudged faithfully and doggedly through the deep, sticky stuff, now warm and yielding from a chinook wind; but once over the summit they hurried down, slipping and sliding, anything to get to the good feed which they knew awaited them in the Brazeau Valley.

Cataract Pass will always remain a hideous nightmare to me. Thoroughly blinded by this time from two days' sunshine on snow, my eyes were bandaged, and I let Nibs follow as best he could, close behind Chief who was in the lead. Now Nibs is nothing if not clever, but he certainly did not take any account of twigs and branches which concerned any other head than his own.

All went well in the open, but the moment we struck timber, bang went the branches, scratch went the trees, and an occasional tear of self-pity fell on the passing landscape.

But if troubles were numerous in the wood, the plot thickened on the snow-laden heights for all. Any sign of trail was completely buried under from one to three feet of dry powdery snow, through which the horses broke to the otherwise undetected boulders beneath. Time and again they fell, almost disappeared, struggled up, and floundered on. The trail-breaker crunched doggedly along, old Pinto plunged and tumbled just behind, the saddle-horses came next in the procession, the snow-blind eyes were of little use in finding where the last hoof had trod, the sympathetic friend just behind was helpless to aid, and the rest of the band, urged and yelled at by turns, completed the forlorn procession. At the summit of the pass was a frozen lake and I believe the sight was a very fine one, but personally it took photographs to prove it later. Over the crest and down, the way was good, bad and indifferent, the "bad" being caused by former enormous snow-slides, which had strewn the way with fallen timber.

It was now the 27th of September, already we had lost three days out of schedule time, the food we had counted upon for this last side-trip was getting uncomfortably low, the main cache was sixty miles away by trail, so the order went forth that we must make a couple of forced marches to the Saskatchewan

Plains, where we could at least get a few pounds of flour and bacon from Tom Wilson before ascending the river to our own cache at Graveyard Camp. I confess to a huge lump in the throat at the thought of doing double duty on the trail practically blind, but to whimper over a pair of eyes seemed weak indeed, with hunger as an alternative for the crowd, so there was nothing to do but to crawl up in the saddle and trust to getting down whole again. Fortunately the predicament was obvious, even to Nibs himself, and the little fellow was led ignominiously the next ten miles by the halter-shank, thoroughly appreciating that something was wrong and treating his burden as though it were a basket of eggs.

In spite of the united care of the family, on reaching Pinto Lake and hearing the welcome order to dismount, there were several nasty blows to remember, sundry buttons torn off, and bruises galore. Everybody was now awake to the fact that there could be no further thought of proceeding, and a day's hard work for the men by remaining, for they must cross the Pinto Pass, whose troubles they had assailed from the other side the year before, and dear knows if they could get a horse across to bring back the heavy loads. But certain it was that beyond that pass lay our cache, and food we must have.

With the sensations of a criminal, I listened to the preparations for the attempted climb next day. The three strongest horses were chosen, and ropes, pack-mantles, and saddles laid out. At 5 A.M. I heard whisperings, the crackling of a small fire, then the snap of twigs beneath the horses' feet, and knew they were off. At 8:30 good eyes, assisted by a pair of binoculars, made out the outline of one horse on the sky-line, in a little while a second, and then a third. For a few moments five black spots dotted the top of the snow-ridge as though taking breath, and then stepped from sight, and we turned about to find the bannock as black as a pot, burned!

As usual, washing and photography filled in the hours, though the semi-blind being rather useless at such accomplishments kept herself employed gathering in a large supply of logs for what might be a very necessary beacon for the home-comers.

The day passed, we ate our lonely supper, listened and waited, but they did not come; washed up our dishes and sat there in the gloom still listening. With the twinkle of the first star, and croak of the frogs in the near-by swamp, we began to throw on the laboriously gathered logs; threw them on till the black spruces stood out like spectres in the glare. Even the owls hooted at us by this time. It grew quite dark, a little breeze sprang up, and suddenly it bore to us a very distant "Yoho!" Everything else was forgotten, on went a log, and yet another, the little breeze brought a nearer call, the preciously hoarded wood was thrown recklessly into the flames, and in a half hour the men stumbled in weary and hungry. "Hungry?" "Yes." "Tired?" "No." (Great relief to the one responsible for so much trouble.) We flew to frying the prepared bacon and potatoes (pridefully adding a couple of ten-inch trout to the feast), while the packs from the three horses were being quickly tossed to the ground.

Tired did I say, and they denied it? With the last pack-saddle removed and halters off, — no need for hobbles, — the three horse which we expected to see scurry off into the dark bush where the leader's bell was distinctly audible, slowly betook themselves a little beyond the pale of the camp-fire and lay down. No use to ask further if the day had been a hard one, — *we knew.*

When pipes were lighted and a little more wood piled on, we gathered round to hear the events of the day. The distance from camp to cabin was fifteen miles. On nearing the game-trail at the top, which we had found and slid down the year before, they came upon a large mass of old winter's snow. In this they were compelled to cut footing for the horses and lead them up one by one to the ice-encrusted rocks which were the last barrier.

Across the summit of the pass the way was easy enough, and the blazes on the east side of the pass, which they had cut in 1906, did away with any trouble at the far end of the line. But there are limitations to horse mountaineering, specially when on the return they were loaded with two hundred pounds of food apiece; and the way being over ice-bound rocks, then fields of frozen snow, and lastly a steep descent through unbroken forest, it had all told on the staunch old standbys Fox, Buck, and Brownie, and they showed the effect of the trip for some time after.

In the shack where they found all in good condition, were two notes from "Jim." We had been out fifteen weeks and this was the first mail we had received in all that time. It was touch and go between that note and a can of freshly-opened maple-syrup as to which we enjoyed the most, but I think the note took precedence. It was written on paper torn from a fruit-can and ran somewhat in this manner: He had started out to stake timber at Fortress Lake and while camped near Wilson Creek on the north side of the Saskatchewan, his horses had crossed the river on him during the night and, as he said, the thermometer being somewhat less than seventy below zero at the time, he did not care to swim the river to get them, so he stood on the bank opposite them for a while, talked to them, told them what he thought of them, and specified where he hoped they would go to next, etc., and then lit out on foot to make some tall crow-hops northward, expecting to finish up his round trip in ten days. The first letter being written on September the 13th and the second one at the same place on the 20th, the distance being about two hundred miles, the "Rev. James" certainly deserves his Indian title, "Wolverine-go-quick."

11: On the Golden Plains of the Saskatchewan

The Beacon in Cataract Valley

THE distance from Pinto Lake via Cataract Creek* to the Saskatchewan River is about twenty-five miles; it has been a favourite highway for centuries, as the well-worn trails show, and the fine fishing at the lake still brings a small band of Stoneys there year by year.

The red hunters' camp-sites, many tepee-poles, and bones galore lined the route; fires for years have swept hither and yon, so it was not altogether an attractive trail after leaving the lake.

Mount Coleman, still decked with the snows which had been our undoing in the Brazeau country, made a great showing in the brilliant sunshine the morning of our departure. Near-by hills, however, soon shut the rugged old fellow from sight, leaving us a fine isolated peak, whose summit at first appeared only as a large knob, which changing to

a wedge as we receded from it, remained in sight almost to the Saskatchewan, and for his guardianship we named him our "Beacon."

From the clear crisp atmosphere of the higher valleys we now plunged down upon the golden Kootenai Plains on September the 26th. Storms may rage north, south, and west, but they seldom invade this peaceful spot, where only the soft chinook winds blow almost constantly, and consequently our arrival was heralded by millions of sand-flies. Into eyes, ears, noses and mouths of man, woman and beast, they rushed. The poor horses, free for several weeks from such pests, were frantic, and rushed ceaselessly about unable to enjoy the grass which was there in abundance on the Cataract Flats* and for which they had probably been longing for the last two days.

Temporarily the wind was not blowing, so a smudge was lighted, and the tormented

* Cline River

* Cline River Flats

creatures crept up and were soon at peace in the choking smoke. Then came the wind at sunset, and old Paul Beaver, a well-known Stoney, and his dog came to call; the horse-bells settled to a quiet "clang, clang" and Paul sat puffing his pipe at our fireside waiting for an invitation to the supper his eyes greedily watched cooking. But our provisions were reaching that point where it was dangerous to invite any guests, specially Indians, to a meal, so we downed all hospitable inclinations, and without a qualm watched him ride away on his handsome buckskin just as darkness was falling.

The next morning the chinook wind was gone and with it the flies, and a howling wind was sweeping from the north with angry clouds everywhere but over our heads, when another kind of a howl went up in the kitchen department,—a fine bannock had disappeared in the night. That brindle cur of Paul's, of course; those half-starved dogs of the Indians, are all consummate thieves.

Just as the tents were coming down up rode Paul smiling and amiable, squatted down by the fire, and solemnly drew forth from the folds of his blanket-coat a dirty old cotton bag. Trade, of course, what had he? Turning it upside down and shaking it gently, out came four turnips for which he wanted as much sugar as he could coax from us. But sugar was low, and a tea-cup of tea satisfying him, we captured the first fresh vegetables we had seen for three months, and Paul rode off with his tea.

As our route now lay toward the sources of the Saskatchewan River, it had to be forded twice, first at the Cataract Flats and again a mile above Rabbit Creek, as the trail is impracticable on the north side between these points owing to much fallen timber. During the mid-summer floods, these cross-ings are a matter for deep consideration, and never at any time a subject to be treated as a joke. As frequently as we had forded both points, familiarity had taught us no contempt for the work ahead of us; a certain ever-present danger, a washed-out ford, a stumbling horse,

* Whiterabbit Creek

are thoughts ever in the mind of one who understands the situation.

I shall never forget the first time we essayed the feat. It was in our early camping-days, we and our nerves were still an uncertain quantity to Chief, and as we wished to make a trip to Wilcox Pass in the very height of the summer, he first prepared the way by charging our minds with tales gleaned from every hunter and explorer who had come to grief in those wild waters in the past ten years, the number of horses drowned, boats upset, etc. As we stood the harrowing stories and still held out for the trip, a preliminary jaunt was arranged for one sunny afternoon. The horses had been selected from a bunch bred in the district as they were known to be good swimmers. "M's" was a little buckskin, mine a huge lumbering bay.

With solemnity due the occasion we dropped over a high bank into the river, and then into a hole where the water promptly surged right up to the waist-line; the temperature being only 42 degrees, there was an unuttered desire for a little warm weather. Almost as quickly as we had gone in we came out on a warm sand-bar, and from that point on, dropped into one arm of the river after an-other, till dripping with water we emerged on the steep bank of the north side. A quick can-ter (fancy anything quick on my cart-horse) over the sunny plains and we struck the river a little farther west for the return trip, not having done any actual swimming so far; all the dread the two tenderfeet had was the bath of 42°. Chief and "M." went in first. The waters at this crossing were not looking quite so peaceful as the first one, and my escort called out,—"Keep your horses' heads up-stream!" In the pounding and splashing Chief did not catch the words, and turning to see what was wrong, his horse lost ground, and the next mo-ment, to my horror, I saw four heads rapidly bobbing down-stream. "Well, Joe," I said, "it looks like the last of our friends. I suppose we must get over if we can and see if there is anything left of them to need help," and with the reiterated warning from behind to "head up-stream" the big bay and I stepped down and in. Giving the old fellow his head and planting my feet firmly down in the stirrups to prevent their natural tendency to come to the surface and float in front of me, I abandoned life, fright, everything, and watched in numbness that angry flood. The big bay never faltered. As the headlong waters struck him I could feel the big body quiver and pause, then move slowly forward, halt again as a fresh surge swept down upon him, and then deliberately advance. Thus were the twenty or thirty yards of that ugly branch of the river mastered, and as we came to the stiller waters I looked up to see the mourned friends, dripping wet, but calmly sitting on their horses just at the point of our emergence, an undisguised grin of amusement on their faces as "they wished they had a camera," (so did I). Thus ended our first lesson in mountain rivers, a lesson which has stood us in good stead many times since.

But now back to the Kootenai Plains—there is no describing them. To appreciate them one must breathe their breath deep into the lungs, must let the soft winds caress the face, and allow the eye to absorb the blue of the surrounding hills and the gold of the grasses beneath the feet. To us, who had been storm-swept, chilled, and baked by turns in the outlying valleys, it was simply heaven. No wonder that the Indians from Morley go there year after year; I only wonder that the whole tribe does not attempt to move in, in a body.

To see the Plains at their best, one should come over the Pipestone trail in August, and look down on the scene from the rolling hills of the south. Then the golden-brown of the ripened grasses floods the valley with light, for miles the river winds and twists from west to east, an occasional Indian shack comes into view, the faint ringing of a bell denotes that a few tiny specks on the landscape are really horses, and the white dots are tepees of the Indians. Here the air is sweeter, dryer, and softer than anywhere I know, and here the world could easily be forgotten and life pass by in a dream.

But on the day in question no one had any particular desire to dissolve even in dreams

while the work of two crossings lay ahead of us. Like many other anticipated troubles, they were passed with the least possible annoyance, and "M." and I with only wet stockings and moccasins, leaving the outfit to trudge along at its usual gait, took a sharp canter across the valley to our prospective camp-ground.

Winding in and out among the yellowing poplars, we spied two tepees nestled deep among the trees. I often wonder when passing an Indian camp-ground, be it ancient or modern, if ever for an instant the natural beauty of a location consciously appeals to them. I have seen not one but many of their camps and seldom or never have they failed to be artistic in their setting, and this one was no exception. Knowing they must be Silas Abraham's and Sampson Beaver's families, acquaintances of a year's standing, I could not resist a hurried call. The children spied us first, and tumbling head over heels, ran to cover like rabbits; mongrel dogs barked and yapped, and above the din and excitement I called, "Frances Louise!" She had been my little favourite when last we were among the Indians, accepting my advances with a sweet baby womanliness quite unlike the other children, for which I had rewarded her by presenting her with a doll I had constructed from an old table-napkin stuffed with newspaper, and whose features were made visible to the naked eye by the judicious use of a lead-pencil. Necessity constructed that doll, love blinded the little mother's eyes to any imperfections, and the gift gave me a spot of my own in the memory of the forest baby; to call her name was to introduce myself. In an instant her little face appeared at the tepee-flap, just as solemn, just as sweet, and just as dirty as ever. She turned and spoke to some one inside, and in a moment out came three smiling, dirty squaws, who looked as though wash-days were not over numerous, but whose welcome was very cordial as they came forward one by one, each wiping her hands on her skirt before touching my glove. Such grimy paws, but such shapely ones they were, so small and dainty, with tapering fingers, that their white sister, bending from her saddle,

Sampson Beaver and his family

envied them. Little Frances was evidently told to shake hands, and promptly put up a tiny replica of her mother's, all covered with sticky dough.

And then we all chattered at once, one in English, the others in Stoney, the only intelligible word I caught being "Yahe-Weha," a name they had given me the year before, meaning the "Mountain Woman." In five minutes they knew where we would camp, that they were invited to call, that their men were away working, and that we had just crossed the river and had come from the north, all with smiles and signs. Then waving adieu we trotted off to take a peep into Mr. Barnes' shack (the only other white resident of the valley besides Tom Wilson), to see if he was home, and then size up the situation for a three-day camp-site.

The four days of September slipped away before we knew it in this ideal play-ground. When I hear those "who know," speak of the sullen, stupid Indian, I wish they could have been on hand the afternoon the white squaws visited the red ones with their cameras. There were no men to disturb the peace, the women quickly caught our ideas, entered the spirit of the game, and with musical laughter and little giggles, allowed themselves to be hauled about and pushed and posed in a fashion to turn an artist green with envy. The children forgot their rabbit-like shyness, and copied their elders in posing for us; then one of them would suddenly remember he was hungry, would rush to the tepee, seize a lump of meat or a bone from a pot swung over a small fire, and rush out again shiny with the grease thereof. Yahe-Weha might photograph to her heart's content. She had promised pictures the year before, she had kept the promise, and she might have as many photographs now as she wanted.

Personal experience has shown me that the Indian has the vanity of his white brethren,

Indian tepees on the Saskatchewan

but he is not going to pose for nothing. I have no belief in their superstitious dread of photography, at least so far as the Plains Indians are concerned; it is simply a matter of fair trade.

The last evening of our stay was devoted to a dinner-party with Mr. Barnes as host, a dinner-party where some of the guests were in buckskin shirts and overalls and some in short skirts and moccasins, where the table had been put together with an axe and the chairs were logs, where the plates were of tin, and the grouse and bacon served from the frying-pan. The solitary candle joined forces with a big open fire in lighting the rough-hewn rafters, the log walls, and the faces of the merry unconventional guests.

With the dinner finished, some one remembered what the cost of a candle (seventy-five miles from the railroad) must be, and conscientiously blew out the light. Then we settled

down in front of the fire, pipes were lighted, and the best part of the day was now to come. A gentle, almost imperceptible pat on the earth floor caused me to turn quickly and peer into the darkness beyond. The sight brought back the life of other days. The door had swung silently open, and from the blackness outside into the red glare stepped Silas and Sampson, in moccasined feet, so quietly that it was just a mite creepy. There was no salutation, they simply joined the group and like ourselves gazed silently into the leaping flames. As Sampson crouched forward on his knees to light his pipe at the fire, his swarthy face lighted up by the bright glow, his brass earrings and nail-studded belt catching the glare, with long black plaits of glossy hair, and his blanket breeches, I was glad for even this picture which in a few years can be no more.

As Silas spoke a certain amount of English and the shrewd Sampson understood all that was said, it was a good time to ask a few questions. Silas had been making a few mild jokes (it is so hard to associate jokes with Indians whom most of us have only met in books), and both of them had been laughing heartily at our lame attempts to pronounce some of their words, so the atmosphere seemed propitious. Beginning, I said: "Silas, do you really let your squaw saddle and pack your horses?" "Sure." (How well he had learned English!) "And let her fix the tepee-poles and put up the tepee?" "Yes." "And get the wood, and cook, and tan the skins?" "Yes, sure!" (He was growing impatient at so much quizzing.) The time seemed ripe for some missionary work which was perceptibly needed along more lines than one, and every one else had stopped to listen. "Now, Silas," I said impressively, "you should be like the white men, you should do the work for your squaw. *We* do not put up our tepees or pack our horses or cut the wood, our men do that." Taking his pipe from his mouth and inspecting me from head to foot leisurely, he said, "You lazy!"

The missionary effort went to the floor with a bang and every one burst out laughing (at the missionary, of course) and she only recovered herself enough to say, "And what do you do while your squaw works?" "This," and he folded his arms, closed his eyes, and puffed away at his pipe. But the rest of them need not have laughed, his look of contempt had swept round and included every man who had so demeaned himself as to be placed in such straits by a woman. The burst of laughter, however, had shown Silas that his company and wit were appreciated, and for an hour he and Sampson positively scintillated with brilliancy, and then, without a word of parting, stole out into the darkness to their tepees, going for all the world, not as two noble braves, but like a couple of scared youngsters afraid of their shadows. And then we too said goodnight and groped out to find our own tents, far

Elliott Barnes demonstrating his camera to a Stoney

more afraid of stubbing our toes in the darkness than in fear of the spirits which the Indians think wander abroad after dark.

One of the greatest trophies we carried with us when leaving the next day for the North Fork of the Saskatchewan was a tiny grubby bit of paper on which Sampson had with much care traced the lake we had tried so hard to find, which was supposed to lie north of Brazeau Lake. He had been there but once, a child of fourteen, and now a man of thirty, he drew it from memory,—mountains, streams, and passes all included. They had to be labelled for our benefit, for he had probably never seen a geography in his life, and it would be hard to remember for a whole year that a very scribbly spot was a pass, and that something which looked like a squashed spider he called a mountain.

12: The Valley of the Lakes, Then Back to Civilisation

AND now for one last flight before our footsteps should be irrevocably turned toward home. James Outram in his book *Heart of the Canadian Rockies* describes a valley he saw from the summit of Mount Lyell. He says:

"An interesting feature was the discovery of the extent of one of the western tributaries of the North Fork, hitherto mapped as short and of very minor rank. It now appeared as a deep enshadowed trough, jewelled with a host of little lakes, and fed by a considerable glacier which apparently descends from Mount Lyell's eastern peak, between two splendid walls of rock that sever it from the great Lyell Glacier on the south and the west branch valley on the other side. This valley has been named 'Valley of the Lakes.'"

And though October had now appeared upon our calendar, we risked yet a few more days, trusting that no serious storms would descend upon the strange pass (Baker, near Field, B. C.) by which we hoped to make our way back to the world, and thus give us trouble at the last. Literally it was the name of the valley that tempted us and appealed to our imaginations.

From the camp at the junction of the North Fork and the main river, we travelled up the east bank of the former for nine miles. Here, as the water was low, we easily made a crossing, where, finding no trail, "M." and I sat down in a slough till the men returned in half an hour to say that they had come across a good Indian trail. As far as the red man is concerned it must have been many a year since his moccasined feet trod that moss-covered way. The trail was beaten and worn, but overgrown and impeded with large fallen trees, and only the blaze of a white man's axe seven or eight feet above the ground showed that a hunter ("Jim," perhaps,) had gone that way in the dead of winter to try his luck with trap and rifle.

No sooner did we leave the river than we plunged into a thick growth of spruce, climbing constantly for two hours. Reaching comparatively level ground, we plodded on through closely grown and exasperating pines, so thick and so nearly impregnable, that even our now depleted packs could not be forced through in many places, until the axe rang out and woke the silence which lay like a pall over everything. So dark and still was this bit of primeval forest, that no sign of life was seen on the way; it seemed that with the passing of the Indian had passed also the need for the little people of the wood; and yet, no doubt, bright, terror-stricken eyes were watching the movements of the invaders from every direction.

After six hours' struggling we gave it up and camped by the noisy river, and the tired horses were driven forth to pick a precarious supper from a timber-strewn slide near by. But where were the lakes all this time, the lakes which had tempted us these many troublous miles?

In a rainy, misty sort of sunshine the next morning, we essayed a climb to look for them. How hot it was when the sun beat down upon a protesting climber, how bitter cold the wind from the ice-fields hidden behind the mists! Climb, climb, as we would and did, nothing of interest developed, till, surmounting the last bit of scree, a particularly boisterous wind nearly bowled us both down the slope we had worked so hard to climb, did dislodge a hat, and as we helplessly stood and watched it soaring away on the wind, there appeared in the valley below a chain of— *sloughs!* They were a distinctly disappointing sight, and I wanted to shake somebody when I thought of the tough scramble with the horses the day before. Then I realised how things were. We were probably at an elevation of 7500 feet. Outram had looked down on them from his recorded height of 11,950 feet on Mount Lyell, and his mistake was most excusable. But just at the moment, hot, cold, weary and out of breath by turns, I was certainly disgusted. We had not even the satisfaction of a view of Mount Lyell (if Lyell it was which poked a white shoulder out of the mist occasionally), so pretending not to mind at all, we turned and stumbled down what we had just so breathlessly scrambled up, and a good supper soon made us laugh at our own chagrin.

There was nothing now to do but return by the same way we had come. *We were going home!* Back to friends, the moving world, and to all that makes life's wheels go round! Were we eager to push on and rush into the maelstrom? No! As day by day one familiar peak after another dropped behind, I think we all grew somewhat depressed. Only as the thought of a fresh boiled egg and a cup of tea or coffee made from material which had not spent its summer bobbing around in sundry rivers, and real bread and butter, struck our imaginations, did we rouse to much appreciation of the blessings in store.

Back down the North Fork, across the Middle Fork, making our way among such mountains as Wilson, Murchison, Survey, and Forbes, was a day's travel, and though we had been over it many times before it was still interesting to us.

Our route now being up the Middle Fork and over the Howse Pass, we realised that we were on quite historic ground, historic at least for those hills. Except for the Yellowhead Pass it was probably one of the most used passes after the advent of the Hudson's Bay trading posts. Across it the Kootenai Indians had brought their furs to trade with the men from Jasper House, as far back as the beginning of the nineteenth century. The plains of the Saskatchewan had been the meeting-ground, from which fact has come the name Kootenai Plains, though I personally prefer the musical name the Indians have given, "Kadoona-Tinda," the Windy Plains. Alexander Henry, Jr., also passed this way one hundred years

ago (February, 1811) with dogs and sledges. He speaks of reaching the pass, gazing south on a vast open country, then seems to have turned on his heel and returned the way he came, and been utterly oblivious to the great mountains all about him; at least he wasted no time discussing them Sir James Hector, surgeon for Palliser's party in 1859, came up the Blaeberry (which has its rise in Howse Pass on the south) and in Palliser's report pays most unflattering tribute to the conditions of the country as he found them. Then there were Mr. Stuttfield and Dr. Collie, who, as late as 1898, crossed Howse Pass and attempted to get down the Blaeberry, and though escorted by one of the best woodsmen in the mountains, Bill Peyto, were unable to make it.

I should add here that from a personal knowledge of Peyto he could have gone through anything if given a reasonable time, but, unfortunately, they were about out of "grub" and it was owing to this uncomfortable condition that the Baker Pass was discovered.

I suppose the very fact of a little trouble enticed us on, and, in spite of Dr. Hector's past troubles and Dr. Collie's unflattering comments on the pass of his own finding, we determined to reach Field, (on the main Canadian Pacific line) if possible, by Baker Pass and Beavertail Creek.*

As far as the Howse Pass we found the way perfectly easy, very interesting, and of a great deal of beauty. So gradual was the ascent, that had we not known of that fact before, we might easily have crossed the summit without being aware of it. Horse-feed at the highest point looked as though it might have been fairly good at one time, but plainly, surveyors had been before us and every spear of grass was cleaned up.

But how we blessed those surveyors, blessed them from the moment we struck a marsh, a pool, a tiny stream—the baby Blaeberry. In two miles that stream became a lusty child, kicking and tumbling over rocks and fallen trees in its hurry to get to the sea.

* Amiskwi Pass and River

—75—

An almost tropical growth covered the old scars of Hector's axe, and left no clue as to which was his, the Indians', Peyto's, or chopping of later date. For us there was only the present, for which we were profoundly grateful.

With a most refreshing thoroughness, those surveyors had laid low many impediments of serious moment, and our home-going looked a matter of mere miles. But alas, our unknown friends had had horses which, like our own, had certainly been blessed with good appetites, and for miles had cleaned up every visible source of sustenance.

For guidance and comfort we nightly, hauled Dr. Collie's book and map (our bible, our library for the summer) from the duffel-bag, reinforced our own troubles by reading his, and tried to remember what Bill Peyto had told us when last we met. We reached the "Hunter's Cabin" as laid down on the map, kept on two miles farther; looked for a second, couldn't find it, then struck into a trail on the left which ran beside a tributary of the Blaeberry ("to avoid a deep fissure in the mountain," Peyto said). Ascending this a half-mile, it suddenly lost itself in huge creek boulders which lay in distressing quantities all about us.

Then a horrid uncertainty seized us all: had we done right to leave the good trail so soon and come by this one? Was this the creek with the rock fissure just beyond it? It was one o'clock, too late to do much fencing round; a fresh blaze on the other side of the stream suggested continuing our course. Peyto said the Baker Pass was steep (how his ears must have burned!), and as what we saw looked as though it filled that bill at least, we went on.

Owing to the tremendous pitch of the hill, "M." and I started first, dragging our saddle-ponies after us; it had taken but a few steps for us to decide that we were glad to relieve them of our weight, too ashamed to let them carry us as long as we had strength to walk. The packs, however, had to be left where they were, and the beasts under them to gain what cheer they could from the struggling brethren ahead. My! that was certainly no pleasure

route! So heavy was the grade, that for three or four miles it was far more like going up stairs two steps at a time, than ascending a hill; constantly springing to reach a higher level the horses were soon dripping wet, and yet nothing but hill was in front of them. For two days there had been little for them to eat, it was now two o'clock, and the call came from behind, "Stop at the first feed you see!" On we climbed, the hours passed, a voice would drift up from below, "See anything ahead?" "No." And on we forged. From ferns we passed to blueberry bushes, and from them to moss; then trees gave out, and with them the blazes we had followed doubtingly and questioningly so long, and at five o'clock we stood at about 7000 feet, in icy mud, the horses, with drooping heads, just clutching the stuff with their toes to prevent slipping into the yawning valley below.

Off to the right a snow-pile suggested Mount Mummery, at its base two valleys met, the one we were following at so great a height, and the one we had doubtingly left. No one had dared stop for a bite all day, no feed was in sight, and night coming on. It seemed necessary to be doing something and doing it at once, the horses could not stand another such day. Little matter now if we were on the right trail or wrong, whether we were hungry or cold, food for the workers was all we asked. A hurried conclave was held, "K." started to explore the remaining elevation, while Chief departed to have a look into the yawning valley beyond, and we were left alone, to watch and wait.

The precious minutes flew, the old sun went relentlessly slipping toward the horizon; Mount Mummery stared at us with icy indifference, the horses ceased to move, or we to speak. A sleepy bird chirped, a rock rabbit popped out his inquisitive head from his hole near by, squeaked, and popped back again, a hawk swept by overhead on his search for prey, and still we waited. Then came a distant yell from Chief, trying to locate us, a hurried scramble up, and the welcome words, "I think I see slough-grass ahead in the valley below, and by going around a gorge near here we may reach it before dark. I'd like to know if it's that gorge which made us come over this crazy hill. Come on!" Come? Well I should think we did! There was not a horse that did not seem to understand that word "grass." The dejected heads came up, we slipped and slid around those muddy slopes, circumnavigated the rocky canyon, struck a mossy gully, and dropped the five to seven hundred feet in almost less time than it takes to tell it.

Coming into the valley from the densely wooded hillside, the imprint of a horse's foot on the edge of a stream was the first welcome sight. The second was, grass everywhere, and lots of it. Packs fell off like magic (even our services were not scorned that night), air-beds were pumped up, saddlery stacked, tents put up, and bacon fried, all in chorus and all in about twenty minutes. None too soon either, for, as the beating on a plate with a spoon announced that supper was ready, the darkness became complete, and we ate with a gusto by firelight.

Where were we? No one was very certain and no one cared. There was plenty of everything for a week, lots of grass, lots of "grub," and sleep that night was a just one if ever such a thing existed.

The next morning, as the sunshine swept across the high meadow and struck the white tent-walls, we woke with sincere, solemn gratitude filling our souls, as we beheld our much-abused horses of yesterday standing bunched up in the distance, knee-deep in grass, sleeping that "comfy," sleep which always strikes a trail-horse just about sunrise.

By nine o'clock one of us had hit a back trail which we had found near our tents, one was exploring a trail south over and beyond the meadows, and two, seeing a nice mountain-slope to climb on the valley's left, started for that.

Three hours' easy scramble brought us to the shoulder of a most respectable peak. "K.''s quick eyes detected a cairn on a mountain south of us; "Mounts Collie and Habel at the head of the Yoho Valley," said he, and then pointed out other familiar mountains in

Mary and Mollie scrambling

the neighbourhood of Field. Climbing a little higher, we peeked into the dearest little pocket imaginable. At the base ran a stream due east, fed by the snowfields of Habel. Between us and it there seemed to be a sheer wall; on the other side the wall was broken, and about half way between the summit of Mount Collie and the river, hung a tiny green lake in the bare cliffs. "This," said "K.", "is the 'Gap' shown on Collie's map," and having been so told, I could see he was right. Climbing to the last snow-clad ridge of this high shoulder, we had a magnificent view of range upon range of mountains in the north which had safely sheltered us for so many weeks; then looked into the valley on our right where wound the Beavertail River, pointing out our way home. But that which interested me most was the frowning summit of Mount

Habel. I had met Professor Habel soon after he made the first ascent of the peak in 1900. He told me he had seen the mountain for the first time when coming down the Kicking Horse hill, under Mount Stephen, had made up his mind to climb it, searched for it for four or five days before locating it, and on reaching its summit, called it the "Hidden Mountain." It seemed so odd that seven years later I should by merest accident be standing so near his goal.

Three days' easy travel brought us out on the Emerald Lake road near Field. Special toilets had been arranged on the previous afternoon; sundry grease-spots had been removed from our skirts, a scarlet neckerchief had been washed, some wool shirts ditto, two or three pairs of shoes, with toes and heels intact, came up from the depths of the duffel-bags, and shaving soap had been liberally laid on. A smile of sincere admiration went round when we collected to behold our united elegance of appearance on the morning we started on our last ride. As for the horses, every one bore his inspection well, not one missing, and all in far better condition than when we left Laggan in June. Is it any wonder their master was proud of their appearance and

we proud to be in such company as I am sure we were?

And then we struck the highway and on it a carriage with people in it! Oh! The tragedy of the comparison! The woman's gown was blue. I think her hat contained a white wing. I only saw it all in one awful flash from the corner of my right eye, and I remember distinctly that she had *gloves on*. Then I suddenly realised that our own recently brushed-up garments were frayed and worn and our buckskin coats had a savage cast, that my three companions looked like Indians, and that the lady gazing at us belonged to another world. It was then that I wanted my wild free life back again, yet step by step I was leaving it behind.

We entered the little mountain town of Field just as the whistles shrieked out the noon hour. How garish it all sounded to ears that had for months heard nothing but Nature's finer notes. Then we grasped the hands of waiting friends, (who told us it was Mr. and Mrs. Rudyard Kipling we had passed on the road,) and fled from the eyes of the curious tourist to that civilised but perfect luxury—the bath-tub.

Old Indian Trails
Expedition of 1908

Mary T. S. Schäffer

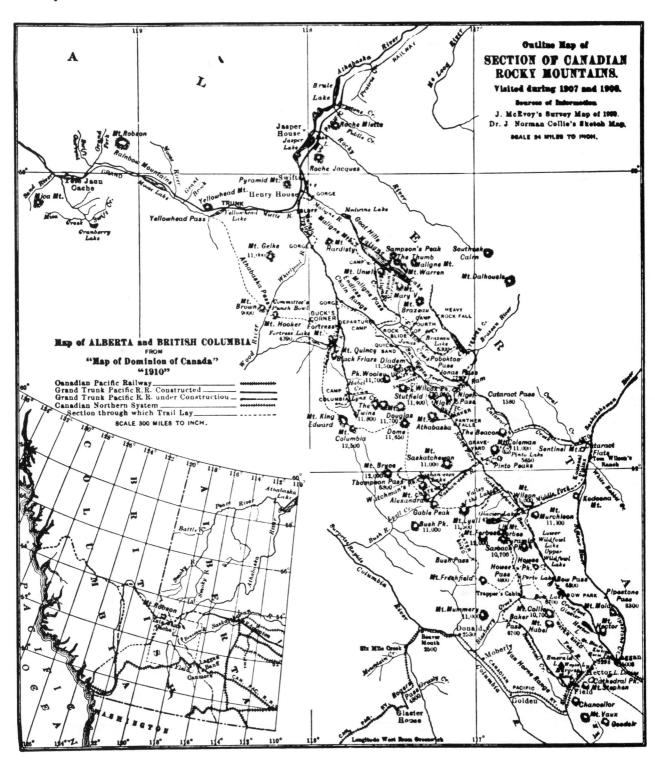

13: The Start

ALTHOUGH the pages of the summer's diary for 1907 had been turned one by one till the last was reached and "Finis" had been written, the memory as well as the camera carried back to the city picture after picture which would not and did not want to be forgotten.

Stowed away in a pocket of the said travel-worn diary reposed Sampson's map of the lake we had tried so hard to find, and in a pocket of our minds the determination to find our way to it if another summer dawned for us. No matter how varied all our interests, all four of us had the same goal in mind the moment there came a chance of pushing toward it.

It is a chronic state of affairs, however, in the Canadian Rockies, that to plan an early trip in them is to court an uncommonly late season, or a heavier snow-fall than has "ever before been known." The truth is, the snowfall is always heavy and the season a comparatively short one. To accomplish anything in distance it is wise to start out the moment the guides think it possible to get the horses over the passes. Prepare to endure a certain amount of discomfort in the beginning with equanimity, and then enjoy any good fortune in weather or otherwise that comes along. Also, no one need ever think he is going to avoid the weather; no mountains were ever made without it, least of all the Rockies.

How often we have been asked, "How do you stand the exposure?" Don't "stand" it, that's all. With a full set of those beautiful canary-coloured yachting slickers, found in all good sporting shops, a cap of the same material, a warm sweater, a buckskin coat, and a pair of heavy boots, absolute independence of the elements is obtained. To reach camp in dry clothing is the key to the situation, for once there a good fire soon puts everything right. We have passed weeks of showery or snowy days in the hills, never knew ourselves to catch cold, and on taking everything into

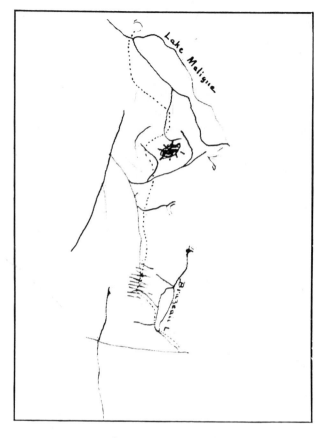

Sampson's map

account could only conclude that nature meant us all to be wild flowers instead of house-plants.

The spring of 1908 crept by like a snail. Some of us haunted outfitting shops, bought shoes warranted "to turn water till worn out," invested in dried vegetables of little weight and wonderful nutritive qualities, and spent hours preparing pinole. This last item we learned of from a practical camper, and obtained the recipe from an excellent book on camping. Ripe yellow field corn is used. It is placed in shallow pans and roasted in an oven as one would roast coffee. It is then put through a good strong coffee-mill and ground very fine. I shall never forget the day that, after hours of labour, I stood and proudly gazed on my completed task—eight pounds of pinole, and a borrowed kitchen covered with fine dust from the crushed corn. I was dead tired, but felt refreshed as I remembered its recommendation: "Two table-spoons of pinole mixed in a small quantity of water will sustain life for twenty-four hours, and consequently is one of the most valuable foods that can be carried on the trail." Knowing that our summer was likely to be a strenuous one, that in the life we were to lead accidents were liable to occur to the food supply at any moment, this hint seemed too valuable to ignore. In imagination, I could see our flour-bags washed away in the Athabaska River, the bacon gone with a drowning horse, and ourselves three hundred miles from a store, sitting around the pinole-bag, every one grateful for the thought which had prompted the addition of this valuable adjunct to our larder.

And right here I might as well finish the history of that pinole. Nothing ever did happen to the food to force so dire an emergency upon us. It was packed for miles and miles till some one asked if we ever intended to use it. So it was tried as a breakfast-food with a little sugar and cream to help it go down. It was not so bad, and the bag came forth the next day with other members of the family trying it. But it had a taste which hung on for hours, its consistency was that of a mouthful of sand, and its grittiness was all over you, inside and out. By the third day every one was politely refusing it, and on the fourth the mere smell of it caused a howl to go up. After that we carried it for a while in case of accident, and as the accident did not come and the odour permeated everything, it was presented to the horses, which, like ourselves turned up their noses at it, and left it on the ground. It may be all right when you are starving, but in times of peace and plenty, beware.

And so while we were busy with pinole and other condensed foods, the western contingent was buying up additional horses, getting saddlery into shape, and attending to all details for a four months' trip into a country as untried as we had yet seen.

We struck Laggan the first of June and for one solid week watched a steady down-pour of rain. The ground, already soaked, refused to absorb any more moisture and left the water lying around in large pools everywhere.

Patience finally ceased to be a virtue, so we decided to move out on the 8th, wet or fine, and on this date, leaving a band of staring tourists to admire our outfit, or otherwise, we crept forth once more into the Great Beyond.

O ye who have never known the joys of the long trail, of the confidence begot of experience, how little you can guess the prideful, excited, satisfied sensations as we gazed upon our new family! There were Chief and "K.", of course (the Life-guard so to speak), our two selves, and two new members,—the Botanist*and his own right-hand man,† the latter to act as chef while we all travelled together.

But the interesting element to us was the horses. A man may be judged in a general way in a short time, but not so a bunch of pack-animals. As the procession pulled out we drew aside on our old reliables, Nibs and Bugler, and watched the new family file by. First came steady old Pinto, then beautiful Dandy, long-legged Fox, Brownie stolid as a mud fence, and Roany who always began his spring work with a burning desire to cut loose from his pack, but quickly fell into line and ended up sensible and gentle. This was called "the old bunch"; then came the "Peyto bunch," many of whom we had had with us two years before. Bessie, a gay and festive lady, who had been noted for airing her heels at sudden and unaccountable moments in the past, led proudly off, followed by Wilcox,—very ancient, very steady, and known as a true friend to the early explorers of the Wilcox Pass country. Frank followed next, a prototype of Fox; then came Buck, slightly nondescript and colourless, one of those poor souls who, always doing exactly right, never gets talked about and thus becomes lost in the shuffle; Splash followed Buck, a brindled-looking lady inclined to stoutness, with one brown eye and one blue one, which gave her such a sinister and wicked appearance it took weeks for some of us to realise she

* Stewardson Brown
† Reggie Holmes

—81—

was harmless and gentle as a lamb. Charlie, a dark roan, who had never seen a trail or muskeg, or been trained to the log-jumping act in his life, carried the Botanist, and for days amused his rider (and any on-lookers) learning to size up the height of a log and take other trail obstructions as they came. We often thought the rider as nervy as his horse when we saw Charlie take a two-foot log with a four-foot leap. But he soon learned. Then there was handsome Ricks from Morley; and sorrel Ginger with a Roman nose and heels built on the plan of strokes of lightning (great respect shown to those heels); pretty, shy, gentle Baldy, still in the teething stage, chewing straps and pack mantles as he went along; Silver, slow, dignified, and strong; Blue Peter, too uncertain yet to criticise; another Pinky, just enough like Pinky of last year to bring up sad, funny memories of our adorable little bag-of-bones who had been sold back to the Indians he came from; pretty Midget who was taken along as an extra in case of an accident; and last and funniest of all, ambling irresponsibly along in the rear, two dubbed Lucia di Lammermoor and Biddy respectively, but who from the first day were known collectively as the "Heavenly Twins."

They were unitedly a bunch to be proud of, as, with their packs averaging two hundred pounds apiece, they passed before us with all the food, clothing, and other effects necessary to six people for a four months' trip into a country where game is plentiful but ever uncertain and erratic. In summing up the family I came very near forgetting Muggins, "Mr. Muggins," under gracious conditions.

After two former experiences, "M." and I had vowed we would never have a dog in the outfit again. But he was there, and in twenty-four hours we saw why he was there, in twenty-four more he had ingratiated himself completely and become part and parcel of our life.

His breed? Part spaniel, I suppose. Breed was not his strong point. He swam like a duck, he kept us in grouse, he never got into trouble with porcupines, he was friendly with all, yet loved but one,—his master. He was

Mr. Muggins

just adorable little Muggins, first, last, and always.

From Laggan to the Saskatchewan River via Bow Pass, the weather and conditions under foot never for a moment permitted us to forget that the season was late and we were early. Muskegs were at their worst and the ground sloughy without much intermission. The trollius and caltha were out in their glory, the cold watery ground being their natural birthplace, while the drier portions were covered with spring beauties and yellow violets, and, at the higher elevations, the snow lilies made the hillsides gay with their golden colouring.

Bow Lake was so covered with slush ice that we were forced to keep out of the water and travel its soft banks to avoid cutting the horses' legs, and a grand snow-storm capped the climax by escorting us up and over the summit of the pass (6700 feet), where there still lay two or three feet of old snow.

As predicted by Chief, beyond that pass were sunshine and warmth, so much warmth, in fact, that we feared high water on the Saskatchewan. No one had any desire to see our food soaked through at so early a stage of the game, or to test any sooner than necessary the swimming abilities of the new horses, so we all promptly proceeded to worry about the weather.

I might say here that this year we had invested in numberless waterproof bags in which had been deposited tea, coffee, cornstarch, sugar, baking powder, dried fruits, etc., so that much of our former anxiety was cancelled, but we were all, with one exception, thoroughly acquainted with the tricks of that river, and would be profoundly grateful when across it.

It was just four P.M., on a hot afternoon, when we stood on its banks, looked longingly to the other side, and held guard over the pack-horses who wished to plunge in and follow Chief and "K." as they went off to try the ford; for, though we had been across that very spot many times before, a ford in those mountains is liable to be here to-day and gone to-morrow, owing to the violent floods which occur after a hot spell, and no one was taking any chances.

Throughout the entire day any moment, that could be spared, had been devoted to telling the Botanist of every catastrophe which had occurred or which might occur

during the crossing. He "must not let his feet fly up if his horse got to swimming, but if they did and he was washed off, to catch his horse's mane or tail and 'stay with him.'" He was perfectly polite and listened with respect as he knelt on the sand, holding back the yelping Muggins, who was struggling violently to throw himself into the flood and follow his master. The men returned, said it seemed all right, and we filed in. I do not remember so much as getting wet feet (one becomes skilled in time in tucking their toes away on such occasions), and we emerged perfectly dry on the sand-bar on the other side. Then there was lots of yelling and I turned to see what was going on. Every pack-horse, as soon as he struck the hot sands, was having a good roll. This was a most unsettling move for the packs and rather inadvisable all round, and I grew so interested watching the proceedings behind me that not till too late did I notice what was doing just beneath me. Then to my disgust I found

his Nib-ship, regardless of his lawful burden, was half way on the same errand bent, and there was nothing to do but leap from the saddle to avoid being crushed underneath. It was then he got his first "licking" so far as his mistress was concerned, when both of us seemed greatly surprised.

Somehow, though we were thankful enough to know we were safely over, neither "M." nor I felt like continuing the discussion of the dangers of the Saskatchewan with the Botanist, and vowed hereafter to keep silent on the subject. He no doubt at that time took us for an easily frightened pair, but by no look or sign betrayed himself, for which we were very grateful.

On the high banks, overlooking the North Fork, we pitched our tents for a few days' stay, in order to permit the Botanist to look into the flora at the Kootenai Plains twenty-five miles down the river, and ourselves to frolic around in one of the most wonderful playgrounds the Rockies possess. With studied care, our tent was placed so that our waking eyes might first rest on the glories of Mount Forbes and the surrounding peaks, while a twist of the neck brought Pyramid, Sarbach and Murchison into view. The spot seemed ideal that night as we sat at our tent-door and called all that vastness ours. The next morning things were slightly different; a gentle tapping on the tent-walls accompanied by a breeze was in evidence. The gentle breeze became a rampant, intermittent hurricane, bringing sheets of water with it straight from the clouds, which now encircled Mount Forbes and pretty much everything else. Our landed possessions disappeared from view and a deluge of rain was tossed in upon what we still owned—our beds and duffel-bags. Clouds of smoke from our fire kept us weeping and spluttering, and, in spite of the elements, we were forced to give up scenery and swing the tent broadside to the gale.

Looking down the North Fork from Mount Wilson

14: Back on our Old Playground — The North Fork

WITH a slight cessation of rain on the 16th, Chief and the Botanist left us for a three days' trip down the river, while "K." and "Chef" went off to Glacier Lake, five or six miles distant. This left us one of our rare days alone, and I for one knew what I meant to do. A most peculiar odour clung to the blankets of my bed. A neatly conducted conversation had brought out the fact that those blankets and some raw bear-skins had spent considerable time in each other's society during the spring, and, though all the water in that camp had to be packed up a thirty-foot bank from the river, the laundry of those blankets was imperative while the critics' backs were turned. Long experience had taught us how to wash our hands in a teaspoon and take a bath in a tea-cup, so the blankets were manipulated with comparative ease in a hand-basin.

Bear Creek canyon was visited the next day, and proved to be an exceptionally fine one for that country where hardly a stream finds its course through the hills without beating its way among great rock-worn cliffs.

And then the Botanist returned safe and sound but with the intelligence that he now knew what swimming the Saskatchewan meant. The snows on the mountains east of our camp were evidently melting much faster than those at the river's sources; our unsuspecting friends made this discovery in mid-stream, twenty miles below us, got a thorough ducking going over, and another when returning. We were very glad to have them both safely back, but the alarmists had been vindicated, and we were not the cowards we had seemed.

As the three tourists started ahead on the morning of the 20th, we turned in our saddles to look with pride on the sight so gratifying to a trailer, sixteen perfectly packed horses slowly advancing, sixteen white pack-mantles moving deliberately among the green trees.

Suddenly a violently propelled pack appeared on the crest of the hill and came charging down among us. It was Roany on one of those wild tears he had so frequently indulged in the year before; his spirits soon infected the all-too-willing Bessie, and, with tail straight in the air, she promptly joined him in his sport. Fearing the whole bunch might take the disease, we three drew modestly aside to avoid the rush. Then we waited, but nothing came of it. The stampede seemed nipped in the bud, and we began to feel that some calamity must have occurred. It appeared that after Roany's rush (which was only exuberance of spirits anyhow), the men counted noses and found the Twins missing. They had been roundly frightened with Roany's scandalous behaviour as he banged into them and tore by, and, like ourselves, turned into the woods to avoid trouble, and had not had sense enough to turn back again. Poor little creatures! They were the only ones of the whole twenty-two that never learned their work; they ended just as they began—always in trouble, just getting in, or being pulled out. Unwilling to be separated, they jogged and thumped and hit each other's packs trying to travel together on a trail just wide enough for one. If two trees standing close together were within a few yards of the trail, it was nothing out of the way to see them both make a dash for it and of course get thoroughly wedged together, when "K." would be forced to go around, and, by yells and perhaps emphatic but unrecorded argument, compel them to back out. In ten minutes they would be at it again. I remember one night we were sympathising with him, for really they were more aggravating than all the muskeg and fallen timber put together, and some one said: "You must find them terribly trying, they are *never* on the trail." Loyal to his charges in spite of such irritating behaviour, he replied: "Oh, yes, they are, they cross it sometimes!"

The travel to Camp Parker, escorted as we were by uncommonly good weather, was more beautiful than ever. With a conscious pride of possession, we pointed it out to the Botanist, who, having already seen much of the country, was willing to admit it was "the finest thing yet." We tested the Big Hill with the aneroid, decided it was about a thousand feet high, were glad when we saw the last pound of grub hauled to the top, neatly stacked in piles at camp, and the horses straying off into the rich meadows of Camp Parker, where they were to have two whole days with nothing to do, for the following day we were to climb Mount Athabaska for fossils.

The next morning, armed with lunches, aneroid, cameras and geological hammer, four of us were off scientifically-bent, accompanied by Muggins, the two at home preferring the joys of laundry, drying out plant-press papers, and making mulligan. What is mulligan? Well, in this instance, it proved to be the final repository for an aged fool-hen, a remnant of dried beef, some stewed tomatoes and corn, and proved a big success at six o'clock that night (but then we, who had been climbing, could have eaten any old boiled stews by that time, so don't take my word that it is a dish for an epicure).

As we climbed, the snow patches grew more and more numerous, and not until after we reached an altitude of 8000 feet did we come upon the fossil outcrop. Here, while we ate our lunch with the wind shrieking around us, Muggins covered himself with glory by killing a small gopher which had persisted in taunting him unceasingly from what the gopher must have considered safe ground, and his hapless little body went into the fossil-bag as a specimen.

After much pounding and hammering on everybody's part, "K.", who had the load to carry, decided that fifty pounds of fossilised corals and shells ought to be enough to satisfy the most enthusiastic geologist, and as every pocket in the party was loaded down also, there was an unanimous agreement to quit, and the descent began.

Near Camp Parker

Several large patches of snow were encountered but easily overcome, then an especially long and steep one intruded itself. It would have been a beauty to glissade, being harder and firmer than the others, but unfortunately at its terminus was a fifty-foot precipice. At first I demurred at risking my neck on the thing, but "K." was really a fine mountaineer, and assuring me that, if I followed cautiously in his tracks, he would get me down safely, I immediately fell in line. "Chef," probably seeing a few rags of doubt still clinging to my movements, gallantly made foot-holes for himself beside those "K." was kicking out, and offered me a steadying hand. I looked round to see what the Botanist might be doing. Denying any claims to scientific mountaineering, there he was poised at the top like some big bird about to take flight, waiting patiently till we got out of the way, when he said he "intended to take a slide down and be caught at the bottom"— a sensible scheme.

"K." was valiantly doing his best, but the constant shifting of his heavy fossil-bag, with frequent spasmodic brandishing of the rifle, kept faith in my original preserver trembling in the balance, while the constant tendency of "Chef's" feet to fly out in front of him, compelled me to liken his help to a reed. Down we slowly crawled a few inches at a time. Suddenly "Chef" gave one wild kick and a sickening whoop, out flew his heels, he thoughtfully abandoned my hand, and went sliding towards the rock-strewn ground and precipice below, grabbing at the snow in vain attempts to stop himself. The hearts of his friends stopped beating for a moment I am sure, till we saw him land on the stones which, though not soft, looked perfectly safe.

Then "K." and, I with depressed minds, crept on, but we had not gone three yards till he too lost his balance, threw out his hands, wildly grabbing at the mushy snow, and went down like a shot, leaving only the most slippery-looking slide in his wake. Both escorts gone without so much as an apology, and more than half of that slope still to cover, things looked desperate for me. Then I started to dig in my heels according to instructions and in spite of adverse circumstances, when a warning voice from behind yelled: "Look out; I'm coming!" Expecting a violent blow in the back I awaited the shock, but he (the Botanist) gallantly swerved to one side and I saw my last hope fly by accompanied by a bunch of plant specimens and the dead gopher. He was received at the bottom with cheers, shouts, and open arms, and I went slowly crawling down. There stood the gallant escorts below me in a row, expectant, grinning, and perfectly helpless. The ridiculousness of it all suddenly assailed me, so with a laugh I gave up and joined my companions in the wink of an eye via the slippery way.

The mulligan tasted delicious an hour later and the air-bed soon felt good to a bunch of untrained muscles. About ten-thirty I woke with a start. Lightning was playing over the hills opposite, the thunder banging on the rocks, and to a sleepy brain the rain was like bullets falling on the tent-walls. Too tired to be bothered, I pulled the waterproof covers close over my head and fell asleep. An hour later I was suddenly wide awake again. Tramp, rustle, scratch, just back of the tent—what was it? A bear enticed by the smell of food, or a horse seeking shelter in the timber from the storm? It was dark as ink outside, both spirit and flesh weakened at the thought of going out to drive off whatever was there. No, the grub-pile must take care of itself, my head went under the blankets, and I was soon asleep again. It was a comfort in the morning to see the stacked food intact, and in a moment of weakness I spoke of the racket outside our tent during the night. To mention "bear" before that family was quite enough to start a run of comments which did not cease till packing began. Then as the mantles were being removed from the great pile of food and saddlery, something wiggled, something backed its way clumsily out and waddled, unmolested, off into the bush; then somebody yelled, "Come on and look at your bear!" That wretched porcupine had been at the bacon, and had done quite a little damage to our valuable material. When we asked Muggins why he had not let us know about the unwelcome visitor, he only wagged his tail and as good as said, "You always scolded me if I went near a porcupine, so don't blame me."

Mount Athabaska

15: The Search for the Unmapped Lake

THE route over Nigel Pass and down the Brazeau River to "Tepee Camp," near the mouth of Brazeau Lake, was like returning to our own again. The old bunch of horses of 1907 seemed to have communicated to the new ones the fact that there was great feed at the latter place, and the moment the river was crossed there was great hustling along. As we pointed out this small corner of real estate to the Botanist, he agreed that in spite of the cold rain,—it was the most ideal camp-ground he had ever seen, and also that the adjacent hills had better be inspected the following day for plant specimens.

They made an interesting climb, though scarce covering 3000 feet, and we found the steep hill-slopes a perfect mass of flowers, with game-trails running in every direction. So fresh were some of the signs that we concluded the exodus of the game had taken place only upon the arrival of our large party in the valley below. Just before reaching the summit we passed over a carpet of the bluest of blue forget-me-nots and flush pink daisies. In some places they lay freshly broken and crushed to the ground, and I could not help wondering a little if it had been given these children of the hills to feel some of this great beauty about them. Alas, I suppose the green grass was all they asked, and to a mother sheep her child would look no fairer for sleeping in a bed of blue and white blossoms on the hill-tops. But they had vanished as the frost from the grass, or the sun behind the clouds; our coming had breathed terror in their hearts.

On the heights we got a fine view of Brazeau Lake, and decided that a gap in the hills west of the lake was probably the pass through which we were to make our way to the lake of which we were in search—the Pobokton Pass. To merely look into it was to be seized with the excitement incidental to reaching new regions to explore, so, after gathering several rare alpine specimens, we faced about,

longing for the morrow to start on our year-old quest.

By 8:20 the next morning (June 30th), the whole outfit was strung along the trail heading for the outlet of Brazeau Lake, and for a land of which we had not the slightest knowledge. We might find sustenance for ten or a dozen horses, but twenty-two was another proposition. On all the previous days Chief had known exactly where he was going to find feed for so large a family; did he have any fears now? If so, his face did not show it, but still there was an absence of joking, there was no whistling in front or warbling of the latest popular song in the rear—that was all.

Crossing the Brazeau at the very outlet of the lake was much easier than we had expected to find it, and as soon as we were over we took up Dr. Coleman's old trail of 1892. A sharp detour was first made to avoid some rock-bluffs jutting out to the water; and then for a half mile on the lake shore we encountered bad going. A few of the old stagers, grown wise at the game, scuttled along close to our heels to have the advantage of the leader's guidance, half a dozen others got more or less mired, and how the foolish, unthinking Twins ever came out alive, no one but their luckless driver in the rear knows, but they did not fail, either then or any other time, to turn up eventually safe and sound.

I think "M's" diary sums up the approach to Pobokton Pass to perfection, as we found it that initial day of our experience on it, and as others will find it unless they cross it later in the season: "The trail was a little fierce, quick changes from burnt timber to rock-climbing, muskeg, quicksand, scree slopes, and mud slides." Late in the afternoon, after much tough work, we made camp at timber-line, where the horses went mountain-climbing for their suppers and we for flower specimens, getting some very rare ones among the rocks.

On Pobokton Pass

With the next day glaringly clear and hot, we crossed the pass which our aneroid made 7400 feet, ploughing through deep snow which the horses hated nearly as much as muskeg. It was a hard climb up and over, and now that I have seen it I should never take the Pobokton Pass from start to finish for a pleasure trip; it is a miserable route, and one only to be used to accomplish an end.

The trail was a very well marked one till, on the second day's ride, it seemed to come to an abrupt end at the river's edge where there had been a large Indian camp at some time. At this point it, became so indistinct that the men looked around for something more promising, and a few old cuttings decided us to take a sharp turn to the right and ascend a steep hill, where we continued to follow more or less of a trail for a couple of hours longer.

The Indians' map told us to leave the valley at the third creek coming in from the right. We had already passed a dozen of them and were now passing another, but no horse-feed was in sight. A short distance beyond, we reached an open stretch, found tepee-poles and stopped for the night. The feed was mostly moss, muskeg, and fresh air, lots of all three; but the lake was getting on the nerves of all the family, and the horses would have to put up with a little inconvenience themselves.

With tents in order, all went off in as many different directions as possible. The feminine contingent came back first, reporting " fine scenery but no pass as far as they could see." "K." appeared next; "he had been to the end of the valley from where the last creek emerged, but that was a matter of impossibility for horses." Then Chief arrived with the cheerful intelligence that " we could still advance; a good trail led down the hill and was probably the real Pobokton trail." Perhaps the river went through some impassable gorge at this point, to cause us to do such an amount of tall climbing all morning. It was a comfort to know we could go on anyhow, certain it was that no one wanted to stay there, and no one contradicted the coolness of the atmosphere. Far, far in the distance, at seven o'clock, we could see the sun just setting in a bank of angry clouds, the wind, which had not been any too pleasant all day, began to howl and sob, and caused us to prevail on "Chef" to leave his baking a few minutes and peg down our tent, as it threatened to go off with our entire belongings. A pocket-handkerchief soared away like a bird, and the collapsible hand-basin had already taken a short flight across the slough in front of our tent.

The morning of the "Glorious Fourth" was ushered in with a crackling fire at our tent-door and a familiar voice saying, "Hot water, thermometer somewhere about thirty!" It took a terrible lot of courage to emerge from the warm blankets, from which position we could note six inches of snow over everything, and every few moments the howling wind would send a fresh supply down upon us. In spite of "Chef's" extra trouble to keep the breakfast hot at our fire, and every one piling into our tent to eat it, the bacon was like candle-grease in the bitter cold, and the coffee barely warm. The packing was worse than the eating. The horses fidgeted and turned to avoid facing the wind, and, what with frozen tents, pack-mantles, and ropes, not to mention stiffened fingers, it was nine o'clock before we could get below the brow of that exposed hill.

For the next two hours the trail led us down a fire-swept valley where the chopping was incessant and heavy. Once more reaching the bed of the stream we again found old tepee-poles and a division of the way, one pointing to the Sun Wapta, the other leading into a notch in the hills with a northern trend. The stream from it really did seem as if it might be the one for which we were looking,

and the opening in the hills the last possible one before reaching the end of the valley of the Sun Wapta, which we had occasionally seen to the north-west of us. The trail here was very steep and rough and, with the thought that we might be coming back over it next day, very hard to keep on following. About half way up the hill, down came the snow, and every one said "Yes!" to the suggestion of stopping at the next suitable place.

The game was now on in earnest. The household was getting into a rather divided state of mind, the opinion not having been unanimously in favour of this particular valley. However, those who did favour it were to have a chance of exploring it. Consequently, Chief and "K." went off the next morning to see what was ahead and the rest of us, as usual, worked each in his own line.

At four o'clock the men returned; had found a good trail, crossed a pass, could see miles ahead, but no lake of any description could be seen. The decision was to push ahead; we always had the privilege of turning back, and the best of the summer was still before us.

The new pass* was a duplication of all other passes, soft and spongy; our aneroid showed the altitude as 7200 feet. Long patches of snow made the travelling very heavy, but the pass was a short one, and, with the saddle-horses ahead breaking the way, we were not long in getting over.

Reaching the eastern slope, I think I never saw a fairer valley. From our very feet it swept away into an unbroken green carpet as far as the eye could see. The botanical department found a rare specimen of *pedicularis*, while Muggins captured a couple of ptarmigan, and then the cavalcade made a quick descent of about a thousand feet, tramping under foot thousands of blossoms of the *trollius* and *pulsatilla* which covered the way.

Two and a half miles below the summit, finding a bunch of tepee-poles—a hint we were now in the habit of taking from the Indians,—

* Maligne Pass

—92—

we made our camp. In the afternoon, I took a stroll up a near-by hill, hoping to be able to report having seen the lake on my return; but no such glory was in store.

The morning of July 7th was a perfect one, the green valley down which we made our way was ideal, and yet in spite of all these blessings we were distinctly dismal. When the outfit was too spread out for us to discuss the quite undiscussable geography about us, we certainly looked our thoughts and rode along in dead silence.

The trail was not well marked this day, but that was owing to the fact that a horse could travel almost anywhere. However, even in face of such depression, we were able to enjoy one particular cut-bank which we followed up to avoid a soft spot on the river's edge; it was a mass of forget-me-nots, great splashes of intense blue, as though a bit of the sky had fallen. Then on and on, up and down hill we crawled for about eight miles, till we came to a halt on the river's right in a fine bunch of spruce. The day had grown steadily warmer, and with it had come the first real instalment of mosquitoes, and, as we ate our lunch of bread and jam and tea, it took considerable vigilance to keep them from drowning in the tea or sticking fast to the jam.

With lunch over, up came the everlasting question: "Where is that lake? Do you think we are on the right track?" "K.", who had grown more and more solemn for days, suddenly jumped up and shaking himself violently said: "Well, it's two o'clock, but I'm going off to climb something that's high enough to see if that lake's within twenty miles of here, and I'm not coming back till I know!" Anxious as I was to go along, I knew he was in no mood to have a snail in tow, and then it was far more important to locate our quarry than that I should personally be in at the death. Besides, it would have taken a goat to follow him when he was as desperate as he was then. With aneroid, camera, compass and our best wishes, he left us,—he for the heights, and we to put in time below looking for flowers and fossils, tormented by hordes of mosquitoes. We found large

quantities of the latter, and, after a short jaunt, returned to camp, where three of us donned the despised "bug-nets" from which we emerged only for dinner.

The hours went by, a smudge of damp moss assisted in slightly allaying the pests, night settled down, but "K." had not returned. We were a dreary-looking crowd. It rained a little. In spite of the hot night, Chief made a rousing fire as a beacon for the climber, and we all sat listening for the first crackle in the bushes. Not till 10:30 did it come, then he staggered out of the black forest into the flaring light, looking thoroughly tired out. He said he had "kept hopping" the entire seven hours and, though tired and hungry, greeted us with the joyful news, "I've found the lake!" Ascending the ridge behind our camp, he dropped 2000 feet to another valley, then climbed a fine peak where the aneroid said 8750 feet. Reaching the top, he looked over and there lay the lake below. The quest was over, all doubts were at rest, so there was no turning back, we could go on. A sigh of satisfaction passed around the camp-fire. Every one had been on a strain for days; "K's" absence on the mountain had added to it; now that we had him and the lake safe, there was no noisy demonstration, just complete relaxation. He was regaled with bacon, tea, and cake; the camp-fire went down, the "bug-nets" went on, and the camp went to sleep.

The sound which woke our slumbers next morning was Chief shouting, "All aboard for the lake!" The expressions on all faces were comical. Every one got off a joke, no matter how stale, every one being in a particularly happy humor. "K." had reported the lake "just around the corner," a matter of six or seven miles; no one minded the mosquitoes and we "hiked" forth jubilant, still sticking to the river's right, though we had a line on Sampson's map telling us to cross to the left. But going was easy, never an axe was used, so why give up a good thing for an uncertainty.

In about two hours, after passing through a little very soft ground, we came out on the shores of Chaba Imne (Beaver Lake), but found our position too low to get much idea of its size, though even there it looked quite large enough for all the time and exertion we had spent on it. As we stood upon its shores, we looked across to the other side, wondered what it all held in store for us, then wandered around while the men looked for a good camp-site.

Indians, of course, had been there, but, unless a prospector or timber-cruiser had come in by way of the Athabaska River, we had reason to feel we might be the first white people to have visited it.

From the moment we left the trail on Pobokton Creek, there had not been one sign of a civilised hand; the Indian is a part of the whole, the white man, with his tin-cans and forest-fires, desecrates as he goes. The unknown has a glamour indescribable; it creeps into the blood; it calls silently, but none the less its call is irresistible and strong.

Yes, the long quest was over, the object found, and it seemed very beautiful to our partial eyes. As some one had to remain and keep the horses from rolling on the hot sands, we individually took short flights to see what was to be seen.

As "M." and I wandered about, we found a number of logs cut by the beaver many years ago; but, knowing the Indian's thriftlessness, I doubt if there was a live beaver left in the valley, for he cleans out as he goes, and is consequently a most destructive hunter. Such carpenter-work, however, explained how the lake had received its name.

In half an hour "K." returned to say they had found feed on the other side of the river, also a good ford, so, retracing a half mile through the previously mentioned soft spot, we all got safely across. Just as Ginger, giving himself an extra hump, sprang up the far bank, he parted company with a fifty-pound sack of flour which fortunately dropped on dry ground, when everybody sighed, "What luck!"

16: A Maiden Voyage on the "New" Lake

THE camp-site just mentioned was a lucky find. How the men ever fell over it I cannot imagine; but they had a Robinson Crusoe sort of habit of falling over the right thing at the right time, and at the moment we scarce wondered. It must have been half a mile back from the river; we rode through fierce scrub to reach it, but once there the horses were as safe as though corralled. The feed was knee-deep and inexhaustible, and we shook ourselves into quarters with the idea of several days' stay.

With the lake now found, fresh food for conversation developed. A high double-peaked mountain, with a very large glacier on its north face, could be seen above the tree-tops about thirty miles distant. It seemed a little too much to the north-east to be Mount Brazeau, while the one that "K." reached in his climb seemed too far to the south-west. Both were in splendid view and kept us guessing.

The Botanist quickly grew busy; he had struck a botanical haven, very rare specimens of other sections of the mountains were there in masses, and other plants he had not seen at all were there also. Dinner passed off with the exciting intelligence that "to-morrow will be devoted to building a raft, as the shores, as far as can be seen, are impassable for horses, and it must be fully three miles to the head of the lake. We will then take tents, blankets and food for three days, and you enthusiastic climbers can fight it out from the top as to which is Mount Brazeau."

Our part of the raft-making next morning was the uncommon permission to wash up the breakfast dishes, and the three men were soon swallowed up in the trees as they went down to the lake, each with his axe over his shoulder. With things snugged up and a huge pot of pork and beans set to simmer over the fire, I too strolled down. It *was* a stroll, too, that took about a half hour to do the job, as the fallen timber made it hard travelling and the sloughs near the lake boot-high.

But we did n't make rafts every day or even reach a spandy-new lake, so the exertions seemed well worth the cause. As I came quietly out to the water's edge, there were two of the men out in the lake busily lashing two logs together, and "K." was just rounding a point gracefully riding a dead tree, which, at that moment, as gracefully rolled over and landed him in the water. He was, however, already so wet that he could n't be much wetter, so he shook himself amidst a momentary smile all round, and shoved his old tree into place.

I found a dry spot and sat watching them come and go for an hour. "Chef," who was an accomplished axeman, wielded his axe with an artistic ability interesting to see; and as I looked at them all, working almost in silence, my mind went back to the first carpenters who had cut logs in those waters,—the busy little beavers whose work was still visible, but whose pelts had been the cause of their extermination.

At six o'clock the three men walked into camp, soaked, of course, but jubilant over results, and announced that H. M. S. *Chaba* would sail for the upper end of the lake to-morrow morning at nine.

A short pow-wow after supper resulted in learning that we were to go in style regardless of our plea that we were willing to rough it for a few days; air-beds, tents, and food for three days were to be taken on that raft.

Personally my sensations towards large bodies of water are similar to those of a cat, and though I begged to rough it, it was not so much to do something uncomfortable as to keep from drowning on an overtaxed raft. With qualms and misgivings next morning, I watched bags, boxes, and bundles carried out and deposited on the upper deck of the *Chaba*, the last two packages being "M." and myself, who were dumped unceremoniously on with the rest of the cargo. The Botanist waded out for himself, as did Muggins, the rowers climbed aboard, and we set sail. Now

that she was loaded, the lower deck looked alarmingly under water, and "M." and I were seated high on a bag of flour, a slab of bacon, and bundles of blankets. To the novice in rafting, nothing could have looked more insecure or unreliable; wide gaps in the logs showed unmeasured depths of green water below, and it seemed as though, with a sudden lurch or sharp turn, we must be shot from our perch into the cold, unfathomed waters.

Determined to put up a brave fight, I clutched my log and awaited a spill. It never came; she rode as steady as a little ship and as slow as a snail. She was propelled by two sweeps twelve feet long; the men took twenty-minute turns at her, the rest of us looking on and silently wondering at the fearful task and lack of complaint. At noon she was paddled as near shore as possible and all hands landed for lunch; Muggins, who sat at the tip end of the landing-log voted the performance a terrible bore, and nearly jumped out of his skin when once he reached terra firma.

Back once more on the raft after an hour's rest, the men slowly pulled the clumsy little

craft, foot by foot, past exquisite bays and inlets, the mountains closed more and more about us, and at six-thirty, as we seemed within a mile of our goal—the head of the lake,—we hove to, and camped by a stream which came from the double-peaked mountain. Landing, we found our new home was a garden of crimson vetches. As the warm winds swept across them, the odour brought a little home-sick thought of the sweet clover-fields of the east in July.

Opposite our camp rose a fine snow-capped mountain down whose side swept a splendid glacier. As we paddled slowly in sight of it, "K." suddenly looked up and said, "That is the mountain from which I first saw the lake." So we promptly named it "Mount Unwin." Though the breath of the vetches remained with us all night, the thought of home fled with the crash of avalanches from Mount Unwin's sides, and the distant yapping of coyotes in the valley behind us. With the coming of the morning, our plans were quickly laid to paddle the intervening mile to the end of the lake, take a light lunch, then climb for the keynote of the situation,—Lake Brazeau.[1]

On one point we had found Sampson's map very much at fault: he had both drawn and mentioned "narrows" about two thirds of the way up the lake.[2] These had never materialised and we commented on the fact of finding Sampson seriously at fault. The raft was growing to be so homey and reliable a vehicle that even the timid now stepped gaily aboard, all but Muggins; he hated that raft, and came aboard sighing and dejected as though he had been whipped, but of course had no intention of being left behind, and away we sailed with a pack-mantle hoisted to catch any passing breeze.

In about an hour, as we were rounding what we supposed to be our debarking point, there burst upon us that which, all in our little company agreed, was the finest view any of us had ever beheld in the Rockies. This

[1] At that time the only established geographic point within many miles.
[2] See Sampson's map.

Looking up Maligne Lake

was a tremendous assertion, for, of that band of six of us, we all knew many valleys in that country, and each counted his miles of travel through them by thousands. Yet there it lay, for the time being all ours,—those miles and miles of lake, the unnamed peaks rising above us, one following the other, each more beautiful than the last. We had reached, not the end of the lake, but the narrows of which Sampson had told us. On our left stood a curiously shaped mountain toward which we had worked our way for two days. We called it "The Thumb"; next rose a magnificent double-headed pile of rock, whose perpendicular cliffs reached almost to the shore. Its height? I've no idea. It was its massiveness, its simple dignity, which appealed to us so strongly, and we named it "Mount Warren," in honour of Chief, through whose grit and determination we were able to behold this splendour.

As we slowly advanced beneath the shadow of "The Thumb," a large fissure, at least 1000 feet above us, became visible, and from it there burst a fine waterfall. So great was its drop that it became spray, waving back and forth in the wind, long before it touched the rocks below, then gathering itself in a little stream,

tumbled headlong into the lake, losing itself in a continuous series of ringlets.

After four hours of tough rowing, we reached the head of the lake, and landed for lunch on an old alluvial fan. None of the higher peaks were here visible, the supposed Mount Brazeau south of us, the uncertain Mount Maligne east of us, or even Mount Unwin; they were all hidden by lower shoulders of themselves.

Like feudal lords (and ladies) we sat at our mid-day meal of tinned-meat and bannock that day. Our table, the clean sweet earth itself, was garnished with flowers, with vetches crimson, yellow, and pink. They spread away in every direction from us as far as the eye could see, and, the warm winds blowing down upon us from the southern valleys, swept across their faces and bore their clover-laden breath to the first white guests of that wonderful region.

With lunch over, we wandered about to drink it all in. How pure and undefiled it was! We searched for some sign that others had been there,—not a tepee-pole, not a charred stick, not even tracks of game; just masses of flowers, the lap-lap of the waters on the shore, the occasional reverberating roar of an avalanche, and our own voices, stilled by a nameless Presence.

We wanted a week in that heaven of the hills, yet back at "Camp Unwin" was only one more day's grub, so, scolding at Fate, we turned toward H. M. S. *Chaba* as she lay indifferently swashing her cumbersome form against an old beached log, whose momentary duty it was to prevent her from drifting off across the lake.

As we came up, Chief had just chopped out a smooth surface on the side of a small tree, and there, for the first time and only in all our wanderings, so far as I can remember, we inscribed our initials and the date of our visit.

Even then I think we all apologised to ourselves, for, next to a mussy camp-ground, there is nothing much more unsightly to the *true camper* than to see the trees around a favourite camping site disfigured with personal names and personal remarks, which never fail to remind one of the old adage taught the small boy in his early youth when he receives his first knife.

And one more name we left behind, not carved upon a tree but in our memories. All day the thought of one who loved the hills as we did ourselves was in my mind, and though she could not be with us, yet did I long to share our treasures with her. On the lake's west shore rose a fine symmetrical peak, and as we stepped cautiously aboard our craft (I never could get over the idea that she would go over with a sneeze), I said: "With every one's sanction I call that peak Mount Mary Vaux." There was no dissenting voice.

Foot by foot we left it all behind—the flowers, the tumbling avalanches, the great rock masses we had named, the untraversed valleys, and the beautiful falls.

The day was dying fast; as we glided by the tempting coves, and swept through the narrows,—now "Sampson's Narrows,"—the setting sun touched a symmetrical snow-tipped peak on the eastern shore of the lake, the dark waters before us caught up the picture, threw back to us an inverted rosy summit, and we named it "Sampson's Peak" for him who had sketched us the little map. The heavy rhythmic breathing of the rowers and

Mount Mary Vaux

Muggins's occasional sighs were the only drawbacks to absolute and perfect enjoyment; but for the tense faces before us and the tenser muscles, we could have looked ahead and aloft and said,—"This is Paradise."

As we came into port under the shadow of Mount Unwin, the sweet odour of the vetches came out to greet us, the sun sank behind the hills, the winds died away, every ripple of the lake disappeared, even the mosquitoes ceased to bother us; The Thumb, Mounts Warren, Unwin, Sampson, and many other unnamed peaks were dyed in crimson, which changed to purple, to violet, then night with its cloak of darkness fell. As the evening's camp-fire was lighted, there came across the water the distant bark of a coyote, overhead passed a few belated duck; except for these there seemed no other life than that of our little family hidden there in the wilderness where "home" had never been before.

The weather on Sunday morning, July 12th, refused to take any action on all adverse signs of the previous evening and burst upon us clear, bright, and best of all, calm. There is little joy in the prospect of a trip on a large mountain lake with only a few logs between you and the depths below, and a storm either imminent or in progress, so every one was thankful. The day was warm, it became absolutely hot; by 8.30 camp equipment and all hands were each in their allotted space, the steady splash-splash of the sweeps broke the glass-like surface about us, and the mountains and islands reflected in the lake, cast about us a fairy-land as we pushed away from them into broader waters. After tying up for a short rest and lunch, we arrived at our original starting-place at 6 P.M., thus ending probably the first voyage ever taken on Maligne Lake.

On reaching land we turned and took a last look at our little craft. Built without nail or spike, held together with wooden pegs and lash-ropes, every ugly line in little H. M. S. *Chaba* was endeared to us. She had carried us far and safely, and now, with regret, we left her there on those lonely shores where other travellers some day may find and use her. Returning to our original camp we found all well and in order, and in an hour no one would have realised we had just returned from a maiden voyage.

The next day the homely duties of washing and mending engaged some of us, while others searched for a trail to the lower end of the lake. The night of the 13th was one of the worst we had ever endured in camp. Heat and a brewing storm brought out every mosquito for miles around I am sure. Donning our hats and "bug-nets," we stowed ourselves away in the suffocating sleeping-bags, expecting the usual change before midnight. Nothing came but more mosquitoes, which hummed and howled and prodded the protecting net till sleep became well-nigh impossible. Toward daylight I rose in my wrath and, with a swoop, switched out a perfect cloud of the brutes, hit "M." on the nose, and woke her unintentionally from a sound sleep—the sleep a marvellous fact to me considering the circumstances.

We then and there vowed to get even with our tormentors, so the minute breakfast was over, out came the netting, nail-scissors, and shoe-thread. While I measured and sewed, "M." hovered over me with a big balsam bough which she kept switching, and by afternoon we could sit placidly in our tents and defy the thousands of impudent little bills presented at our front door.

17: The Tribulations of the Investigator

THE next day between showers camp was broken, and we soon hit an old Indian trail bound for the lower end of the lake. This trail, in places, must be from five to seven hundred feet above the water, over high cut banks. From the moment of finding it, the distance of eight or ten miles was both interesting and very easy and but little cutting was necessary. At the lake's outlet we found that a comparatively recent fire from the north had burnt an area of about half a mile on the western shore, the only blemish in the lake's whole twenty-mile length of exquisite green.

On a high bank overlooking the mouth of the lake our three tents were soon pitched in the burnt timber, the beds were pumped up, the fire-place arranged, the horses turned out to feed, our lake lay spread before us, and life looked as serene as the sunshine about us. We investigated the outlet, which, though showing considerable volume, looked calm, and it seemed a more or less easy crossing with a swim of only a few yards in the centre of the stream (which was probably not more than fifty yards wide). After a smooth flow of about two hundred yards, the water plunged over a steep, rocky bed and we could hear it pounding and roaring as it rushed on its way to join the Athabaska. As "M." and I sat at the water's edge, we sized up the situation for a short and exciting swim to the other side on the morrow, for it was across there we could see fine feed, and there seemed a strong probability that the trail to the Athabaska lay that way.

Considering our aspirations, the next move seemed a more or less providential affair. Not that we were in the habit of rushing headlong into deep rivers, still we might have ventured; there was certainly nothing terrifying in appearances in that placid body of water, only a few yards of it where, through its crystal clearness, we could plainly see a horse would be far beyond his depth.

Returning to camp for lunch, "M.," in an idle moment, got out the binoculars and sat silently at her usual stunt, gazing at the mountains opposite for any geological phenomena. After a few moments she said in her quiet way, "I see goat." That was enough. The poor binoculars, which were always "catching it" for their inability to perform their proper functions, were eagerly sought by the masculine element, who soon announced two goats and a kid, and in a few moments two nannies and two kids. As soon as we could locate them, they could be quite easily seen with the naked eye leisurely strolling over the grassy slopes a couple of thousand feet above the lake.

"K." decided that a stew of kid was not to be despised (no one craved elderly goat after our former experience), so stuffing some clothes, the binoculars, and the camera in a waterproof bag and mounting Ricks, a strong swimmer, he dropped over the bank to the well-marked ford and started in. Knowing he would have the swim which "M." and I had been hoping to take for the fun of it, I went to the edge of the bank to watch the proceedings, little thinking what was coming. I was astonished to see the horse protest violently at being put into that nice stream, and astonished still more to see that in a few yards the shallow-looking water was sweeping to the top of the saddle. Then, to my amazement, I beheld the ever well-behaved Ricks thrashing and striking the water violently, then suddenly turn over backward, and "K." shoot out of the saddle. Craning my neck still farther, I saw "K." swimming for shore and the horse, with head under and feet up, being borne quickly towards the rapids only a hundred yards below.

Camp in burnt timber

I turned away. One of the best horses gone and "K." perhaps washed into that awful maelstrom before he could get out!—all for a bit of fresh meat! Telling the others what I had seen, we stood there dumb for an instant and then, oh, the relief! Through the willow brush they all returned, Chief leading a draggled, crestfallen horse, and "K." just behind with a very puzzled face over the whole performance.

Soaked and shivering, he waited till Dandy (also a strong swimmer) was brought in, then returned again to the river, this time hitting the water a little above the first attempted crossing. But no more watching for me; I viewed the affair by proxy now,—keeping out of sight and noting progress in the countenances of those who had more nerve.

I was watching "M.'s" face. It suddenly stiffened, she leaned forward in a tense attitude, then without turning, called out:

"Dandy 's gone under! "K." has been tossed off and is swimming to shore!" Then: "Dandy can't right himself, he is drowning!" Chief, who was standing near, turned away, saying: "There is a dead horse for you; his foot is caught in the halter-shank!" I could not look; our beautiful, willing, gentle Dandy lost in that horrid river! I thought of all his virtues, just as I had been thinking of "K.'s" the first time he was pitched off and before I knew what a splendid swimmer he was. And all for an old yellow goat! Then looking at Chief's face again, I saw it eased of its set expression as he said, "He 's swimming, he 's up, he 's out!" and I rushed forward to see Dandy, only five minutes before bright-spirited and handsome, slowly emerging from the water, scarce able to drag one foot after the other, yet it was Dandy *alive*, but on the far side of the river. Head down, the rifle still hanging from the saddle, he stood there alone. "K." determined to swim across immediately to get him, but the family vetoed any more risks in that river, and Chief suggested lashing together a few logs and rafting over.

After two such experiences the mild-looking outlet of the great lake could hold but one solution, there must be an undertow, so to speak, the force of which was so great that the moment a horse carrying man, saddle and rifle, was caught within its vortex, it bowled him over.

With plenty of dry timber lying around, the men were soon chopping, hauling, and lashing together logs, and we, desirous of doing something to relieve the tension, proceeded to dry some of the numerous soaked garments which festooned the surrounding bushes. Then we suddenly realised something was amiss, an ominous quiet pervaded the atmosphere, and, looking up, we realised that the other twenty-one horses were hitting the back trail, the tails of the last two or three just disappearing beyond a rolling hill.

Here was something useful to do. Shod only in canvas sneakers, I flew to head off those aggravating horses. After a mile's chase, I arrived at a point of vantage and paused a moment to watch the speed at which those hobbled horses were getting over ground. Old Pinto was leading, his bulky, stubby body sawing up and down, as he rapidly put distance between his all-too-willing followers and their legitimate abode.

Then I found myself on the wrong side of quite a deep stream (as well as my temper), so grasping the only weapon I could find (a club), I skipped down, sprang into the water, and landed, a figure of Vengeance, among the surprised bunch of culprits. Impudence succeeded surprise, and a look of " What have you to say about it? " came over their faces. "A good deal!" And I shook my weapon at the greatest sinner—Pinto. With the kittenishness of an elephant, he skipped just out of reach and remained so all the way back, and to this day has not had the drubbing he so roundly deserved. The others, absorbing Pinto's defiance, promptly spread themselves over the landscape like the sticks of a fan, utterly ignored the trail, and made themselves generally disagreeable. Heated, exasperated, and with soaked shoes, I finally landed them back at camp.

The men were still working desperately on the raft, so the rest of us, coaxing in the few unhobbled horses with salt, soon put a quietus on rapid locomotion, and the salt put a quietus on our driving them beyond the camp limits. They hung round nosing into everything and kept us busy driving them out of the pans and grub-boxes. In the midst of our efforts, Baldy, a four-year-old pet, was spied behind a bush calmly making a meal on a piece of laundry. I think he was cutting his second teeth, and lovable though he was, he had been more nuisance on the trail than a puppy in a drawing-room, chewing the straps, ropes, and pack-mantles of any of his pals who chanced at the time to be sharing the trail with him.

As clothes did not grow on trees in that land, some one had to rescue that shirt, so some one started for Baldy, whose flight through the forest was made plain by the bright bit of waving colour. He was finally rounded up between two trees, the thoroughly masticated sleeve was drawn from his throat, and in time the labourers knew that some of us had not been idle.

At last the raft was completed and " Chef " and "K." pushed out into the lake, making a wide circle to avoid the current. Dandy, who had never moved in the hour and a half since the catastrophe occurred, saw them coming and gained heart sufficiently to sample the grass around him.

With bated breath, we watched the bulky old raft piloted safely past that uncertain exit and into shore on the other side. Dandy was reached, the saddle and the rifle were removed, and then he was invited to recross the river. Poor fellow, after so recent and miserable an experience, he had no desire to again place his life in jeopardy, and rushed up and down the bank to avoid his rescuers. It looked for the moment as though he would have to be left there, but a little incident turned the scales. Just as matters were beginning to look hopeless, two of his special chums came to the bank opposite him and coaxingly whinneyed to him. Hearing their call, he plunged in, sank utterly from sight for a moment, then his nose and ears becoming visible, he struck for our side and in a few minutes every one was patting and making a fuss over him, and in our hearts we were saying, "A well named river, 'Maligne.'"

As the sun went down that night and the slanting rays fell on the far green slopes, the once coveted bunch of goat was still strolling peacefully about, but had no longer any charms for us.

The following day was devoted to looking for a trail to the Athabaska, "K." being rafted over to the east shore for a search on that side, while I, in a moment of aberration or overzeal for the situation, followed Chief on the west side as he scoured the country for miles, looking for a possible way out for horses. At every turn we were met with burnt timber, ravines, and unsurmountable walls of rock, till, after six hours' trudging, we turned back weary and discouraged. Flowers new and rare bloomed everywhere, but I would n't have undertaken to carry even a match by that time, and camp looked pretty good to us when we struck it at 5 P.M.

"K." returned with a better report. He had found an old trail on his side of the river, but much cutting would have to be done before it would be passable. However, it was enough encouragement for us, and we woke the next morning to hear lots of chopping going on; some one had begun bright and early to reinforce the emergency raft,—we were to cross to the other side that day. Nobody was specially jovial at the prospect, considering how near we had come to losing two good horses the day before, and, but for the fact that he was a strong swimmer, a good man also. But the Athabaska via the Maligne, could be only thirty miles away at the most, while, by the only other route, it was over one hundred.

As Dandy had made his return journey safely when freed of all impediments, it only remained to be seen if the smaller horses could stem that bad river; if they made it all right, we and all our belongings were to be rafted over where horse-feed was plentiful.

With breakfast despatched, all minds turned to the horse-drive. Hobbles were removed, "K." went down to the water's edge on Nibs to give encouragement to the others, while Chief on Dandy shot here and there through the fallen timber trying to force the other twenty to follow. Pinky, reaching the water's edge first, held the key to the situation and refused to budge or even touch that river, and as none of the others claimed his position, he just stood there betraying no sign that he heard any of the rumpus behind him, or that he, with the others, was "going to catch it shortly." "M.," with a collection of cameras, stood on the bank, running the risk every few moments of being bowled over into the water by one of the fraternity slipping away from the main bunch and banging into her. It soon proved useless; Chief could drive them to the edge, but there it ended. Fresh tactics must be tried. "K." came up and, with Chief, drove the whole bunch down to the old ford.

I looked no longer. Some one was liable to be drowned; even the Twins grew dear as I realised we might never see them more. I stood out of sight and waited; the yells and threats ceased; there was a dead silence; then up from the water came a snorting, blowing and splashing; I rushed over to "M." just in time to snatch up one of the cameras and train it on the draggled-looking horses as they were emerging on the far side. Old Fox had led off and the others had followed according to disposition. The Twins, on whom so many doubts had settled, went sailing and bobbing over in the same reckless and irresponsible fashion in which they did everything else.

Then down came the tents, all the baggage was hustled and tumbled to the water's edge, the old raft made five or six trips, and we landed on the beautiful meadows on the other side.

As a storm threatened, and I was n't much success at carrying flour and bacon into dry quarters, I offered to go in search of the horses who had silently stolen away while every one was busy. The offer was accepted and Muggins and I went off to look them up. In a few minutes we had picked up their trail; the threatened storm disappeared, the sun burst forth, and on we walked. Fine meadows, dotted with ponds of clear water, followed each other with great regularity, but not a sign of the horses. Their tracks led us on over one knoll after another, it grew hotter and hotter (so did I), then, while Muggins was after a grouse, I heard the distant clang of the bells and, climbing one more knoll, looked down upon the twenty-two sinners. Momentarily they cared nothing for all that luscious grass, but, bent on having a lark after their cold swim, were enjoying a regular picnic. A sortie of a mile or so got them just where I wanted them—ahead of me, then, cross and tired, I started for them with a club. In a trice they were off to the hill from which I had first spied them; then Pinto threw his tail in the air, fifteen or more followed suit, and before I could move they were out of sight and were thundering towards camp. Tired as I was and utterly deserted, the uncommon frivolity was so ridiculous that I sat down and laughed, then sauntered back home and arrived in time to see the culprits getting their deserts—hobbles.

That evening as the sun went down, it cast a most gorgeous colour over the lake. The white summits of Warren, Unwin, and Maligne changed to rose, then, merging into a violet tone, slowly disappeared with the coming of night.

Around the camp we discussed the probabilities and possibilities of reaching the main Athabaska by this route. "K.", who had made the only inspection, dwelt on the fearful amount of down-timber, but, with his accustomed grit, and, knowing that the only other route meant quite a hundred miles, advised the attempt of cutting a way through. "Chef" was to take charge of camp and the useless members of the household for two days, when one of the choppers would return and let him take his turn at the front.

The morning of July 20th was hot and clear; Chief and "K.", with their axes and two days' grub, pulled out of camp about 7.30. Nobody said much; you learn to take a great deal out in thinking on the trail, and both sides of the situation were doing their full quota at this particular time I'm sure. We had been in similar straits before, and "M." and I at least knew what it all meant. Hard labour with heat, flies, and mosquitoes by day, and a camp-fire and no blankets at night, are not the most joyful conditions to contemplate or endure. Camping and exploring are great fun until you reach the point where you must see others suffer for your hobby, and then, if you possess even the smallest amount of conscience, you feel most mortally mean and uncomfortable.

As we watched the faithful disappearing in the distance, gone without a murmur or complaint, we both felt "pretty low in our minds." The day passed with nobody in camp active except the bugs. By noon the thermometer registered 90°; a breeze from the lake sprang up and blew away the mosquitoes; "Chef," in looking after the welfare of the horses, got a couple of grouse, and we all agreed that they should be roasted for the workers. Prepared and cooked before the wood fire in the reflector they make a wonderful addition to the daily fare of bacon. The Botanist went off for a stroll to investigate the hill-tops where we had seen the goat, and on his return brought with him specimens of an exquisite alpine bluebell which he said grew in great profusion above tree-line.

We did not expect our men that night, nor did they come. As the air in the mountains always grows cool with the departure of the sun, we sat wrapped in our buckskins watching the rays of an aurora and thought of the absent ones as we tucked ourselves away for the night in our blankets, for once despising our comforts as we knew they had only a fire before which to turn and turn about in order to keep warm.

A similar day passed, except that the evening brought in a weary pair heralded by Muggins, who seemed glad to get back home where every slice of bacon was not counted. Reports were not encouraging; they had cut about five miles, but the burnt district seemed limitless and the nearer they got to Medicine Lake the heavier was the timber. The previous night had been pretty cold, and, what with working all day in the heat and stoking their fire all night, they were going to arrange a different plan of campaign.

At dusk the horses strolled in, apparently just for a visit, got a little salt all round, and strolled off leisurely again to the meadows.

The next attack on that wood-pile came the following day, when a horse with tent, blankets and food pulled out and the entire masculine contingent, accompanied by the Botanist, who was to bring back the horses, were off.

What a grand day that was in camp, not a soul to pry into our domestic efforts! I had been bothered with the old familiar odour to my blankets, the efforts to rid them of it on the Saskatchewan had not been successful, and I had vowed to wash them again the moment no one was looking. When I saw the last of those four men I knew what was going to happen.

With a lake of clean water, with soap, energy, and sunshine, I saw a chance of eliminating some of the annoyance; and washing as the wash-ladies of foreign lands, the blankets were soon sweet and dry in the hot sunshine.

Then the Botanist returned at sun-down with the information that the chopping that had to be done was something terrible; the horses came in for their salt, clouds all steeped in deep rose decked the sky, so trouble and beauty met.

Seven miles away our men were working to cut a trail through to the Athabaska, and we sat there by the lake dreading the hour we had to leave it all. But it had

to come. On the fifth night they walked in weary and worn, and black as crows from the burnt timber, reporting "that weeks of labour would not put us through, and the longest way round would eventually be the shortest." Disappointed as we all were, it was a lovely night in our home; forest fires from the south veiled the distant peaks with a smoky softness. It was tensely quiet, not even the lap-lap of the water from the shore. Then the pall-like stillness broke. A queer, wild laugh came over the water again and again; it was the loon calling his mate.

The following morning the horses were put across the river, the raft took us and our baggage safely over, and we camped for the night on the western side.

On the morning of July 24th, a tattoo on the tin wash-basin at five o'clock woke every one for an early start. It had rained hard in the night, not a sign of haze or smoke had been left in the air, and everything was as dazzling as water could make it. By seven o'clock, leaving the poor discarded raft to its fate, we said farewell to the only kingdom we could call our own. With the last of the night's storm-clouds rolling away from the high peaks, with shadows and sunshine racing in mad confusion across her rippled waters, the lake was just as fair and beautiful as the day we first met her. Then we turned the corner, she was gone, and we hurried along. How we did hurry too! The horses, in spite of their packs, cantered along remembering the camp-ground ahead of them, and as we came into Chaba Camp, Bessie's joy burst all bounds, and she went bucking and scampering around in a most absurd fashion. But oh, the crest-fallen expression when orders from the rear drove them on: down went their heads and they marched the next seven miles solemnly to Camp Eureka.

18: The Joys of Pobokton Valley and the Sun Wapta

JULY the 27th should have been Friday and a black one at that, instead of which it was Monday—and blue. As grumbling aloud is out of order on the trail, I poured out my sentiments that night to the long-suffering diary thus: "Hobson's Choice Camp. Thank goodness we are here, though goodness knows it is little to seem thankful for!

"Leaving Castillea Camp with only a two-mile drive to Pobokton Creek, and about six from there to the Sun Wapta according to the map, and with Dr. Coleman's trail of 1892 to assist us, no one dreamed of trouble. So off we started with far brighter prospects than usual in taking an untried course. We had reckoned on three hours' travel, but had reckoned in blissful ignorance.

"From the moment we struck the Pobokton, troubles assailed us. Muskeg, a few yards of good going in green timber, log jumping, more muskeg, much cutting, a good stretch, a bad stretch, followed on the heels of each, till at 5 P.M. there came a regular jam! We could plainly see where Dr. Coleman's axe had been used down the whole valley, but since his trip many a wind had swept that way, and the advance was cut off by a game of giant jackstraws. In a thick bunch of pine the men left us and went off to reconnoitre and chop. The tired and hungry horses stood around dejectedly, a few straying off in a disheartened sort of way, to nibble a few spears of grass which had the courage to grow on that dreary hillside. As it was hard to keep track of the whole twenty-two in that thick timber, we tied up the worst stragglers, occasionally rounded up the others, and spent the rest of the time listening to the distant sound of the axes and wondering if we ever had been quite so miserable before.

"Everybody was hungry and I added neuralgia to my woes. The sun was fast descending to the horizon and, scanning the heavens, 'M.' and I concluded that a good downpour would just about complete our discomfiture. So we thought till we heard a wind coming down the valley. It grew louder, then swooped with full force into the dead pines among which we were standing, with a creaking and cracking enough to make one shudder. We untied the horses to let each have his chance to jump, and just about then came the welcome call, 'Drive up the horses!' No one hesitated, but just drove, and for five hundred yards there was some pretty tall jumping. Then we struck green timber once more, somebody in the lead stirred up a hornet's nest, and there was great exhibition of speed for a few moments. Reaching the river there was no favourable crossing to the good feed on the other side, so here we are to spend the night."

Thus ended one of our few dreary days. Three miles of trailing the next morning brought us to good feed and to a point where we were to part company with the Botanist, "Chef," and nine of our horses.

They carried many letters and messages to the outside world for us as well as our best wishes for their safe crossing of the Saskatchewan, which at that time would still mean swimming. As "K." was going with them for a few miles he shouted back the familiar caution, "Don't meddle in the kitchen while I am away," so we promptly went to work and made some fish-cakes. Then Chief thought he would get in some fine work, and when I came back to camp half an hour later with a pail of strawberries, there was the loveliest fruit-cake just going into the reflector. The moment arrived to turn it, and we all stood watching the performance. (No amount of time or numbers of bannocks or cakes on the trail ever cause the interest to pall when the turning operation takes place.) The deed was done, and the reflector being pushed gently and breathlessly back to the fire, when—slip! bang! went the hot puddingy dough into the ashes! Muggins, who had been greedily watching proceedings, was invited to partake, was nothing loth, and seemed none the worse later on.

Not to be done out of his treat, Chief flew round to duplicate the dish and have it out of the way before "K." returned. In his hurry for some water, he picked up the enamelled fruit-kettle (one "K." never allowed us to use), and rushed to the river. But fate follows the evil doer. As he reached for the water, the force of the stream knocked it from his hand and away it went! Regrets were useless. We got the cake and it was good, but the memory of the lost pot lived with us the rest of the summer. For the fruit had to be stewed in a tin pot, while any left-over puddings became rusty after standing a few hours, and "K." referred resignedly at such times to the enamelled pot which was lost through disobedience. It was all quite painful, still we survived and can firmly deny that there can be any evil effect from eating acid on metal—in spite of scientific proof.

With our horses now numbering thirteen and our family reduced to four, we proceeded on the 30th down the east bank of the Sun Wapta, hourly comparing the route with the one taken on the west side of the same river the previous year.

It was a toss-up which was the better of the two; I think we considered there was a little less muskeg, and a little less chopping, and a little less trouble generally where we were. Still it was "nothing to write home about," it was all quite mean enough.

The trail had not been used for a long time, and there were spasmodic searchings in the indistinct places for it, while at one corner the river had carried it off bodily, and left us facing a raging torrent, all other advance cut off apparently by an impenetrable mass of fallen trees. Off came the axes from the saddles, the men disappeared, and "M." and I remained guardians of the horses, which, in our limited quarters, left four of them standing well on the edge of nothing, and no other spot to stray to but the river. We two communed silently with nature, the horses apparently did likewise, for fully twenty minutes. Then came the familiar call, "All right, we'll move up a bit!" So well did the horses understand, that, without a hint from us, they pro-

ceeded to get into line and slowly move on. All but Silver; he, poor fellow, had got so shunted in his restricted quarters that his back was to the river; he was sound asleep, and the impetuous Peter crowding past him for fear of getting left, caught on his pack, and the sleeping Silver was bowled head over heels into the water. The awakening was a rude one but very effectual, and he went swimming hither and yon trying to get out of the rushing river. He was finally rescued from a nasty log-jam and walked out on dry land carrying our duffel-bags, which we thought surely would have shipped an abundance of water. We examined them and to our joy and surprise found them intact, so tied them up, repacked, and pushed on to find fresh mud-holes and other obstructions.

On August 1st we merged from the Sun Wapta valley and, following the undulating hills of the Athabaska River, came into camp on her rugged shores. From here we were once more entering new country to us (a pastime much more interesting than covering old ground), and these wide-open benches on the south side of the river proved very fascinating.

We had at last traversed the full length of the Endless Chain (named the previous year), and found at its farther end a busy little creek by which both white man and Indians had camped in earlier days. Not having done our full day's travel in miles, and feed apparently plentiful anywhere, we lingered only long enough to prowl through the willow-brush interspersed with grassy spots, and found the ground covered with huge wild strawberries. There had evidently been a very recent banquet there, for logs were ripped and torn in every direction,—old Bruin had been feasting on ants as well as berries. Camping a couple of miles farther on, it took quite a little courage for "M." and me to return the next day and pick berries, as we did; we were only spurred on in our good efforts by the knowledge that our men were spending a hot day in the bush cutting a trail through a bad stretch of timber. But we accomplished our task by keeping up a loud conversation to warn Mr. Bear that we were around.

Falls on the Sunwapta

The following day's travel was as delightful as turning the pages of an old book. The book was the trail, the pages turning as we crossed streams, brushed through forests, passed old camp-sites, read the significance of blazes on the trees, or pushed our way through recently fire-swept country.

At one point, after a tough scrimmage on a rough side-hill, we entered a cathedral of spruces. So dark, dim, and silent was it, after the glare of the burnt country behind us, our eyes at first scarce took in the surroundings. Then we found ourselves in an Indian's winter quarters. Under the great black boughs he had built himself a tepee of poles and covered it thick with spruce boughs; against a tree leaned the boards on which he had stretched his marten skins; a pair of discarded snow-shoes lay near by, and at the door of the te-pee an old broken tom-tom which he had evidently used to scare away the evil spirits during the long winter nights. The picture was a depressing one, the thought of the lone hunter and his lonely nights breathed through every sign; some one bunched the straggling

horses quickly together and we moved on again to a meadow nearby, which was simply a mass of gold, white, and crimson flowers, where the horses waded up to their necks in flaunting asters and other autumn flowers; what a contrast it was, all within a hundred yards!

Climbing a low, sharp hill, we found ourselves looking down on the Athabaska rushing silently by. From every direction radiated well-marked game-trails, bunches of white wool hung on low branches, a favourite salt-lick without a doubt, and we wished we had time to hide nearby and watch the coming and going of the game whose tracks were everywhere.

By this day's experience we were beginning to consider (barring mosquitoes, sand-flies, and such minor details) that travelling down the Athabaska was not such a bad matter after all, and looked forward to the next day's drive with interest and pleasure.

Starting off cheerfully in the early morning, we soon reached a sharp bend in the river, where, swinging to the left, it plunged through massive walls two hundred feet high into a narrow canyon, which seemed to wind along indefinitely into the hills beyond. It was a very fine sight, but, on searching for our previously well-defined trail, it seemed to have died a sudden death.

For six miles we groped around the base of Mount Hardisty, over small fallen timber which cracked like pistol-shots under the horses' feet, and then stood guard over our steeds while the men searched for a way around a deep gorge, and at last, after hours of climbing on the interminable rolling hills in the hot sun, we made camp near a slough, which supplied fairly good horse-feed and, as usual, an abundance of flies.

Mount Hardisty, one of the few named mountains in that country, where hunter, trapper and prospector have travelled for many a year, brings to mind no joyous thoughts of the trail,—just heat, sand-flies, and weariness. Scenery we had to perfection. Away to the west of us lay the gap of the Whirlpool River, up which we had time to travel only in thought. For it is at the head of this river stand

Mount Hardisty

Mounts Hooker and Brown, printed on all maps up to ten years ago as two of the highest peaks of the Canadian Rockies. They had been reported by David Douglass, the English botanist, when he travelled through that country in 1826, and up to 1894 had carried off the palm as between 16,000 and 17,000 feet high. Dr. A. P. Coleman, visiting that pass in 1894, climbed Mount Brown, promptly reduced its altitude to 9000 feet, and thus left Mount Robson (at the head of the Fraser River) to carry off the laurels of the eastern slope of the Rockies. The Whirlpool itself has its rise in a curiously named little lake—"The Committee's Punch-bowl." Inquiring of an old-timer of the country the origin of the name, he said: "In the old days when the factors of the Hudson's Bay posts of the interior met those of the coast, a com-

mon meeting-ground was chosen; it proved to be the little pool at the head of the Whirlpool, and thus the name."

All these facts passed through our minds, but the summer days were passing, we had many miles to go, equally other interesting things to see, and reluctantly gave up the Whirlpool trip for that year.

Through the gorge below us flowed the swiftly-rushing, muddy Athabaska winding away into the indefinite distance among hills of which we had no slightest knowledge, and a rift far, far to the north-west suggested the possible valley of the Miette River, the highway to our Mecca—the Yellowhead Pass. Would the way be kind to us, or the same as yesterday and many other yesterdays?

Dr. Coleman's report had left much vagueness, much to be surmised. On one point only were we clear, that was,—"buffalo prairies" had to be crossed, prairies where grass for the horses would be in plenty; perhaps the coming day, August 6th, would see us leaving rock-ledges and burnt timber behind us and we be wandering in vast elysian fields, for the word "prairie" certainly represents miles of open country to most minds.

For four miles of our way, having at last struck a real trail, we climbed up hills and slid down them, encountered annoyances of various kinds, then rode for an hour through a regular park where our horses crushed great bunches of strawberries under their feet, and where we occasionally sprang from our saddles, filled our hands with sprays of the crimson fruit, and sprang back to nibble at them leisurely as we rode along behind the packs. And then we suddenly emerged from the timber and struck the finest bit of feed we had seen for many a long day, where purple pea-vine, goldenrod, and bluebells grew to enormous heights in the tall grass. The horses, at the sight, kicked up their heels and were ready for lunch at once, but a masculine voice behind ordered every one on to the river's edge, where tepee-poles pointed out the camping-ground.

The next day's travel was one of great beauty as we wandered through a chain of small grassy meadows, where flowers were gorgeous and where recent fires had wiped out the way to go, where streams of indefinite depths and crystalline clearness twisted their way through great bunches of willows, where the men made innumerable sorties trying to recover the lost trail, and we stayed with the horses and munched strawberries till they returned with the same old story, "Can't imagine where that trail has gone."

And still in our ignorance we kept looking ahead for the "buffalo prairies," little dreaming at the time that our pretty open sloughs were the "prairies." (I 've often wondered who named them.) Going, however, was perfectly easy, and, with the Athabaska only a few hundred feet to our left, we decided we could not go very far wrong, so wandered blissfully on.

Then we awoke to the fact that a high bluff had intruded itself directly before us, which forced us to turn to the right and climb probably a hundred feet; again we advanced, a rocky fissure came into view, and the performance was repeated; a third time our tired horses were forced to ascend the rough hillside till we reached a bold and prominent point so far above the river that we could see for miles around us. A tiny thread of white in the green timber to the west seemed as though it must be the Miette River flowing from the Yellowhead Pass, while other stray threads just ahead showed where the Athabaska had split into many channels.

Bewildered as to which way to go next, the men again left us to explore, while "M." and I took up our usual duty of minding the horses.

The sun shone bright and clear over the great wild panorama. Did that western valley hold our dream—were we at last to reach it? The Yellowhead Pass and Mount Robson,—were they there? Where were the hundreds of prospectors, surveyors, etc., who, we had heard in the spring, were flooding that country? Was there no voice to rise out of all that wilderness and tell us which way to go or where to cross that swirling body of water?

Our questions asked in silence came as silently back to us. The sound of our guides' footsteps on the rocks died away; Muggins put up a covey of partridges and tore off after them, his barks growing fainter and fainter. Yet there we stood alone with our patient beasts, only a little wind from the north keeping us company and, for the moment, blowing off the tormenting flies. Then out of the vast solitude came a sound so refreshing, inspiring and exciting that even the tired horses raised their heads and we listened. Again it came, very faint and far off, but still it was true—a horse-bell sounded across the river! Some one besides ourselves was travelling in that wide valley.

It doubtless seems rather silly to even mention excitement from the mere tinkle of a horse-bell. But it was so. Two months had gone by since we had seen a face, heard a voice, or had news from any other world than our own. Even now our men were gone and only we caught that rare, musical note, for it came to us on the wind, sweeter than any opera note I ever heard. We scarce breathed lest we miss the sound of that old brass clapper as some stray horse moved slowly about in the distant forest, little dreaming what an object of interest he was to two lonely women perched high on a rock-bluff a mile or two away.

Suddenly a rifle cracked and we fairly jumped with surprise. Had the people over there seen us—we and our horses against the sky-line? Were they red or white? Would they ride into the open and signal to us? Questions, questions, and no answer. No sign of a horseman, no sign of a tent or tepee, just the silence and the soft winds floating by, and yet we listened. Then we awakened to the fact that far below us Chief was yelling for us to start the horses down the bluffs. Brave old-stagers, they understood. Just a word, they fell in line and slowly crept down without a moment's hesitation or misstep, and we slipped into an ideal camp-ground in the bend of the Athabaska right opposite the mouth of the Miette. "Ideal camp-ground" it certainly was, and others had found it so before us. With all wind cut off by the hills behind us, the horses could not feed for the flies, but chased up and down till darkness sent their tormentors to bed.

With camp fixed up, the men went off to look over the next day's march, while I climbed over the bluffs for another look toward the Yellowhead.

Darkness brought the men and much depressing information to be digested with supper. 'The lost trail had been found after a long hunt, located a couple of miles back in the hills; our own advance by the river's edge was cut off by a rock wall (which only game could scale) scarce two hundred yards away, and, to get out, we must retrace our steps over the rock-bluff down which we had travelled that day.' Hard lines, but the lines of him who insists upon penetrating a country he does not know.

We stole rather dejectedly to our tents that night, leaving a bright camp-fire at the door where the horses promptly gathered and stood around in the pungent smoke.

19: Rock-Bluffs, Gorges, and Residents of the Athabaska

THE diary at this point speaks my mind better than any after-thought. It starts: "Friday, August 7th, Rock Bluff. I wonder why so much that's uncomfortable happens on Friday. The sun rose this A.M. without the sign of a cloud. On the netting, stretched across our tent door, were hundreds of flies, batting their senseless heads to get in,—a great day for us when we invented that net. Just as 'hot water' was called, we heard the horses galloping in and making a frantic rush for our fireplace, where they had found relief the evening before from the stinging gnats. Our trials and our joys, lived out together for so long, may make us love those horses very dearly, but with the glaring sun in the tent, about a million flies all over the horses, waiting to attack us the moment our noses reached beyond the confines of that patent curtain, while fifty-two iron-shod feet pounded and kicked up sand and ashes, is a situation trying to the sweetest disposition, and we could have loved them better at a distance. Impatient with conditions, I reached out for a towel and wash-cloth which I had left lying overnight on the tent-rope. Luckily the towel was there, but Bessie had got ahead of me with the wash-cloth. Nine-tenths of it had disappeared; the other tenth hanging from her black mouth told the tale. At breakfast, Chief, with a rather grim countenance, announced the fact that, before making the long detour to reach the trail in the hills, he meant to tackle the rock-bluff ahead of us. Personally, the suggestion made me shudder even though I had not seen the spot, but the set of his jaw was quite enough for me—it was no child's play he was attempting.

" By nine o'clock we were packed up and off, crossing an arm of the river to an island, and back to the south shore again. Bessie was in a rather bucky mood (not at all unusual), and 'M.' suggested it might be the wash-cloth lying heavy on her conscience. Fortunately, she was in the rear as we made a short stiff climb to a precipitous grassy bank, where a well-used game-trail gave comparatively good footing. I was coming slowly along on Nibs just behind Chief, who was leading Dandy, and was quite unprepared for a sudden plunge and kicking in front of me, till Chief called out: 'Hornets' nest; back out and try higher up!' We certainly did 'back out' without waiting for second orders. Dandy's position was most disconcerting; a hornets' nest plays fearful havoc on level ground let alone on a precipitous slope overhanging a wicked river, so, as I was next in line, I ascended several feet above, struck a parallel game-trail, and, keeping a top eye open for another hornets' nest, re-started the procession. Travelling slowly along, I spied a huge fellow sunning himself on a low rock by the trail. I sneaked quietly past him and the whole pack luckily got by without raising his ire.

"Then we reached the sticking-point. As I looked over, I confess I shuddered at the thought of putting horses over such a place. To be sure a game-trail was there, but that was no comfort, for goat and sheep can go easily where no human foot can follow.

"The pack-horses were solemnly tied up, 'M.' and I held the saddle-horses, while Peter, the least useful member of society, was led forth and prepared for the experiment by having his saddle removed and a rope attached to the end of the halter-shank so that Chief might be down at the bottom and, through the rope, give the poor thing a little courage. 'K.' was behind him for the same purpose.

"For once Peter had things all his own way. They dared neither pull at his head nor hurry him from the rear. For a moment he looked bewildered and astounded, and then, taking in the situation philosophically, and realising what was expected of him, he stepped forward and made a desperate plunge; his front feet, striking the rock about half way down, gave him just the impetus for the final leap which landed him safely below. Bugler was the next and went over nicely, as as did Nibs also. Then 'M.' and I, sending our cameras rolling down ahead of us, got down ourselves and photographed the rest of the bunch doing one of the neatest horse-stunts I have ever seen.

"With the horses safely down, saddlery, bedding and food came sailing after, and in an hour we were fixed up in camp with only a memory and a few films to recall the event. Hours of travel had been saved over the high hot hills and we wanted to praise the engineer of such a feat, but as he disliked a fuss, I decided to go and pick gooseberries for a pie instead.

"The day being yet young, 'K.' was to go on down the valley and see if by any chance he could locate 'Swift's.' In Mc-Evoy's Government Report, he mentions this true pioneer of the country and on his maps locates the spot where Swift may be found.

"We had seen quite enough of the river by this time to know that our horses could never swim it with their packs, and so thought a safe way of getting over was with Swift's boat. But how far away was Swift's, and then had he a boat, and would we ever be able to let him know we were on the south side of the river? Life has been resolving into interrogation points these past few days. So taking some food in his pocket and telling us he might not return till morning, 'K.' has left us and started off."

Evening and a glorious moon arrived together; it was too warm to need a fire, but a signal was lighted which would show up our little home if the absent one was wandering back late in the night. Ten o'clock came; he should have reached Swift's by that time. We extinguished our beacon and fell asleep

thinking of "K." as having put up somewhere for the night comfortably. At five o'clock the next morning the thud of a horse's feet was heard, and "K." came quietly into camp. The history of his experience again answered a long-asked question: Why had Maligne River been so named? Leaving us the previous afternoon, he soon struck a well-marked trail and, passing two or three small lakes, reached the Maligne near its mouth. Though it was shooting past with terrific force, a well-defined trail led into the water and out again on the other side, so he forced his unwilling horse in, but quickly retreated; no horse could make it at that time of year anyway.

Remembering McEvoy's comments on the conditions farther up the Maligne, he tied Pinto up, walked up about two miles, found a narrow canyon, dropped a tree across, and decided that, though difficult, it was possible to bring horses over. Rather than make the long return trip, he tried to put a tree across the river lower down. After much cutting it fell, fell in exactly the right spot, but the great volume of water caught the boughs and, as though they were straw, hurled the tree into the Athabaska only a few yards away, carrying with it the hope of making a short cut back. His solitary sandwich was eaten, his clothes still damp from the first attempt to get over on his horse, all his matches wet, no coat, the moon, which had lighted his efforts, slipped relentlessly behind the clouds, and he was forced to endure complete discomfort till early dawn shed light enough for him to cross the logs at the canyon. However, he had seen a bunch of horses and knew some one must be not far distant.

After he had had breakfast and a couple of hours' sleep, we were on the move to the mouth of the Maligne to await further developments. Soon after leaving camp, we struck the long-lost trail, which looked as though it had just come down from mountain climbing. It wound past the blue lakes of which "K." had told us, in which we saw large pike fish near the shore. Quantities of tepee-poles proclaimed it a favourite fishing ground, but, as our meat supply was plentiful, we preferred pushing ahead to investigate the next situation.

Just about noon we came on an open prairie and could see conditions on the north side of the river which we so longed to reach. Opposite us lay all that remained of Henry House, an old North-west Fur Trading Company's post. Built as a rival to Jasper House, located twenty-five miles down the river, the site was close to the water's edge, directly opposite the mouth of the Maligne. All that was left of it were the remains of two chimneys and a few charred logs. As I looked across at those silent sentinels, back came the pictures of bygone days when the forest had been cut down around the site to avoid the enemy, when the beaver pelt was currency, when the Indians gathered there to trade the furs they had just brought over the Yellowhead Pass.

All gone—the Indian, the beaver, the old log-house, just we modern people wishing some magician might raise the curtain of the past and show us the traders white and red making their journeys in the dead of winter, with dog-trains, over the frozen river. As I looked, a soft wind swept through the branches of an ancient spruce above my head, the little whispering sounds came down as if to tell me they had been there watching the doings at the old post in the old days, but alas, it was not for me. I could not understand the tongue of the rugged forester, so stole silently back to camp and watched the glorious sunset.

All evening our talk turned on the well-defined trail we could see back of Henry House, on the distance to Swift's, on our chance of signaling some stray surveyor working close by on the Grand Trunk Pacific route, so our minds were naturally bent, even in sleep, on our hope of soon seeing some one.

During the night a slight shower woke and then lulled us to sleep again. About three o'clock dawn was breaking, the birds beginning their morning songs with a first sleepy twitter. A fly, a mosquito, or perhaps a mind, still dwelling on the probabilities and possibilities of the future, woke me. I sat up with a start; "M." was wide-awake listening

too. Far away sounded our horse-bells, but they were an old tune by this time; a distant roll of thunder drifted up the valley—it was not that. "Did you hear some one call?" I asked. "I think I did." Then to our straining ears came a long call; a second, then a third sounded. "Some one has seen our tents and is calling us from across the river! Why don't the men answer?" "M.'s" eyes were big as saucers. Finding my moccasins, I crept to the door of the tent, crawling from under the "bug-net," and listened. Again came the sound, but this time from the opposite direction and far back in the hills,—a long clear note. All remained quiet in our guardians' tent,—dead to the world no doubt with the strenuous work of the last ten days. Sorry to wake them, but fearing to miss something, I listened once more to make sure that my ears did not deceive me, then called sharply: "Chief! Wake up, don't you hear those voices calling?" A sleepy voice came back: "For heaven's sake go to sleep; it's only a coyote!" Coyote! I slipped foolishly back to the tent feeling exceedingly small and tenderfooty.

As described, the cry of those animals was "dismal," while this was a high clear note; so, muttering excuses and self-apologies, I crept into the blankets, dreading the laugh that I knew would be my portion at the breakfast-table.

At seven o'clock the men were off to cut a trail around the canyon and "M." and I were busy housekeeping.

At noon, while at lunch, we took an inventory of our morning's labours. A thin and meagre-looking bannock testified to our unaccustomed energies in that direction, a fine batch of fish-cakes made us hungry to look at them, while our efforts at a cake resembled a Chinese puzzle more than an article of diet. The, last made of apricots, prunes, currants, figs, bacon-fat and sugar, all bound together with graham flour, seemed a poem to our partial eyes when we scraped the "gooey" stuff into the reflector, and a woe-begone-looking mess when it came out. But, with the return of the hungry trail-cutters, I noticed it disappeared like the dew from the grass.

With the advent of the diaries late in the afternoon, we discovered that the day was Sunday. No church-bells rang. There was the distant wash of the river mingled with the lazy ring of the horse-bells, a fitful bee blustering around, an occasional wind sweeping up the valley heralding its approach by a whisper in the distant tree-tops, then sighing musically in the poplars overhead. It came laden with the aroma of ground-cedar and brought to mind odours of long-ago Christmas trees. For the time forgot, a Sabbath peace fell with redoubled force over our little home. No church spire built by man could compare with the great rock walls of the Maligne; no organ could speak so soft and low and true as the Athabaska winds, no incense smell so sweet as the warm breath of the spruce and cedar. A perfect Sunday.

To one who loves it, there can be no monotony on the trail, small events are exciting and larger ones become thrilling, so that to us Monday was a record-breaker for action. Every one was out early, "M." and I eagerly anticipating the Maligne gorge of which the men spoke enthusiastically. Bearing away to the right of the trail, we were soon climbing over a hill covered with flowers, and entered the fresh-cut passage made by the men the day before. Fallen in though it was, they had found a way which had been used many years before and, to avoid extra work, had followed it as closely as possible. It led us along some very steep and narrow paths. As the canyon came into view it was really very beautiful, about the finest one in all that country, where canyons are so numerous.

The climb became steeper as we advanced. Striking a sharp ridge, the trail clung to the very brink of the black chasm and showed a sheer drop of at least two hundred feet. The sight, and its close proximity, caused a little shiver to go through even our hardened nerves, especially at one point where it seemed like ascending a ladder into nothing.

Overhanging it and high above this great amphitheatre, we rode; down below the waters boiled and thundered; in pantomime we pointed to the streams issuing from the various strata, tumbling into large worn holes and from there plunging into the river in the deep canyon below. Then the amphitheatre closed to a narrow fissure, the thunderous roar was muffled, and we made our way through the last bit of timber and came to the edge of a very small stream.

The powerful river which, only two miles away, was impassable, had, somewhere nearer its source, dropped almost out of sight, and only in the canyon just passed, had it gathered its forces together again for the last plunge into the Athabaska. Muggins was at first inclined to swim over but was given a free ride, and we were soon thankful that one more problem was solved.

Having climbed about five hundred feet, we now had the pleasure of descending the same. Leaving the river, we came out on bare hills which gave us a fine panorama for miles around. The Miette, in the west, faded away into nothing towards the Yellowhead Pass, and the Athabaska trailed away to a silver line and was lost in the hills to the north-east.

Of course we looked for Swift's, and "Swift" became the sole topic of conversation. Sliding and slipping anywhere down the slopes, we soon reached the river-flats and came across a fine bunch of horses whom I felt like asking if they knew Swift. However, we all stared at each other and our little party continued down the river where travelling was easy.

About 1.30 we came out on a knoll, and there lay Swift's. I wonder if three or four log buildings, a little fencing and a few acres of cultivated land ever caused much more excitement—not to any of us, anyhow.

No one seemed to be moving around, we could see no boat, and the glasses showed no trail, so we decided the crossing must be lower down. Reluctantly we went on, hating to lose sight of that straw of refuge.

When we had gone a mile or so below Swift's, the trail led us directly to a second bunch of shacks surrounded by wheat-fields and a small garden of cabbages, potatoes and turnips. On the other side of the river lay two dugout canoes lashed together. This must be John Moberly's, a half-breed of whom we had heard. Chief rode up to the house to investigate, but came back with the woeful intelligence that no one was home. This was enough to try the most sanguine spirit, but reading a crude notice on a tree at the river's brink, "Here 's the crossing," we decided to camp right on the spot, and our possessions were accordingly dumped there. "M." and I proceeded to take count of the situation while camp was being made. It was a mussy spot and showed signs of recent habitation.

Over the door of the log-cabin hung sheep, goat and deer horns, and a tiny moccasin and an old shoe were tossed where the small owner had used them last. Peeping in the windows, quite free of curtains, it looked just as lonesome and free of comfort as the average shack which the breed inhabits. The true home of the Indian is certainly the tepee; when he takes to a house, he is sure to construct a dismal failure, from our point of view. Returning to the tree and again reading the notice "Here 's the crossing," we sat down to study it all out. Perhaps it *was* a crossing for anything that could swim three hundred yards, or coax over by will-power those canoes reposing so tantalisingly across the river.

With the packs and saddles removed from the horses, "K." decided to fire a couple of shots with his rifle before getting lunch. Nothing materialised. Consequently the horses were turned loose, the tea was made, and we sat down to lunch, wondering how far Mount Robson and the Yellowhead Pass were from us.

A grating, thumping noise from over the water suddenly arrested our attention and we beheld a man loosening the queer-looking craft and about to make his way over. It was Swift. Chief went to welcome him. "M." and I, in our excitement, forgot our unconventional garb and when he came up to join us, felt no reminder of our extraordinary appearance in his greeting. "Women in your party?" he is said to have exclaimed. "Well, well, whatever brought them here? Prospecting or timber cruising? No? Now, look here, I 've been in this valley thirteen years and they 're the first white women I 've seen around these parts. Are you sure they aint prospecting?" He was courtesy itself. He told us "his woman" had heard the shots, so he came down promptly, knowing that Moberly and his family were away hunting.

Two trips of the dugouts carried over all our household goods and provisions, then the horses were rounded up to be put across. This being a more or less painful operation, "M." and I discreetly withdrew from earshot. Swift and the men drove the poor brutes to the point where they must take to the water, no boat for them. From where we were standing, we saw them plunge into the water amid a perfect pandemonium of yells and sticks and stones. Old Fox led bravely off, but the moment the heavy current struck them, Dandy led a gallant retreat. Again they were driven in and again they returned under the same escort. They were then started off for the third time and, as they had had about enough of that shore reception, they continued to follow their leader. Across a wide expanse of muddy water they swam, looking more like a string of ducks than anything else. It was a long swim and the current heavy, so that not a back was visible, their noses and ears being the only part of them above water. Slower and slower went the little procession till, one by one, we counted thirteen dark objects creeping up the bank on the far side. Then, with a sigh of relief that our horses were over, we proceeded to sigh for ourselves at having to cross in those crazy-looking dugouts. This was accomplished safely in spite of a squall that struck us with great force in mid-stream and dry land felt pretty good when we got there.

By the time we could look around not a horse was in sight; Swift's two little girls were standing there glued to the spot, and not a word or a smile could we extract from either of them. No wonder. Later we found we were really the first white women those children had ever seen; that they had been sent to tell their father to hurry home as a surveyor wanted to buy some potatoes, and that he was sending them back with a message frilled in his own inimitable fashion, that "two ladies had arrived and he was going to visit them and get all the news, potatoes or no potatoes." It made us feel like a travelling circus.

Chief now started off in search of the horses, as did "K." also. The lowering clouds brought signs of rain, and Swift started for home. Then it really did rain. We covered our possessions as well as we could, made a fire which was small enough to go in your pocket, owing to the scarcity of fuel, then stood and shivered and felt pretty miserable standing there wet and alone on the banks of the wild Athabaska. Finally a scampering thud announced the return of the entire family, hobbles went on, tents went up, a slim supper was cooked. So scant was ground space that even the wet saddlery had to be piled in where our wet beds, wet duffel-bags, and wet clothes reposed. So gathering to my arms a nice hot-water bottle I crept under the blankets and the Athabaska's annoyances were drowned in dreams.

Accepting Mr. Swift's invitation to camp near his home, we strolled leisurely up the next day, were met by our host, who was leading a very small boy in a very large hat, whom he introduced as "my son Dean Swift," and who used his eyes to effect to see those "first white women."

We had travelled far and had thought of ourselves as going farther and farther toward the end of nowhere, so that the unexpected civilised influences, into which we suddenly plunged, struck us strangely. Our tents were barely up when a hospitable procession was seen making its way through the poplars. First came Mr. Swift carefully balancing a pitcher brimming with new milk, little Lottie followed with a pail of new potatoes all cleaned and ready for the pot, while tiny Ida brought up the rear with a basket containing a dozen fresh eggs. Later came Mrs. Swift carrying the youngest child, and, though her English was limited, we managed to get along nicely and returned the call in the afternoon.

That pioneer's little house was very interesting. Thirteen years previously Swift, and his wife had penetrated here to make a home. By degrees, he had brought in his stock from Edmonton over three hundred miles of as bad a trail as can well be imagined,—cows, horses and chickens. His wheat-field was yellowing, the oats were still green and waving in the soft warm wind. By a mountain-stream he had built a mill for grinding his flour, and a large potato-patch was close by. His buildings were of logs, sound and solid, made entirely by himself, his residence composed of one large room. Here we were welcomed by our hostess who showed us how comfortable a family of six could be in so small a space. Two slept in a good-sized bed, two in a sort of box, the baby in a home-made hammock, but where the sixth was stowed I never found out unless it was under the table. Everything was as neat as a pin. The chairs were of home manufacture and covered with skins, and it was all a lovely study of what may be done with next to nothing in the land of nowhere. But when they offered to take us in too, during our stay, we simply marvelled, and rolled our eyes discreetly around to see where even these hospitable people could possibly have discovered a corner in which to deposit us for the night. Seeing none, and being rather attached to our own comfortable beds, we decided to decline their kind offer.

Then Mrs. Swift (oh, we women are all alike!) unearthed a box from beneath her bed and showed us a half dozen gowns made by herself, most of them her bridal finery, and, as we looked on the carefully treasured garments, I realised—be it mansion or shack—there is sure to be stowed away just such a precious horde around which a woman's heart must always cling. Then came her fancy-work which she did in the short winter days and the long evenings by candle-light, and we began taking a deep interest. She had quantities of silk embroidery on the softest buckskin I have yet seen. Her silks she dyed herself, and her patterns were her own designing. There was a most delicious odour to the skins which she said was through their being tanned

Swift's homestead

by poplar smoke. Gloves, moccasins, and beautiful coats, we took everything and wished she had more; it was a grand afternoon's shopping for us all, for the lonely Athabaska woman and the two white women who had seen none of their kind for many a long day.

That night we had fresh eggs for supper, and Mr. Swift and the little Swifts came to spend the evening with us.

20: Bound for Mount Robson

TO waken in the morning to the crowing of roosters, the lowing of cattle, and the distant chatter of children, were strange sounds indeed to us who had lived so long with the winds, waters, and birds, that we had to think twice where we were when we first opened our eyes. Then in answer to the rattle of a pan at the kitchen fire, we dressed and hurried out to the creek for a hasty scrub before the big eyes of the three small observers should light upon us.

Every one stood around interestedly at packing time and Mr. Swift paid Chief the compliment that, of all the outfits he had seen pass through, his was in the best condition. As it was now fully two months since we had been on the move, to see every horse round and fat, every hoof well shod, every back sound, and every coat sleek and glossy, we certainly did feel proud of our horses especially when we met other outfits.

Leaving our kind host about 9 A.M., we headed for our last goal, Mount Robson. The day was warm and lovely and the trail a good one. On our left we passed Henry House and promised ourselves a visit to it on our return. An hour later we met John Moberly and his family returning from the hunt which had been a very successful one. Though there were several horses loaded with hides and meat, it looked far more like the moving of an orphanage than the return from a month's hunting expedition. John, with a small child in front of him, headed the band, two grinning kids on one horse followed, and so on till Mrs. Moberly brought up the rear in a dignified manner, carrying a small infant under one arm. In all, they counted eight, and I wondered how many white mothers would go on such a trip and look so placid on their return. She smiled a pleasant smile at our greeting and we each passed on our way.

From the day we struck the valley of the Miette, we realised what the trails were. We had never seen a really bad one before.

John Moberly

Our horses were in good condition, but what must the way have been to the footsore and weary? For years it had been a highway for trapper, prospector and surveyor, yet no one seemed to have taken time to remove a solitary obstruction they could possibly get around. We did likewise and grumbled at our predecessors.

The hills were steep and stony while the valley was exceedingly soft. The bones of many a worn-out servitor strewed the line of march and we wondered how it was to fare with our own before the set task was accomplished.

Our second day's travel on the Miette was but a duplication of the first day's conditions, up over high rock-bluffs, then down into the sticky muddy bottoms where willows grew rank above our heads.

Out in the open, where the sun beat down fiercely upon us, there was considerable relief from flies and mosquitoes, for in the willows, they swarmed upon us in millions.

Swift had attempted to describe a specially bad corner on this second day's drive high among the rocks, and had advised our taking a low trail, which, though soft, would be better than following the dry trail at this dangerous point. Not being specially fond of wallowing in the mire, our leader, at the parting of the ways stuck, to the rock trail. It was a more or less unattractive spot, but much more dangerous to horses which had *not* spent practically all their lives at trailing than to our own seasoned stagers. At the critical point, the trail led to the brink of a forty-foot precipice, where the horse and his burden must swing sharply to the left, running the chance of miscalculating the room for his pack, smashing into the rocks, and being bowled over into the abyss below.

I peered over as we came to it, saw many a bleached bone to verify Swift's warning, then followed the line of cautious ponies passing safely down the hill.

Out in the open, the trail was bordered with raspberries and large black currants; fresh beaver cuttings were seen at frequent intervals; flowers familiar and strange were there, and we came into camp on Derr Creek just as tired as our horses, after having had a very interesting day's ride.

Prospectors, from now, on grew numerous and to us, who were so long accustomed to an unconventional garb, quite annoying from the "dress-up" standpoint. From a social point of view we could have asked nothing more, as courtesy, politeness and kindness were showered upon us by all we met.

It was with great curiosity that we started on the next drive which would take us over the Yellowhead Pass. As the pass is only thirty-seven hundred feet high, we found McEvoy's statement (that it is hard to tell when you cross it), quite correct. On the west side a recent fire had swept across the fine timber, through whose gaunt standing trunks we had our first glimpse of Yellowhead Lake, which lies at the base of Yellowhead Mountain (9000 feet). To eyes accustomed to mountains of higher elevations, these lower hills made a rather unimpressive scene.

As we travelled the north shore of the lake, we found it had been fire-swept again and again,

and the timber being Douglas fir of enormous growth, some of us had all we could do to keep in our saddles as our horses went careering and jumping over the huge fallen trees.

Just as we sat down to supper that night, which was spread on the shore of the lake, and in fact right on the trail, the sound of a strange horse-bell announced the coming of more strangers—a half-breed and a French prospector, and they had almost to step over our table in order to get past. As they camped but a short distance from us, when everything was fixed up for the night, Chief and "K." strolled over to see them, leaving "M." and me alone in our grandeur. It was grand too. Our fire, built on the very edge of the glass-like lake, was reflected in the black depths yawning beyond us; the wind died down; over the water came the faint sound of the strangers' horse-bells; then the weird laugh of a loon pierced the darkness with a taunting, ridiculing sound as though calling, "Ha-ha! Left alone, left alone!" and in its wake came the cry of a coyote, which was answered by two or three others on the distant shore. The loon laughed again derisively, the firelight danced cheerily on the walls of our tent, and a few stars peeped down through the black boughs of the spruces above our heads, leaving us to feel but an infinitesimal part of the great whole.

The morning of the sixteenth was Sunday, the signal for rising was not our usual gong, but the cry of the coyotes answering one another around the lake. By eight o'clock we were off, passing our neighbours' camp and making our way around the lower end of the lake. In the first break of the hills beyond Conical Mountain, we came upon a muddy, bustling stream, the Fraser. Tearing down through rocky walls it seemed a perfect miniature of the great river which the traveller by train first sees from the high banks at North Bend on the Canadian Pacific Railway.

Alternate stretches of fallen timber and stony hillsides, Grant Brook, and finally the swiftly flowing Moose River were our portion for the day. Similar to the days before, we found it a great spot for berries of many varieties, the most prevalent being a low-bush *vaccinium*, or blueberry, which grew from ten to twelve inches high. The bloom on the black fruit was like the blue frost on a plum, and the ground for miles was so overgrown with it that it had a blue tinge rather than green. At specially thick spots, we would stop and pluck two or three bushes and refresh our parched mouths for the next ten minutes with the delicious fruit.

Saskatoon bushes grew high above our heads and, as we passed beneath them, seemed to reach forth their graceful boughs and offer their long racemes of purple berries as a gift to the stranger. The big crimson raspberries tempted us to stop, but we nibbled from them all and passed on, pitching camp on the banks of Moose River, where, in a few minutes, our camping-friends of the night before joined us. They dined with us that evening, and I question if a stranger stepping up suddenly could have told red man from white, so sun-burned were we all and so worn and weather-beaten our clothes.

In his broken English, the Frenchman told us of seeing our outfit on the Athabaska and of signaling us with a rifle-shot as he thought probably we were some Indians he was in search of; thus unexpectedly, was answered a question we had often asked ourselves, "Who was it had fired that shot back on the Athabaska?"

The next day's travel around Moose Lake would well deserve a veil thrown over its memory. Swift had spoken of the lake's wonderful beauty, but we had seen so many fine lakes already in that country that we had not been specially impressed with his remarks. As our trail friends pulled out of camp ahead of us that morning, they informed us the trail ahead was "pretty bad," and it certainly fulfilled our expectations. We fairly crawled along for an hour and a half, when a glint of silver through the trees showed us we were nearing the lake. It is a fine stretch of water seven or eight miles long, with a colour of milky green, as it is fed by the turbulent Fraser. The far shores were a soft unbroken mass of forest, a rest to our eyes, weary with the charred conditions under foot

for so many miles. The hills beyond rolled away in soft undulations, but at the time, we were thinking far more of the length of them than of their artistic effect.

Trail on the north shore there was little or none for long stretches; sometimes the ghost of one wound round the pebbly shore, then it would take a notion to dodge up into the wood, wander round a bit up there and return hopelessly to the shore again, only to repeat the same performance all over in a few moments.

Instead of realising the real beauty of that charming sheet of water that day, my mind was not only on our horses, but on those which had gone before and must come after before the coming railroad, the Grand Trunk Pacific, would be a fact. Many had been sacrificed, many were still to be sacrificed, on that hard, barren bit of trail around the shores of beautiful Moose Lake. The sad truth was ever present.

In the hot sun, that lake-shore seemed to stretch twenty-seven miles instead of seven, and we dragged into camp at four-thirty after a strenuous eighteen miles, and one of the party was quite ready for bed by seven o'clock. I believe there was a magnificent aurora that night, but no auroras made any impression on my mind—I had other affairs that took my attention.

The last day's travel to Mount Robson was a great improvement on anything we had had since leaving the main Athabaska.

The moment we started, the valley began to narrow and close in on the river. At places where we could gaze down upon the water fighting its way through huge rocks, we blessed the steady little feet beneath us picking a way so calmly over the treacherous trail, for a slip or a stumble meant the river two hundred feet below.

As the trail left the river and settled down to winding through the timber once more, the family wondered "Where is that old mountain?" Suddenly Chief called out, "Here she is!" and we hurried forward. There "she was," sure enough. No doubting the highest peak in the Rockies of Canada—she spoke for herself. To our weary, sunburnt eyes she

Mount Robson

loomed refreshingly up from behind a hill, cold, icy, clean-cut, in a sky unclouded and of intensest blue. The mountains rising far and near were but worthy of the name of hills, leaving Robson a noble massive vision to the pilgrims who had come so far to see her. We gazed, and our hearts grew hot within us as on every side we saw black tree trunks strewn, ghastly reminders of careless, indifferent campers of other days.

Crossing the Grand Fork of the Fraser we camped in green timber where, if the feed was scarce for our horses, at least there was a lovely setting for the beautiful mountain. When darkness had settled down and bed seemed the most wonderful of all inventions, "M.," our most enthusiastic star-gazer, called us to see an aurora which was throwing ribbons and arches with wonderful rapidity across the summit of Mount Robson and dyeing her snow-fields with a constant change of colour. But tired eyes refused to remain open for even that wonderful display and I soon crawled out of sight, leaving "M.," the aurora and the expiring camp-fire to sit it out together.

21: The Tête Jaune Cache

THOUGH Mount Robson had been so long our Mecca, now that we were within reach of Tête Jaune Cache, it seemed a pity not to see that historic point. Who Tête Jaune really was, is a myth. A fair-haired Indian, he is supposed to have had his cache of furs somewhere on the Fraser River. Milton and Cheadle say the true cache was at the Grand Fork. But being a matter of a hundred years ago, and the history of that country being largely handed down by word of mouth, few of the real facts are obtainable. All our knowledge of the present cache in the summer of 1908 was, that it was the meeting-point for the surveyors of the Grand Trunk Pacific and prospectors, that an Indian village was on the far side of the river, and that Swift had told us that "his friend Mr. Reading lived there and that we were not to miss him as he was a fine man." Not an especially interesting list of items, still it had been a much-talked-of point and it seemed foolish not to satisfy the last grain of curiosity.

With inward trepidations, the following day "M." and I climbed into our saddles, wondering if we were to regret this last drive, if we were to taste at last of the wilderness-fruit in its rawness, to be frightened to death or murdered (tenderfeet to the end!).

These last twenty miles were a duplication of all the annoyances under foot for the past five days, and it was late in the afternoon as we swung sharply to the right on the river's edge, looked across that muddy torrent, saw a number of tepees and drying-racks on the far side, and heard Chief say: "We are coming to the Cache."

Then "M." and I, with our hearts giving an extra jump at the thought of meeting the roughs and toughs who were supposed to have already poured in here from every direction, looked down from a hill on the city of Tête Jaune Cache as she was in 1908. What we saw was a tiny log shack and a tent pitched beside it, both enclosed by a fence, with a few spurious efforts to grow a little garden stuff just inside the fence; a little beyond was another tent. Near the shack stood a terrible-looking man clad in rough khaki, his hands in his pockets and his eyes glued on the strangers with a stony stare; by the fence lounged our travelling companions of the day before, who had arrived before us, and out from the far tent strolled two more nomads with unkempt hair, grizzled faces, ragged clothes and moccasins. In that quiet village, they had heard our outfit coming and the population had turned out to see who it was. Strange to say, those who got in ahead of us had never thought to mention there were women coming behind, so that the apparent hostility which froze the blood of the two scared ones, was a case of pure astonishment, and everyone, for an instant, stood dumb in his tracks.

I speak for no one's sentiments but my own; but for the time being it seemed to me my hour had come. They looked awful, and stood so terribly still as we slowly filed by them into the open. (It was only later that I wondered how much charity and faith might have been mustered on the spur of the moment to welcome us, and realised that we were probably quite as rough-looking in our travel-worn garments as those we rushed to condemn.)

It was only a momentary pause, and was quickly broken by the first terrible party mustering a pleasant smile (unmarred by a razor for weeks), coming to greet us cordially, showing us where our horses could pasture, and offering us his own yard as a place to pitch our tent. There wasn't a tree in it to shelter us from the eyes of the curious, so Chief politely suggested moving back a little from the residential section to a place which our host sarcastically explained was "where all Indians camped." This was rather unnecessary information, for rags, bones, goat-hair and hides stared us in the face, and yet we chose it in preference to the too close association of the city limits.

Our tents were scarce in place when Chief came over to say: "The cordial gentleman was Swift's friend, Mr. Reading of Philadelphia, and he 's just brought a five-pound trout for you ladies." While eating lunch, another long-haired brigand passed our camp and in mildest tones said, "Good-afternoon, ladies." We began to feel better, and deciding that a little water on our hands and faces might still further enhance the situation, I asked Chief if he thought it was quite safe for me to go to the river to wash. As he thought it was, I got soap and towel together and sauntered down to the banks of the Fraser, keeping one eye open to run if any of the terrible men showed up. Instead, out came the pleasant, khaki-clad man; we introduced ourselves, and, in a few minutes, found we had dozens of mutual friends in Philadelphia, and so the terrors of the Cache fell away.

As Mr. Reading presented his friend Mr. Finch I grew still more disgusted with myself and my habit, in spite of the many lessons I had had, of judging the men of the hills by their clothes, little heeding how I might be judged by them in return. Inviting the two gentlemen to dine with us in the evening and help to eat their own fish, I continued my journey to the river, and there washed away the last troublous thought of the Cache. As I bent over the water, I heard a gentle splash, and around the bend and close by my bath-tub came an Indian in his cottonwood canoe. It was a pretty picture, and I felt far from home, till leaping gracefully from his craft he came toward me smiling, holding in his hand a small bag of very crude manufacture (at the most worth fifty cents), which he told me I could have for the sum of ten dollars. Enough. I had still some distance to travel to reach the innocent wilderness.

The following day, August 20th, we lay over to rest our horses and ourselves, after the hard road we had been travelling so long, before returning over the same. Mr. Reading had unearthed the ruins of a tiny shack near the river, about seven feet by ten; it must have been very old as the logs were spongy and rotten, and as we prowled about it among nettles as high as our heads, we wondered if this could possibly be the original Cache. Hardly, it looked too much like work to be of Indian manufacture.

There were the remains of old fire-places nearer the river, but these were probably in existence in the days of the Canadian Pacific Railroad survey, and we walked back to camp again leaving it all a conjecture.

After lunch Mr. Reading visited us and invited us all to dinner, and, with our permission, he would invite the entire population of the town to meet us—in other words, the two prospectors who were camped close by. This was exciting. In view of the festivities and late hours we might keep, we drew down the "bug-nets" and each took a nap, which passed away the afternoon nicely, and were awakened hearing our host borrowing crockery for the feast.

Being our first and only dinner-party the entire summer, costumes might naturally be supposed to engross a good deal of thought, but that 's the joy of having only a duffel-bag,—there was little to think of. Asking "M." what she would do toward gracing the festive board, she replied succinctly: "Wash my hands and face, and get a fresh leather shoe-string to tie up my back hair." For myself, I recollected having a gorgeous violet handkerchief with a green border, which a kind relative had presented me for camp use, and which I had dutifully carried in my bag for many hundred miles, awaiting an opportunity to use it. It had never lost its pristine newness, owing to my dread of startling the horses if I ever flashed it on the trail, but the time now seemed ripe for bringing it forth. Decorated with it, another round my neck, and a pair of brand-new moccasins, we joined our men, fresh from a tussle with the razor and a cracked mirror, and strolled down the hill to the beat of the dish-pan—the signal that all was ready.

Our host and the two prospectors stood smilingly awaiting us at the dining-room—a little six by six roof projecting from one end of the shack. A real table hewn from logs stood beneath, around which ran a continuous bench.

After introductions, the gentlemen all stood respectfully around while the ladies, with skirts on, attempted to get their feet over that bench and under the table. For some time we had heard them preparing the meal and so curiosity and appetite were both at high-water mark.

It was a delicious meal, for you must remember that most of the condiments had been packed on horses for hundreds of miles. We had fish (just caught that afternoon), fried potatoes, and bacon and beans. Pickles, tea, coffee and cocoa were added to the list, and some cheese which had seen better days, and then they passed the bread and butter. There was something a little strange about that bread till they explained it was "sour dough," and I was rather glad we had stuck to bannock on our trip, which is merely flour and baking-powder, while the "sour-dough" is a fermentation and tastes as though it meant you should not forget it. I did not ask for the recipe; to have experienced the fact that such a concoction existed, was enough.

We were such a curious little company gathered together in haphazard fashion in so far-away a corner of the globe, that, while jest and merriment went round, I watched us all, myself included, to note what a stranger might have thought. His eyes would surely have opened at the ease with which the use of a butter-knife was dispensed with, to have noted that the various courses reposed in their original pans, and pots stood on the ground awaiting a "long arm" for second helpings; that our clothes were badly in need of repair, and that the plate which had held our bacon and beans and fish must also hold our dessert of stewed peaches and tapioca pudding.

I called "M.'s" attention to the fact that when she was asked to have a second cup of tea she gazed into her cup and deliberately threw the cold remains on the floor behind her, and she retaliated by noting that when the dessert came round I forgot all my early training and peered into the pot saying,—"What's this stuff?" But barring these few lapses, we two sat on our log seats and received the courtesy of host and guests not to be surpassed in the most civilised regions.

Even Muggins had found the situation not to be trifled with; when dishes were pushed back empty and heads shook "no more," and the remains were scraped into a little pile for him, he refused to touch them till he glanced his big brown eyes up at his master and received the permission "All right, go ahead."

And then we clambered out from the table, boxes were found for seats, pipes were lighted, and as the curious, not unmusical sound of the tom-tom came over the water from the village on the other side, we realised the Indians were having a feast also. Some one spoke again, and some one said: "Hush! What is that?" "The first jumping of the salmon. They should have been here before. Do you hear them splash?" We heard. Again we all sat listening to the splashing of the visitors "who come every year up the Fraser as regularly as hay-fever," so our host said.

Just as we were departing, the other guests suggested Klondike lemonade, and, from their precious horde, mixed citric acid, sugar and ginger, and we drank there in the hills to a meeting in civilised lands.

And I judged from the sentiments of one as she raised her tin cup to the toast, that all hearts wished the civilised days might never come, but rather the toast might have been: "Here's to a life of unnumbered summers in the mountains, with stars above by night, sunshine and soft winds by day, with the music of the waters at our banquet." Civilisation! How little it means when one has tasted the free life of the trail!

22: Going Home

THE next day, loaded with mail and messages, we said good-bye to our new friends and groaned inwardly at the thought of the miles of rough travel in store till we reached the Athabaska shores again, where on our course southward, there would be better footing and better feed for our horses.

A constantly increasing volume of smoke, drifting from the south, settled the scenery for the first day, and downpours of rain the next two finished the smoke, the scenery, and everything else. For miles we rode along in oil-skins, our hats at proper angles to shut off as much as possible the uncomfortable little cold rivers which seemed to find their way down the back of our necks, and we reached camp only to spend the afternoon drying things out before a huge fire.

The long, dreaded drive round Moose Lake began, however, in sunshine and we congratulated ourselves. But the day was not done. As we neared the upper end of the lake, a glimpse through the thick forest showed an inky blackness in the sky in the far distance ahead, and we went scurrying along to get out of the thick timber before the storm might strike us. Whoops and yells from the rear made everybody hustle; no time to mince or loiter over logs—they were taken at a bound. All was going well, every one was sailing along nicely, when that spoiled, greedy Nibs spied a specially nice bit of grass just beyond a high log. Nobody's fault but his rider's; over he skipped, swerved to the left to get it, and jammed her between an unyielding tree and the saddle. The pain was excruciating; the result lasted for a year after, but at the time, a distant mutter of thunder, the ominous silence and pause which come before a storm, the close proximity of the dead, standing timber, put self out of mind. Reaching open ground, we donned the now ragged slickers. Our horses knew what was coming as well as we. They looked anxiously around having probably heard the wind before we did, or perhaps their acute ears had caught the sound of some distant crashing tree. Nibs shivered a little, as the wind shrieked through the trees as through the rigging of a ship in a gale at sea. I decided that I preferred my own legs to those of my pony, and so got down. We had never faced a gale like this together before and I was mean enough to doubt my little friend. With a wild blast the storm struck us, first pelting us with large hailstones, then following them up with a drenching rain. The poor defenceless horses refused to face such a storm, and turned their backs upon it.

With the first onslaught of wind, a dead tree fell with a bang within twenty yards of the outfit; fifty yards away the huge trees swayed, rocked, bent, then fell like a volley of musketry—fully two hundred of them. Nibs shuddered, and I shuddered too as it was all too close to be comfortable. The fusilade stopped as quickly as it began, the wind fell, the rain poured down in torrents, the lightning played and leapt across the summits of the hills towards which we were travelling, and the awful crashes of thunder left nothing to be desired in the way of effect. No, it was not nice and we did n't enjoy it one bit.

Then came the order to advance—to advance into the very heart of that recent artillery-ground, and off we started, inwardly most reluctant. For once, in spite of the injured member, I preferred my own locomotives to those of my horse, and following the leader, we were soon swinging around and jumping over the freshly fallen trees. Nobody needed urging, every horse knew the danger as well as ourselves, not a tree was cut, and only fear helped some of the packs to clear the *débris* without an accident. We hurried across Moose River into

our old camp with some one calling, "Here we are again all wet and happy!" Quite true; for with tents up and a roaring fire our troubles were soon drowned with a cup of hot tea, and clothes were soon dried before a huge blaze. The injured leg was bound in cold compresses, mental note was taken that the bone might be injured, but as there was n't a doctor within three weeks' travel, there was n't much use in adding worry to the already annoying pain.

Often and often have I been asked, "What do you do when taken ill on the trail with no doctor?" This being our only accident in five years, I can only say: "Do without, and trust to the healthy life to keep things straight." For three weeks the leg was slung in a rope from the horn of the saddle, its progress kindly inquired for each day by the family, and in the night, when blankets pressed upon it, fretted over by its owner. Like all other worries, it was wasted energy, and it got well when it got ready.

At the time of our passing, there was certainly no newspaper published in the Moose Lake district, nor, to my knowledge, at present writing, yet two years after that rather uncomfortable storm, a passing stranger remarked, "So you are one of those caught in the big storm of 1908 on Moose Lake." Talk of walls having ears! For universal knowledge of every one on the trail, the wilderness takes the palm.

August the 30th found "M." and me hurrying off ahead of the outfit to make a "sachez" at Henry House, see that historic point, and then join our party before we once more arrived at Swift's hospitable home. Few would think to call a point historic with only a hundred years resting upon its shoulders, but in this great land of Canada, where for ages the valleys have been sleeping, where only the birds sing, and the Indian, moose, and elk have passed to wake her, one hundred years is quite a little time to be able to trace the first coming of the outer world. There was little there to satisfy our curiosity. Two chimneys, built of stone and clay, rapidly returning to their original constituency, stood on the original site, but perhaps were the remainsof what was known as Athabaska Depot, used as a base for supplies when the Canadian Pacific Railway was surveying the Yellowhead country many years ago. Embankments marked the traders' home or surveyors' winter quarters. The timber around had been cleared away for a considerable distance to expose the treacherous Indian on his approach, or for fuel, or building purposes, perhaps.

We left it in its silence by the river where in the old days, the guardians of the fort could see for miles the coming or departing guests, joined our party as they went by, and in fifteen minutes were once more in camp at Swift's, eating fresh eggs that night for supper. It seemed almost disloyal to the bacon to enjoy those eggs so much, for bacon is about the only food on the trail of which one never grows really tired. Trout palled till we wanted no more, there came a time when grouse failed to enlist any enthusiasm, but bacon on the trail is bacon to the end,—blessed be the man who invented bacon!

In the evening we went to Swift's home to return sundry calls and obtain any drifting news, and spent a rather interesting time. The following morning, "all set," we said, "Good-bye; will see you when the first Grand Trunk Pacific train comes through," and passed on, knowing we were coming to the beginning of the end. As we crossed the Athabaska, we realised that next time we came that way our horses would not have to swim for it, all would be made easy with trains and bridges; that the hideous march of progress, so awful to those who love the real wilderness, was sweeping rapidly over the land and would wipe out all trail troubles.

With the passing of each day, we said a long farewell to, some peak, some gorge, or lake. Storms swept across our paths, snows blinded us on the high passes, and the autumn colours gave the warning, "Winter will soon be here"; nothing, however, staunched the inward cry, "The play-days are dying one by one!"

One night they piled the logs higher and yet higher on the camp-fire at our door. The night was cold and frosty. Up through the black spruces, whose boughs were tipped with the crimson glare, we gazed on the stars twinkling above. Except for the distant tinkle of the horse-bell, and the snapping of the fire, there was no sound. Each one of our little household was busy with his own thoughts. Then through the silence of the forest there came a cry; it sounded again, a long-drawn weary note. I looked at Chief,—"What is it?" "Don't you know? 'T is the night train signaling at Laggan." *The last day's play was done!*

Where Old Friends Part

The 1911 Expedition
to Maligne Lake

Mary T. S. Schäffer

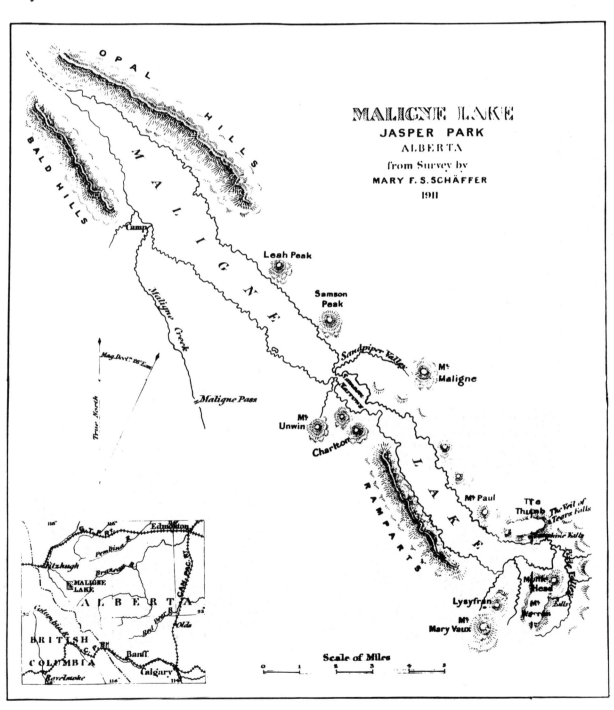

MALIGNE LAKE

JASPER PARK
ALBERTA
from Survey by
MARY F. S. SCHÄFFER
1911

Scale of Miles

In the spring of 1908 a small party of six — three guides, a woman companion, a botanist, myself, (not to mention twenty-two horses and the dog) — unnoticed by a solitary soul, slipped quietly away from civilisation and were lost, so far as the world was concerned, in a sea of mountains to the north.

Our quest was a mythical lake spoken of by the Stoney Indians of Morley, many of whom had never seen it themselves, though Samson Beaver, one of their number, said he had been there when he was a small child, having been taken on a hunting trip by his father. He said it was a great game country and they did not want the white man in there; but the Stoneys are dying off fast and in a few years will need their hunting grounds no more. The Crees of the north also had known of its existence, but they are being rapidly driven back by the white man, and this little pocket of rich game country must soon go the way of all the game country of this continent.

All who are interested in that particular corner of the globe today know of Lake Maligne, though few of the present day have looked upon her beauty. She was found after a three weeks' search; a whole happy week was spent on her shore and then our little party bade her adieu and made a detour of one hundred and seventeen miles to reach the Athabaska River — the direct route down the Maligne River being so utterly choked with fallen, burnt timber that even five days of heroic cutting failed to make an opening wedge through it. The trip to the Athabaska had been to see, for the first and last time in its untouched, unsullied charm, a valley filled with historic lore.

For several years Canada and Canadians had been talking enthusiastically of a second trans-continental railway, the Grand Trunk Pacific, which we knew was well on its way, wriggling and twisting like an enormous python, from ocean to ocean. Not being interested in railways, and being very much interested in countries which had hitherto scorned the attempts of railways to penetrate them, our little party fought its way through all the hardships of down timber, muskeg, and swollen waters of the Pobokton and Sun Wapta valleys, for the sake of seeing the Athabaska, the Miette, and Fraser River valleys before the iron "python" should insinuate itself thus far. We did see it too, saw it from Swift's Crossing to the Tête Jaune Cache — the muskegs of the river-bottoms, the stony hillsides (so hard on our poor, patient beasts' feet!), the great Douglas firs strewn upon the ground (the result of ancient forest fires) over which the horses leapt and

stumbled, the great lakes, Yellowhead and Moose, the named and unnamed mountains in ceaseless array — to the right and to the left, before and behind — a hard road, but one fraught with the mystery and glamour of old Indian and trapper days, when "H.B.C." was king, and when the Indian lived the life his Destiny had planned for him. When on our homeward way we said "Goodbye" to it all, mile by mile, we knew it was forever — as we saw it in those days. Prospectors and surveyors had left their imprint every foot of the way, the dreaded change was bound to come, and come soon.

As I write, two summers have flooded those valleys with sunshine, three winters have choked them with snow, but nothing has held back the tide of "improvement" foretold by the harmless-looking line of white pegs, and many are they who rejoice in the fact. Not so ourselves. With every mile over which we hear the "python" has worked his way still further into the hills comes a fresh pang of regret that, inch by inch, our pet playgrounds are being swallowed up.

With all the time and seasons fled, however, there still lived in my own mind the memory of the beautiful lake and an ever increasing desire to see it once more before it too fell under the fatal breath of "improvement," to see if it still remained as lovely in reality as in my imagination — so the duffle-bag was packed, and with two companions who had never seen my much-vaunted lake, we sallied forth to the wilderness very early in June of 1911.

Into the town of Strathcona our train puffed and shuffled one starry night, disgorged her weird collection of passengers — the like of which is only seen in a "new" country — disgorged our precious camp equipage, spitting it contemptuously into the surrounding darkness, and left us wondering which way to turn next. There seemed no alternative but to scramble into an ancient stage whose odoriferous little oil light was about the only point of brightness visible, and it seemed to beckon to us from the surrounding gloom; and as a reward we were bumped, and thumped, and pounded downhill, uphill (very up) and with a final flourish, landed into the very heart of one of the most modern up-to-date, wide-awake cities of the northwest — Edmonton. Rooms, such as they were, were obtained, with a muttered, "You can be thankful you have these. If you were a man, you might walk the steets." (Once more thankful for being a woman.) And though the morning inspection of the water pitcher suggested a mud bath, and an inch-thick mattress reposing on a bunch of tight wire springs had received a set of very weary bones that night, we were compelled to accept them. There were at least a dozen unaccommodated, heavy-eyed travellers seated in the rotunda below, only too eager to take what we might spurn. The city was filled to overflowing with incoming strangers; no one cared for our opinion, so we accepted our fate — the mattress and mud — silently, and wished for the day and the hour when the long trail and its comforts were ours.

For three days we waited impatiently for a trunkful of trail necessities to turn up, and were forced to listen with small comment to a freshly imported English woman's opinion of the vaunted American method of checking "luggage." Then, begging, borrowing and buying all we could to fill the awful void, we rose at the dreary hour of 5:30 one chilly morning and stole forth, lugging our own belongings as best we could to the station — a matter fortunately of only a couple of squares. As we beat a retreat from the hotel, whose business was so rushing that there was no necessity to increase the thickness of their mattresses in these days of comforts or lend a helping hand to those freighted with duffle-bags, cameras, plant-press and blankets, again the personal comments of the nice little English lady came to mind — and somehow I did not blame her. But with said belongings once deposited in a safe place, no more thought was given to them or to the inhospitable hotel — we were bound for new highways, we were to ride the "python's" tail; we were to learn by experience the difference between entering a country locked away from the world and the same one when the door was swinging wide open for the first time.

What is termed in the northwest, and what the Englishman first visiting this corner of his realm takes for gospel, was awaiting us — a first class car. It was clean as a whistle, and smelled suggestively of disinfectant. As the crowds poured in, we had reason to believe it *was* disinfectant, and felt grateful to the new road for its forethought, only hoping it had been as copiously applied as it smelled. Tales have been rife since railroading began that in the early stages of their existence you want to keep very much to your own society for fear of getting into worse, so we all sat bolt upright till our backs ached, then gave it up and trusted to the disinfectant.

We could not help surmising who and what each traveller was, where he was going, and why he should go there. One gentleman in a suit of most decided stripes and very high-gloss shoes looked like the opulent owner of a chain of saloons in the new land, though later I had to disabuse my mind of such a heinous idea, saloons not being tolerated along the line of construction; another, quiet, alert, his hat tipped at an angle of forty-five degrees, I took for an expert at cards; a rugged, burnt, genial face beamed at us from across the aisle, his blue overalls and cowhide boots proclaiming him a native returning to his own again. Mining engineers, surveyors, a bunch of French Canadians, and a lady wearing a hat that looked like a Christmas tree and carrying a three-foot band-box filled the car to brimming proportions. It was only 6:30, and we were all sleepy, cold and breakfastless — not the best conditions through which to view our fellow men most charitably. As we surveyed our lunchbox with chilly eye, we asked the brakeman what we all knew to be a silly question, "Is there a dining car attached to the train?" And all bounded when the prompt and cheerful answer came, "Sure! Be ready in ten minutes, I'll come and call you," and off rushed that remarkable brakeman. True to his word, back he whisked in the stated time and, as though to avoid a stampede of the other hunger-driven individuals, he whispered, "Come." Led by our new friend, and followed by the small boy of the party only half-awake, we filed out as inconspicuously as possible, though even in that jumping-off part of the world, where one would naturally suppose that slouch hats, short skirts, and buckskin coats had their original being, we caused heads to turn and eyes to open.

As oil and water refuse to mix, or sheep and goat to range on the same mountainside, so did we discover a different grade of occupants in the next car where disinfectant seemed much more imperative than in the one just vacated. Still headed by the wiry little brakeman who authoritatively ordered the aisle loungers to their seats, we cut our way through cigarette, pipe, and cigar smoke, and emerged triumphant in the "dining car." Alas for our advanced ideas of dining cars, only the eight front seats of said car were devoted to the inner man — or woman — the rest of it was filled to overflowing with consumers of the "weed."

But we were to learn what a real brakeman's duties consisted of on this road-to-be. Without a moment's hesitation he accosted the smokers (of about as many nationalities as numbers and twice his size) and in good old English ordered "all smoking to cease while ladies were present." He seemed so small for the job, so utterly inadequate to cope with those great, brawny sons of many climes, that I felt a moral certainty we would be picking him up in pieces from the aisle before the meal was over.

To our suprise — you are always being surprised in this new land — the table was clean, the plain dishes, chosen for rugged service, equally so, and a little bunch of wild flowers set in the center of the table in a bottle, whose original label "ketchup" still clung to its side, appealed to the flower-lover of the party.

Our order given to the waiter, who was as friendly and civil as our recent body-guard, our attention was arrested from the passing scenery by hearing him yell above the racket of the train,

"Once the ham and eggs!

Three times the bacon and eggs!

Four times the coffee!"

In due course, accompanied by paper napkins, it was set before us — hot, done to a turn, and the coffee delicious. Paying him the moderate sum of 50 cts. per head, receiving in exchange for a modest tip a genial smile and bow, we turned to run the gauntlet of the gaping foreigners, and found our small brakeman, still intact, at the head of the procession to lead us back to the "first-class" coach.

Till 12:30 the little, unpretentious train pulled and puffed and wound its way through country long famous as the worst possible example of muskeg. All the old campfire tales of those who had dragged their weary way through it in the past came to mind, and it was entirely self-evident that many a poor packhorse had there found his final grave after a vain struggle to drag his load to a drier land. Some day, however, it will be a great country, but it will have to be through financing an enormous drainage system. Watching it closely as we were being rushed through it, I was reminded of a conjuror's trick I once saw. The master of tricks held a little white bunny in each hand; before my infant and believing eyes, he mauled them together, and lo! out came one big rabbit. I thought if the Grand Trunk Pacific drainage proposition could be mauled with the Canadian Pacific irrigation department, Canada would be the possessor of a very fine rabbit.

While meditating, down came the rain; the general factotum — our brakeman — yelled "Edson," and we and all the other pioneers tumbled forth in a downpour. By this time a friendly engineer, whom we had first met in Edmonton, began to feel alarmed for our umbrella-less condition, but seeing us quite ready to plow through the deluge and the city mud without flinching, he admiringly offered to escort us "to the best restaurant in the city."

Composed of muskeg in all directions, of a new board-walk to span the same in spots, a sparse house here and there decorated with those funny false fronts so common in all new western towns, and as non-deceiving as an old lady's chestnut frizzes, and any number of vacant corner lots quoted in the Edmonton papers as "2,000 and up," Edson failed to appeal to us as a permanent abiding place, our one idea concentrating itself upon a hot meal.

Waving his hand toward a humble dwelling whose roof was of canvas and through whose polished window we read the request "Come in and try us," our conductor and we straggled in, bearing Edson mud and Edson rain all over a spotless linoleum floor, the small boy bringing up the rear, still clutching the despised lunchbox which we dared not leave behind for fear an hour of dire necessity might catch us in the end. A table covered with spotless white oilcloth received the four hungry grown-ups, while the small boy mounted to the counter, where pie and cheese and doughnuts catered to his more primitive appetite. An old, snowy-haired Mammy served us with great dignity, and her soft, low intonations carried me back to Dixie. So thoroughly did she captivate me that, on leaving, I asked her if she had been long in Canada. "Nevah wus beyond the bohdah, mahm." "Then I suppose your people came over in the 60's at the time of the Rebellion?" "Ahm suah Ah cayant tell, mahm. Mah fathah was Guhman, and mah Muthah wus a Spaniard, so Ah cayant tell whut they would be doin' in the United States." I looked at the snowy, kinky hair, at her warm, brown complexion, then over her shoulder to the kitchen beyond where a strapping black man (who looked as though he might be the German-Spanish lady's husband), was listening complacently to the recital of his wife's complicated ancestry, and much as I admired the meal she served us I admired her more. It takes a woman of the world to carry off so fine a situation as well as that, and to think I should find this perfect specimen in the "wilderness."

Slopping back in the mud and the muskeg, we reached the station where a yet more primitive train than the last one stood waiting to carry us to the end of the steel — to Hinton. There was no doubt in our minds of the relief we felt at being able to ride those last sixty-five miles by rail instead of the very recent form of getting through the ever-prevailing muskeg (packtrain) but — I confess I took one look into the single, crowded passenger coach and wished I had made arrangements to be sent through by freight.

It was only a train for carrying the flotsam and jetsam which pour always into a newly opening country — the thousands of labourers employed on the road, the

—134—

seekers after mineral wealth, the surveying outfits of a great corporation. Tourists, such as we, were neither expected or wanted (their day in that country is still to come); we were merely tolerated, so we meekly took our position on the platform, hoping in some way to melt the heart of the owner of a caboose which was attached to the rear. Thanks to the mining engineer, it was quickly rumoured round that "friends of the president of the road were aboard." Magic rumour, if somewhat untruthful! But I am sure if he had been there to put his nose inside that coach, he would have instantly pardoned the fib. In less time than it takes to tell it, the door of the caboose swung just wide enough to let us through, then went shut with a bang and a spring lock. A genial host awaited us, the caboose was ours for the rest of the afternoon and, being attached to the end of the train, we soon had a pretty good idea of how railroads looked and felt before they were real railroads. By turns the track was straight and twisted, mostly twisted; melting snows and spring rains had played fearful havoc with rails laid during the previous fall and winter, and the nearer we drew to Hinton, the more profound became our education in this special line of work. The last ten miles we took at creeping gait, the caboose owner explaining that "the engineer holds the throttle in one hand, the emergency brake in the other." Comforting information.

Suddenly there was a commotion and then a yell. Had the expected come to pass after all the caution so evident: were we not to see Hinton till the small hours of the morning, after all the throttle and brake business? O no, the small boy, in spite of all the admonitions, had done what all small boys have done since car windows were invented, poked his head out of the cupola window and lost his hat. The mining engineer had saved every situation that day, and he proceeded to save this one. Leaping from the caboose, he chased wildly back after the hat (we were then bumping gently along over ties jacked up with spruce and poplar, the leaves still green upon their boughs), and as speed was the last matter to be considered, no one dreamed but that the feat would be accomplished. The hat was grabbed up and the race to the train begun when, with that curious turn of affairs so common in life, the engineer opened his throttle just a little, and then began a real race the memory of which will surely recur to the small boy whenever he is inclined to disobey orders in reference to heads again. He got his hat in the end.

With that excitement over, and the hero plied with a cup of hot tea, our thoughts wandered to the scenery again. We were nearing the mountains; we caught a glimpse of shimmering silver far in the valley below; the caboose man said it was the first sight of the Athabaska River. The patches of silver grew more numerous, and then continuous, and looked from our point of vantage like a great straggling ribbon slowly unwinding itself from ranges and ranges of purple mountains which were rapidly fading into the shadows of the night, and the caboose man said, "It's not far now to the jumping-off place"; so we began to look up tossed-aside Stetsons and buckskin coats. Then someone called, "Here's Hinton! Pile out!" We "piled," fairly falling into the gaze of a huge bunch of foreigners who, with their day's work done, had probably sought the only excitement to be found in the neighbourhood at that time of day — watching the coming of the daily train. We must have been a totally new element in the country, from the way heads and eyes turned, but not a rough word or rude look escaped them. Those are two things a stranger, especially a woman, need never fear at the great opening door of Canada. Be the army gathered from where it may, and it gathers there from every corner of the globe, voices are lower and actions more respectful than one may expect in the streets of our culture-proud cities, while the vocabulary has been expurgated of much that one feels is in ordinary daily use when women are not present.

Out from the mass of unnumbered nationalities yelled a bona fide bus driver, "All aboard for Prairie Creek and the Mountain View Hotel!" We saw our tents and blankets and the duffle-bag take a flying leap from the baggage van into the waiting mud, and then — O joy! Out of that sea of unknown quantities loomed the familiar face of Jack Otto, our famous old guide from Field, B.C. He was riding a handsome sorrel, and his welcome smile, as he quickly rescued the blankets from the Hinton soil, was worth all the "Mountain Views" in creation.

Turning our backs upon the little train which had carried us safely over ooze, muskeg, quicksands, Christmas trees and jack pines for sixty-five miles, we climbed into the "Mountain View" bus — a farm wagon if it had gone by its legitimate title — and were rolled and joggled and bounced about two miles further in churned prairie mud till we drew up with a flourish at the principal hotel of the city of Prairie Creek. Out climbed the band-box, seen in the morning, with the lady still attached to it, out tumbled a fat man who looked as if he would never fit into any room of the

"Mountain View," out stepped the mining engineer, whom we pitied from the bottom of our hearts when we looked at the external appearance of the hotel. Then with a "Geddup, you there, Ginger and Mustard!" on went we.

Reaching the "city limits," we were soon bumping and rocking over a pathless waste strewn with fallen logs interspersed with old bottles and tin cans which acted as milestones on Civilisation's march, and then were greeted with the welcome sight of a brand new tepee half hidden in a cluster of spruces. It was dusk; a fire inside the tepee lit up the white walls, and a short distance from this picture a bright fire in the open showed a man bending over a frying pan, and a little breeze brought to us that best smell of all camp odours, the smell of frying bacon.

With the bacon, potatoes, peas, tea, jam and some homemade fruitcake stowed away in a once very empty spot, a bit of free advice given to the as-yet-uninitiated that she had better keep the most of her clothes on if she wanted to keep warm till daylight (for the air in these Rockies penetrates like a darning-needle about four A.M.), we tumbled into our blankets, our last thought being for those who must take their much-needed rest in the confines of the "Mountain View Hotel."

To those who have seen and know construction towns — and they are doubtless about the same the world over — please skip a few lines. To us it was all spandy new. Just as we were dropping into oblivion that night, there had come, wafted from the mushroom village below, the sounds of many gramophones in as many keys and as varied physical conditions, each sounding as though it were trying to be cheerful long after life was practically extinct.

When Jack went down to do the last shopping the next morning, and we to see if "sneakers," stout shoes and a few other valuable adjuncts of camp-life could be bought to tide over the coming of the belated duffle-bag, our eyes were open to take in the new phase of life. The gramophones had all been wound up again and were desperately doing their best, though it seemed to be to the empty air as there were but few listeners about and those few sunning themselves at store doors and poolroom entrances. No one apparently noticed us as we waded in boot-high mud from shop to shop, finding courtesy everywhere, and a line of goods that would teach an Edmonton department store a lesson. Later, when we knew more about some of the residents, we learned they could almost have given us our family history for two generations back. Trust the indifferent-looking pioneer to be wide awake; never judge him by the face he shows you; he is never asleep, and there are a few occasions on record where he has been known to waken the traveling easterner with a terrible jar.

All was orderly and quiet (barring the gramophones); a little girl rode by on her pony with a tiny terrier perched behind the saddle digging his claws into the pony's rump to avoid a slip; a few pleasant-faced women, leading little children by the hand, strolled in the sunshine and mud; in the shops there was a hurry and bustle, every one was preparing to ship to the next important town, to Moose Lake — Prairie Creek would soon be a city of empty shacks. We were glad we had seen it just as it was; when next we came, doors which had hidden home life, or life which would not bear the light of day, would be swinging wide into the winds, to the sunshine and the storms. It would all be a sad little story told in gaping windows and tumbling logs.

Gladly leaving the rubbishy little town to finish its pathetic history, we hurried back to camp only to find our own house on the back of a horse, a pot of tea waiting for us, and the order "to mount" when the last drop was drunk. Leaving our first wilderness home, we filed forth at noon, wondering what the trail had in store for us, for the trail is a book and every day a chapter. We were feeling the excitement of the start which was to bring us to the head of the "python" in a couple of days; there, leaving him to finish his way to the Pacific, over the Yellowhead Pass, we would be privileged to leave all progress concerning railroad construction behind and bury ourselves for many a day in valleys where "pythons" could not penetrate and progress was unknown.

Jack had regaled the lunch hour and other odd moments by telling us that the afternoon's march led through the "green timber," a remark which shed but small light on the work ahead of us. We started forth, occasionally passing heavily loaded freight wagons whose every plank groaned and rebelled under its load; passed a Cree village where, when we tried to photograph the untidy spot, the inhabitants scuttled like rabbits to their holes; passed abandoned construction camps; passed an isolated eating house where all the S's in the numerous signs were turned wrong way about till we wondered how anyone had mustered courage to enter there after reading them; passed along the rolling, flower-decked hills on a very good road and wondered what Jack meant by speaking so painfully of "the green timber."

Then we struck it — full in the face! The highway looked so attractive under the dark spruces ahead, after the glare of the warm hillsides, that we felt it had been somewhat slandered. Just at the entrance we saw considerable mud, and suggested it was rather thick. "Just you wait," muttered Jack. Then we saw two light teams emerging from the gloom with something like black sponges festooning the wheels — mud, mud! Seeing our expressions, the driver on the lead called out, "O, it's lots better than it was a month ago!" What must it have been that "month ago"? For us on horses, it was an easy proposition; it was the heavily loaded outfits which suffered. All teams were traveling in twos, with four horses to a team, thus enabling the men of one team to unhitch and help the other when in trouble; and certainly they seemed to be in trouble most of the time.

Again and again we passed bunches of steaming, struggling horses, men yelling, whips snapping, but always the undercurrent of patience surprised us. And then we arrived at an especially bad hole where the rear end of a huge wagon had dropped most discouragingly into an enormous hole while the front end stood most defiantly high in the air brandishing a mattress, and the horses, as though the last spark of courage had burnt out, stood dejected and knee-high in mire. "See them boards sticking up there?" said Jack with a quizzical smile. "Them's the boards the Government give us to make the boat for Maligne Lake. I wonder if they'll come out of that mess whole?" It was too discouraging a question to me. I passed round the "mess" and went on where I need not look. All the time Jack kept saying, "O, this ain't so bad. Why, this spring it took these men just five days to make these five miles of green timber." "Green timber!" There it was; we knew at last what he

was talking about, and the story of it all was written every inch of the five miles. It seemed as though there were not five yards on each side of the road that some poor wayfarer had not out-spanned for the night; it was a story written in abandoned tent-poles, discarded tin cans, worn out clothing, and patches of young oats springing up where innumerable weary horses had been fed.

It was a relief a little later on to hear Jack call, "only a half mile more of this," and a short distance beyond that point, coming upon another outfit, my sister called back, "Do look at this handsome team of horses ahead." I looked: three men were walking, a driver was holding the ribbons, the horses were tugging slowly through the mire, ruts, roots, stones, as all the rest had done, the great wagon pitching high then low again, like a ship wallowing in the trough of the sea but, unlike the other outfits, they would draw but half the usual distance when the beautiful beasts were allowed to stand and blow. We passed them in one of their pauses, and one of the men, hearing the remark flung back at me, grinned from ear to ear, then said, "Do you think them horses look good? So do I. I paid just $800 for that pair. They're all I have in the world, and you bet I ain't goin' to let 'em be killed in this rank bit o' country." He spoke the words of a feeling which seemed to dominate the actions of all the teamsters we passed. In spite of the fearful physical conditions, we saw not one case of cruelty, and a stock of patience displayed which one could scarce expect in that great army slowly toiling westward.

Camping at the far edge of the "green timber," far into the night we could hear the soldiers of fortune passing slowly by, making for a better camp than we had chosen; but our civilised bones had been too weary to go further, even for the tempting water which Jack said was "only two miles beyond." Soft muscles have their limitations on the trail, and we were growing a little wise as to the length of Jack's miles; they contained about three times the material of any eastern mile.

The next morning, made over new by ten hours' uninterrupted sleep in that wonderful air of the Rockies, the three "tourists" were up and off, leaving the packs to come along at their leisure. It was a great day for any one loving the trail. The weather was perfect. Far ahead we could see a picturesque mountain which we knew must be Roche Miette; we ambled along, guessed at the names of the streams crossed — as we had not armed ourselves with a map — slipped by the teams we had heard lumbering along in the night, and noted quite a number of men who seemed to be coming from the opposite direction on foot. They had a draggled, weary, discouraged look about them, very different from the alert appearance of the faces set the other way.

The small boy saw a board nailed to a tree by the roadside and rode over to read it. Even his little head took in the significance, the pathos, the sarcasm of what was written there. We joined him when we saw the smile on his wee face, and over his shoulder read the crudely pencilled, misspelled lines which had doubtless come from a full heart, "To the land of milk and hony, go west, ye fools." And we knew they had been written by one whose face was set to the east, who was taking back to his abandoned home a burden greater than the one he had brought into the new country, a disappointed heart. Outwardly we smiled and yet we knew he needed pity more, and that there had been many before him whose thoughts he had so tersely expressed, and many who would come after.

Then we rode on through the flower-decked land which looked so fair to us who had horses to ride and food to eat, and a great wild country to call our own for the exertion of getting there. Someone picked up a little, worn purse from the middle of the road with a pitiful sum of money in it and we hoped it had not belonged to the man who had been looking for "milk and hony." And then we came riding out on a pretty "open" all dotted with tidy shacks whose location and appearance gave us the impression that it might belong to our friend, the mining engineer.

We rode politely round to what appeared to be the living-shack, and were not at all surprised when a smile (attached to the familiar face of the engineer) came to the door. While going through the greetings common to such an occasion, we were conscious (though we did not wink an eyelash) of a second personage making a wild dash from the back of his shack and, in view of the world at large, taking a bee-line across lots to a second shack. I had "been there before," and with my knowledge of previous situations knew that the razor must have been lying untouched on the shelf for many a day. Obliviously we talked on, dismounted on being asked to stay to dinner, examined the cinchas of the saddles, put in time, and at last the engineer burst out laughing, saying, "It's no use, the moment Johnson saw you coming he said, 'Hold onto them, Morris, till I get the house fixed up a little and have a swipe at my razor. I don't want the first ladies that ever visited us here to find us in such a muss.' So I am 'holding onto' you; please don't mind, this is a great event to us."

But the holding process was of short duration; we were two ladies too many for Mr Johnson's curiosity, and he emerged unshaved and unshorn, his toilet put off for another day, and was soon telling us he had been at the Jasper Park Collieries for over a year and would certainly like to have a photograph of the first ladies to visit his hermitage.

A little later, having inspected the "office," which in spite of apologies looked to us as neat as a pin, we heard the musical sound of a triangle, and were asked if we minded eating at the same table with the miners, for they had no other place to offer us. Our appetites had reached such a condition, we minded nothing, but when we reached the dining room we found there was nothing to mind. I think they must have specially scrubbed those miners for the occasion; there was certainly nothing about them to lead us to believe that any one of them had ever touched a lump of coal, and as for the dining room, it would have shamed some of those eastern architects who plan "bungalows" for ladies' magazines into retiring from business.

We foisted ourselves over rustic benches nailed to the floor, faced a long deal table covered with white oilcloth and burdened with a meal fit for the gods, and, in spite of hunger, could scarce eat so busy were we mentally fitting up and decorating that fascinating mountain shack with Navajo blankets, skins and heads.

A little later we said "goodbye" and went on our way still looking for "the wilds." For some distance east of the Jasper Collieries we had lost sight of the grading of the new road; but once more making our way to the shores of the Athabaska, we came upon the army of labour, and a well-defined trail led us to — the ferry! To my two companions a ferry seemed quite the proper thing, and of course under the circumstances, a very necessary one; but to me, who had stood on those banks only three years before, who had looked across that wild body of water to the fair, unbroken prairies beyond, where only the Indian trail marked the way, it was an ugly sight. The great, picturesque bluffs that hung above our heads had been scarred and maimed by dynamite to make room for the "python," the wreckage of camp-life strewed the nearby forest, and there before us came creeping an ugly scow, clinging to a wire stretched tightly overhead, trundling her awkward way through the Athabaska's rebellious waters. Three years before, our horses, with sticks and stones, with blows and emphatic remarks, had been forced to swim that wild flood, and we to cross in an Indian, cottonwood dugout that bobbed and danced like an erratic cork on the turbulent waters; today we went over with — "horses 50 cts per head, men 25 cts." The old ferryman shook his head when we asked him if women went free; he said they hadn't made any arrangements for women, so for once in our lives we had a man's privilege, and paid our quarter.

Our main outfit having passed while we were enjoying the hospitality of the Jasper Collieries, the sight that greeted us two miles beyond the ferry looked very restful. Beyond the wide, grassy flats, buried almost from sight by tall spruce trees rose the white wings of our tepee, from which curled a column of blue smoke and a little further away drifted the smoke of the second campfire — a cup of tea was waiting for us after the fourteen-mile drive.

Jack had camped within a mile of the old Jasper House site, an old Hudson's Bay Post within ten yards of the main highway (the railroad from the ferry having kept to the other side of the river), and again we had the chance of studying at close range the life which gathers in a newly opening country.

All afternoon the teams rumbled by. Not being accustomed to so much society while on camping tours, I seemed to give my family considerable amusement by dashing forth at frequent intervals to see who was passing, though the family profited if anything out of the ordinary came into sight. They always passed in twos; they were always heavily loaded and always very quiet. In one of my sorties, I found that friends, so to speak, were going by — on top of an extra heavy load sat a man and woman, she with a face that told of hardship, poverty, loyalty, all the wordless misery which goes to make up the life of the pioneer woman. I had not seen her before, but behind her, perched high among the precious household possessions they had dragged so far from home, sat the little girl from Hinton, and

clutched in her arms was the small dog which I had seen taking a free ride on the pony's back the day before. Of course the child had noticed us in Hinton, tourists being decidedly out of the ordinary there, and I sent her a smile of recognition; the serious little face, already copying the expression of the mother, returned a weary smile, then the team disappeared in the forest beyond. And the world goes on singing the praises of the pioneer, the "*man* who opens the door." Could he open it if the woman did not hand him the key? Not from what I have seen.

The next morning was utilized in visiting the ruins of Jasper House, a "walk of only a half mile." The day was intensely hot and, of course, we did not reach the place off-hand, but must go at least a mile out of our way. It lay by the river's brink, hidden from our camp by a long stretch of thick timber. Once there, there was little enough to see. All that marked the historic stop were the remains of some chimneys, a few logs tossed upon the ground, and a short distance from these, the ruins of an old graveyard. Walking over to this, we found a few staggering and fallen crosses crumbling behind an equally crumbling fence, which told where those who had fallen asleep in the wilderness had found a last home. Perhaps many a heart, sick with longing for the home and faces they would never see again, rested beneath the flowers which, all about us, rocked in the sweet wind unmindful of the day. Then across our reveries swept the distant roar of dynamite — it was the lash of the "python's" strength against the obtruding boulders which had so long guarded the Athabaska's waters, and I shuddered for the future peace of those nameless graves.

Tramping back to the camp in the heat and the dust, we let our minds drift into the past, carried there by the picture we had just left. Our tepee looked wonderfully cheerful and comfy in the dusk of the spruces, and a cup of Jack's tea helped to dispel the gloom. As we sat around waiting for supper a little later, we heard a stage whisper through the tepee walls from Jack, "For goodness' sakes! Come and look at this!" Not desiring to miss anything, we flew to see what had excited him so. It was one more of the tragedies of the road. Two men were passing the camp on foot. The dust of the highway was too thick for us to have heard them coming, and as they shuffled by, they were indeed a pathetic sight. One was very tall and slender, the other short and very stout. The latter was on the lead; were they well dressed, no one would ordinarily have taken the slightest notice of them. The stout one was about "all in"; his shoes were slung round his neck by a string, his feet were tied up in gunny-sacks, his coat in a wad on his back. Behind him came the slender one who, having less to carry, was helping his less fortunate friend along with a stick which he was shoving from one end, prodding the other into the middle of the stout man's back. It was just one of those sights at which you laugh, and then — sigh. I longed to call after them to "stop and have a cup of tea," but knew if I gave tea to every deserving wayfarer that passed us, my family would go thirsty in a week, so we let them pass on, and thought, "To the land of milk and hony, go west ye fools."

The next drive we knew to be a long one, so the sister and the small boy and I had the saddles put on our ponies immediately after breakfast the following morning and set our faces to the west, hoping to see the packs before the end of the day. Jack had said something about "making twenty-two miles," which I told him was quite too long a drive for the small boy (we were out for pleasure, and I have no love for twenty-two mile drives) so I quashed any such ideas by saying we would start early and keep going till we were either tired or found a good campground. Away we went, and in the end made Jack's desired distance, by riding briskly, loitering, feeding the horses and then ourselves, a drive of beauty and interest.

First we passed through some fine timber where the road was *good;* then mounting one hill after, we at last looked down on Jasper Lake, and far into the distance where the Athabaska wandered aimlessly along the valley bottom, parting the hills peremptorily on each side of its torn and flood-rent shores. Now and then we passed, ambling along on a calico pony, an Indian half-breed who stared at the two women and small boy as though they meant the beginning of the end, and again it was a couple of teams panting and straining up the steep inclines. We crossed beautiful crystal mountain streams where each pony had to bend for a drink, and ever and anon our way was decked with masses of flowers, interspered with discarded tin cans and patches of young oats. From the superb heights we again dipped down into the valley, into a wide, low prairie, which will surely some day be utilized for mountain farms, and again started to climb. Ahead of us went toiling yet more wagons. They looked like all the others we had seen, except that owing to a lack of axle-grease, one of them was protesting violently, its groans being audible a quarter of a mile away. As we came up behind them,

the lead team just starting up a bit of narrow road blasted out of a stony cliff, the pitch of which would have been considered impossible to one less determined than these men fighting their way into the new El-dorado; the great rocks and holes ahead would have made the average teamster hesitate — not so these people, and we paused to see them take it.

The wagon was loaded to its utmost capacity, a man walking beside the team was holding the reins and yelling encouragingly, "Avaunt!" A woman's form was silhouetted against the intensely blue sky, and I could see her body sway and pitch with the plunging and jerking of the unwieldy load; a little girl behind her, with a familiar-looking small dog in her arms, clutched a table lashed firmly to its fastenings; and as we drew nearer I recognized the friends to whom we had nodded the day before. We rode up alongside of the struggling team; I looked into the face of the woman; I shall probably never know who she was and we shall perhaps never meet again, but she was one of the universal sisters, her way was as stony as the hill she was climbing and my heart went out to her. Her face was hard, weary, discouraged and hopeless. She hardly noticed us, unless it be in her inmost heart to compare her life with ours. I longed to say something which would raise the cloud from a face that was once pretty, but there seemed nothing adequate to the occasion. Nodding to her, I called out, "I wish I could take you with me on my fresh little pony over this stony hill." The driven face lit into one of almost beauty, and she shyly said, "O thank you for that kind thought." Then closing the window of brightness as quickly as she had opened it, her head went down. We rode on by, wishing, wishing it might have been in our power to do more than toss her a word, and for the rest of the day I thought of her and of all the other women who had given up life and home to follow the fortunes of their husbands into a new land where hardship stalked at their heels, disappointment, death perhaps. But so it has been since our ancestors first touched this continent, and it has been the women who were the true pioneers, the women who suffered. One of the vastest continents of the world has been meekly and silently conquered by women and, even at this late date, few men know it. Such is the history of our land from Hudson's Bay to Florida. There can be few more such armies sent into the wilderness, for the wilderness will soon be gone; the sight has been a sad one, yet I am glad I had the privilege of seeing it and knowing what it meant.

That afternoon, after paying a short visit to Swift, a white man who had made him a home in the warm, fertile valley of the Athabaska eighteen years ago, after following torn and rent mountain sides where the new road was pushing its way, after covering the entire twenty-two miles which Jack had laid out for us, we came to a halt and rest on the banks of the Athabaska, to rest in a bunch of sand dunes. O how dirty we were, and they were, and everything was! We had breathed dust and sneezed dust all day, and now we were to sleep in dust, but when I heard a grumble which spoke my own mind, I mustered the moral courage to say, "It is pretty awful, but we had better be thinking of those women who will be toiling along far in the night, behind those fearful loads." The very mention of them hushed our last thought of self-pity; their hard lives were too vivid in our minds.

Still hearing the rumbling of the great wagons passing in a continuous stream to the westward, the following morning we shook the dust from our blankets and our feet, washed our faces of the same, and prepared to perch ourselves on the lacerated banks of the Athabaska to watch that most exciting event of the trail — the driving of a lot of untrained, unwilling, and violently protesting horses into a river, the possibilities for disaster as evident to them as to us. The bunch was driven to the treacherous shore where an old stager was caught, a halter put round his neck by which he was gently led to the water, and then we all took a hand in "whooping" the rest in after him in the vain hope they would take the hint and follow behind. For Jack was bending with might and main to the oars, shoving his boat as rapdily as possible into the middle of the river, the second guide tugging at the halter of the unwilling Buck, almost finding a watery exit from the world thereby, and the rest of us yelling our little best and rushing at the heels of the hesitating. But it was no use, they knew we were not "onto the job," and, having reached the end of the stream to please us, they proceeded to put up their tails and scatter all over the sand dunes to please themselves. It was a humiliating defeat. The small boy accused the shore contingent of not beng sufficiently fleet-footed. We told him he had got in our way and interfered with the proper display of skill; we were none of us in a fit frame of mind for argument; we had all grown hot, tired and more dusty than ever and threw up the job — cross at ourselves, cross at the contrary beasts — and concluded that "the old horses weren't ours anyhow, and it was up to Jack to get them over."

Like everything else, there is a knack of driving horses into a river. I could tell you exactly how it is done, but it takes a language I do not possess and a quickness learned by practice. To add to our discomfiture, down from the mushroom village behind us had come two ladies to see the drive. We did not mind their coming, but their apparel was such an aggravation; they both looked as though someone had just pulled them out of a band-box by the head, and there in their immaculate white gowns they stood, a horrid reflection on our camp garments all covered with Athabaska dust, our faces red with the blistering sun and unaccustomed energies, and our tempers as ruffled as their starched skirts. But they had been so thoughtful as to bring us a loaf of homemade bread which helped materially to soothe us, and we did not tell them of the envy which possessed our souls. With patience the horses were got across at last, we and our saddlery were shot over via the boat, and the last load to come was the lumber which had been seeing so many ups and downs in a freight-wagon from Hinton to Fitzhugh.*

A chain of small lakes lay but a few hundred yards from our point of debarkation and, where the fishing was said to be of the best, they dumped the lumber down for the night, put up the tepee, built the camp-fire, turned the horses out to grass, the small boy went paddling (thus scaring away any fish in the notion of being caught), and we to washing the dust of the trail from our grimy garments.

With supper over, we strolled on the shore of Deborah's Lake, watching the sunset colours playing on the mountains to the south. Even at 9:30, when common sense called us to our sleeping bags, we looked from our open tepee door and saw the faraway peaks stained crimson with the dying lights; the shadows grew to a royal purple, and the waters of the lake seemed too brilliant to be translated by any palette. No one wanted to go to bed, but there was heavy work for the morrow, and the small boy received a very emphatic invitation before he betook himself to a small bag — his personal property — in the men's tent.

Our heavy, restful sleep was broken the next morning by hearing an unaccustomed sawing and chopping over near the cooktent. Poking out an inquisitive head, I saw Jack trimming the boat boards till there was not an extra square inch to tote over the next thirty-five miles of trail to Lake Maligne, our destination. These cedar planks, kindly donated by the Canadian Government, were sixteen feet long, eighteen inches wide and a little

* Jasper

—141—

over an inch thick. These were the sides of the boat. There was a big bunch of much shorter cross planks, but they did not count as did the larger ones in the question of transportation over a new trail, over a high pass reported to be covered with eight feet of snow, over miles where the trail gang had so far been unable to cut any trail at all. How Jack was ever to get those long "gangly" boards over those thirty-five miles to their destination, to the fair waters of Lake Maligne, with any one — or two — of the outfit of new horses with whom we had been getting acquainted for the last few days, was too much for my comprehension. Most of the workers had never been to school before, and to think of strapping a sixteen foot board to a poor beast, which even resented a packsaddle because of his ignorance, seemed suicidal to the boards and the horse alike.

Just as we mounted our steeds to ride out ahead of the outfit we saw a horse led up to which we had not been thoroughly introduced — Jonas by name. He was apparently just "plain horse," nothing extra about him to have ever made us notice him specially before. How we were to take off our hats to him in the end only the next three days were to prove.

"What's to happen to Jonas, Jack?" said the small boy. "O, he's goin' to carry the boat." With a careless fling across the adjusted packsaddle went two great bags of hay, one swinging well down on each side of him. Jonas' face never showed a quiver, he never budged a leg. You might have thought he had been carrying great slabs of wood all his life. I still failed to see how he was to do the job entire, but I saw later. We rode off pitying Jonas sincerely.

We had gone scarce half a mile when, directly in front of us, we met an angry "fool-hen" strutting and parading. We all paused and looked at the hen; she fearlessly stared back at us and then flew to a low limb at the side of the road. "It's a pity to kill her," I murmured, "but fresh meat would taste good, shall I kill her?" No note of objection coming from behind, I jumped down from Maud (which in itself was a feat, for I was short and Maud was tall) and hunting round for a proper stick, took aim, as I had seen the men do, and "let drive." The "fool-hen" wagged her head as the stick flew at least a foot above her, evidently decided that though not dangerous, there was a bare chance I might hit her if she sat there long enough, so flapped her wings and discreetly flew into the entangling branches of a tall spruce.

Then and there I lost permanent prestige with the small boy; he never risked the life of another bird in my

hands again, and though I have no recollection of his ever hitting one himself under the same circumstances, at any rate he never let me frighten them off.

It was a day of grouse. We saw all sorts and varieties of them, but only shot at them with the camera. Mother ducks, trailing their young families of eight to ten chicks out for a swimming lesson, were numerous on the small lakes we skirted. The trail was nicely cut out, we could not lose our way, so sauntered on through green timber at one time, burnt timber at another, admired and gathered many a rare orchid, and lived, lived the story of the trail.

Slowly and quietly surmounting a long hillside, where the ground was covered with gaunt, fire-scarred trees, we silently reached the summit and started on the down-slope, when my sister unexpectedly had a long-expressed wish gratified. Twenty yards in front of us stood a beautiful black bear. The moment we spied him he was busy tearing up a rotten log — looking for ants, a most toothsome dainty of bears — and his fine, glossy pelt was vibrating with his energies. What a sight he was! We could look right into his little, startled, pig-like eyes for an instant. We three paused on the hill top, our horses craned their necks, the bear gazed at us one moment, and then — ants, logs, all else forgot, he was off down the valley with the speed of the racehorse. Over logs and intercepting bushes he bounded, his trail marked by the glistening pelt quivering in the sunshine, then, diving into the distant forest growth, he was lost to view.

We all sighed, the inquisitive horses straightened up their ears, we tightened up the forgotten reins, and, with the small boy muttering "I think I could have hit him if I'd had the *22*," we went onward to our night's destination — Buffalo Prairie, one of us at least very thankful the *22* had not been round to raise the ire of our recent acquaintance, though we might have had the lost "fool-hen" if it had been on someone's saddle. Hot doughnuts, hot biscuit, blancmange, fried ham, and boiled potatoes, however, did much to drive the memory of the hen from our minds and send us all to well-earned repose.

From Buffalo Prairie Camp to one called by the government trail gang "Windy Camp," the trail was quite as full of interest as all the previous miles of travel. Our party rode out entire that day, as Jack said there were a few indefinite spots where one might go astray, and we had no desire to hunt trouble. Quickly leaving the bed of the valley behind, we mounted long, rilling mounds covered with the first spring flowers. The cottonwoods were just in their first leaf and the air was heavy with their sweet odour. All the world about and for miles away seemed full of joy, all but that small portion which was right there under our noses — Jonas and his trouble (the boat) stalking ever before us. As Jonas summoned an expression of "what's-the-use," his burden was lashed to his unprotesting sides, a rope looped across the front ends of the boards. Jack assumed the position of steering gear and, Jonas acting as pro-propeller, the pair took the lead of the small procession, and we saw our fad for measuring a "new" lake in the far wilderness being fought out to a finish before our eyes. For, in case I have failed to mention it elsewhere, our visit at this time to Lake Maligne was to learn her length and breadth, and study her valleys and mountains.

Leaving camp at 4900 feet we were soon ascending the long hill of which Jack had told us; with slight intermission the way led upwards, always upwards; for three hours we climbed steadily and, though the distance accomplished was not great, the aneroid read 6400 feet at Windy Camp. The panorama the entire way was a splendid one, and many an old friend seen on the expedition of 1908 reintroduced himself — Mounts Hardisty and Geikie and the valley of the Whirlpool being well-recognized points.

Of course it blew at Windy Camp, though not sufficiently to keep down the mosquitoes that night, and everyone was glad when the order came to "march" next morning in spite of Jack's dubious opinion as to our ability to get through the deep snow on the coming pass.

Jonas led off with the boat as usual, for, if relegated to the rear where we need not have beheld the painful sight, his impetuous nature invariably interfered with the steering gear, and Jonas was sure to come charging ahead, unmindful of the one whose duty it was at the time to assist him on his journey and save his head from being battered to bits. The sight of him under the best conditions was trying, for when the boards were not striking the inoffensive horse in the cheek, or nearlyknocking the steersman down, they were slipping from the guiding ropes, going fore or aft according to the lay of the land, and having to be shifted back into place. Nearly anyone would ask, "Why didn't you lash the boards between two horses and avoid so much trouble?" For the simple reason that we had only one Jonas in the family and that in a new country, such as the one in which our horses had been picked up, they are not yet being trained to carry boats over high passes and are consequently incompetent for the work. No, the only thing that could be done was being done, and Jonas and the men in turn must suffer for the cause of science.

A mile from camp trouble assailed us. It was June 17th, and the winter's snow should have been gone, but as it was not, we were perforce compelled to plow through it. Jonas had been relegated to the rear that the saddle-horses and pack-animals might break the way for him. The new outfit had probably never been required to make its way through drifts six and eight feet high before, and it was self-evident that every horse was "green" at the job. No matter how nice a path Jack and Unwin beat carefully down for them, they would turn and twist with a horrid perversity, get "balled up" and have to be dug out. We circled every patch circleable, but the ones to go through were legion. A mile from the summit, where the last, hard ascent began, Jack rather excitedly called our attention to two tiny specks on the skyline and, though he remained sweetly non-committal and suggested they might be a horse or two men, we knew he meant "sheep," and sheep they promptly became. The lady wearing the red sweater was asked to remove the same for fear of frightening the game, but refused on account of an icy blast which was blowing straight from the direction of the sheep. The binoculars were applied to the doubtful subjects and the announcement made: "They are the thinnest legged sheep I ever saw." There they stood, immovable, like sentinels guarding the far-away summit.

We crept closer; all yelling to the horses ceased; we

came to great fields of snow where the men patiently helped the obstinate and untrained horses through in silence. We were stalking those sheep — wild mutton has no equal — and none of us had any desire to miss so fine an opportunity.

Even we with our saddle ponies had our troubles in getting through the huge drifts for, leading them with long lines, we yet ran the risk of their plunging forward on us. In places we found a partially dug out trail, a trail the men ahead had shoveled out a few days before, and took to it as well as we could. Then we came close enough to analyze our two immovable sheep — only to find them a pair of abandoned shovels which had been hewn from a tree and, in case we needed the same, left standing conspicuously in the snow. I noted a curious fact a little later; the starting of the "sheep" rumour could not be laid to the door of a single member of the party, and no one had really thought them sheep after all.

Upon reaching the summit of the pass, a pair of cold-stiffened fingers groped for the aneroid and read the altitude as 8100 feet; laughingly we named the pass "Shovel Pass" and went on our way down the heather and snow decked slopes till, weary and wet and cold, we halted by a stream for a night's well-earned rest. A couple of ptarmigan, not quite so quick as Unwin's *22*, provided us with a supper fit for the gods; our exertions of the day, a delicious sleep.

Poor Jonas' troubles thickened the following day for the valley was wet and spongy, and we had come to the end of the trail gang's work. Held back by the cold spring, they had been unable to get over Shovel Pass much before us, and the work beyond was very heavy. There was only one spot on the day's march, however, which will forever be ineradicable, and that was where I saw Unwin drop over an almost perpendicular thirty-foot bank, hanging desperately to the front ends of the boards, and Jonas, who couldn't see an inch in front of him to tell where to put his feet, stumbling blindly after. As I peered over at them, it seemed as though this spot must surely be the Waterloo of Unwin, Jonas and the boat, and it would be such a pity when we were so near our destination. Giving them time to complete their descent, I then slid down on my own two feet, leading the sliding Maud behind me, and arrived at the bottom in time to see Unwin sailing round the corner still clutching the bobbing ends of the boards and Jonas showing no signs of fresh bruises.

Toward three in the afternoon we rode into view of the lake, about six miles distant, and I eagerly watched the faces of those who had never seen it before to see if an impartial eye would behold the beauty with which I had vested it three years before. The signs were decidedly favourable. From this point, where we had at last come up to the trail-makers, they rushed frantically ahead of our outfit, slashing a tree here, tossing a fallen log there, anything to get Jonas and his load to the end of the journey, we naturally being a mere detail in the rear. At one point, after all the trouble of getting him and the boat thus far, I thought we were going to lose them both. Within two or three miles of the lake, a mountain stream from the Bald Hills descends with such rapidity that it could easily carry off his feet a man who attempted to wade it. Jack mounted Roany, behind the small boy, and sallied across and though Roany was quite capable of seeing the child over without further assistance, it looked well to have Jack on the spot in case of accident. There could be no helping hand for Jonas. Jack returned and, adjusting the boards as evenly as possible, told him to "go in there," and, with that prompt obedience which had been so marked a characteristic of him all through the trip, he went. The stream was scarce ten yards wide, but that was wide enough for trouble; Jonas stepped cautiously among the big boulders, the boards swayed uncertainly forward, his foot turned on a rolling stone, he stumbled, then recovered himself, but the boards had pitched into the water, they caught on the far bank, the wrench threw him to his knees, he went down, his head under water, the boards pinning him as in a vice. Jack leapt to the assistance of his favourite and Unwin jumped in to help; a violent pull, the poor old fellow was up and out on dry ground before it was too late, and we all drew a long breath. Such are the trials of the trail.

Once to the shores of the lake you can well understand that it was Jonas' pack which came off first, and stock in Jonas, which could be had for the asking a few days before, was no longer on the market.

For the nonce our tepee had to be pitched on the corner of the lake which had been swept by fire many years ago — the only blemish to that wonderfully lovely face which, unseeing, looks ever heavenward. The entire masculine contingent then turned its attention to the building of the boat, leaving otherwise idle hands to get the meals, keep the fires going, etc.; and when housekeeping was slack we strolled down to the shore to watch progress. She grew but slowly, for the rain came down in torrents daily, specially when they were ready to do the calking. Then one day she was finished, a thing of beauty in our eyes, and as the men slid her

gently into the water, the small boy solemnly broke an abandoned vinegar bottle over her bow, saying, "I christen thee, H.M.S. *Chaba the Second.*"

We were to look later at the mouth of Maligne Creek and find all that was left of poor little abandoned H.M.S. *Chaba the First,* which had been used on our first expedition to the lake — a bulky, ugly, clumsy raft, but very dear to us whom she had carried, safer than we knew at the time, on our first voyage of the then unexplored waters.

The moment the exciting launch had taken place someone went out to round up the horses which had not been living on the fat of the land — the good feed we knew was on the other side of the lake. We all knew there would be trouble getting the now-worldly-wise across the self-evidently dangerous outlet of the lake which, though only twenty or thirty yards at the utmost, is a nasty treacherous stream. The horses were all driven to the shore and there that part of it ended. Then someone got in the boat, and the bell-horse of the trail gang, Wall-eyed Sue (you would really wonder what there was about her to attract the other horses),

was led across. For once Sue's attractions failed to draw the crowd, and Maud, the belle of our bunch, was led over in the same way; they made a strong combination, and eventually the whole lot was swum across.

Then began a perfect camp-life on the shores of Lake Maligne. The tepee made a home which has no equal in the out-of-door life. But a small fire is needed in them to keep out ordinary cold, thus avoiding a constant chopping of wood, and the smoke thereof keeps out the pestiferous little mosquito whose number is legion in the north country during June and July and a part of August. In our outfit we carried two air beds and a couple of cow-skins. In the evening when the frosty air began to filter in through the lower part of the tepee, the skins and blankets would be stretched on a rope which had been looped from pole to pole, and there, all gathered round the fire on other soft blankets, the men with pipes lighted, tales were told of the winter's hunt and trapping stories till the small boy's eyes grew big in the fire-light glare, and a wail would break forth if someone mentioned "bed." Be the tales as fascinating as they might, by ten-thirty the same small boy would be

H.M.S. *Chaba the Second*

poked into his sleeping bag — well tied and safety-pinned to keep him from being found in the open in the morning — the fire allowed to crackle itself into ashes, and we would drop to sleep listening to the flapping of the tepee-wings, to a nighthawk swooping by, to the lap-lap of the waters, in the far distance a loon calling, or a duck skimming over the water with a plaintive cry and perhaps, if it were very still, we might catch the monotonous notes of the horse-bells back on the green slopes of the Opal Hills. Beautiful? Of course it was; healthful, restful, peaceful, and the whole kingdom ours! We reveled in it for one whole month.

It was not wholly a play expedition, however; there was a bit of interesting work which had brought us so far. Not long after our discovery of the lake, I had been telling of its wonders to Mr. Dowling of the Canadian Government Survey. He said, "Why not go in there with instruments and measure it?"

"*Me* measure a lake? Why I couldn't measure a pond, much less a great lake like that one!"

"O yes you can, it's very easy; I will lend you the instruments, and you will find it a most interesting thing to do." I thought to myself at the time, what next?

The way opened, the day came which brought the instruments and all details for the work, instructions so easy that the most stupid could not fail to pluck up courage to at least attempt it; and that was how we came to have so many days on the shore of the lake. Anyone who has ever picked up a set of tools with hands and head totally untrained for the work can imagine the trepidation that stepped into H.M.S. *Chaba* with me the day on which I fixed the log at the stern for the first time, as I took my first reading through the sight of the compass and felt that a doubting and grinning sister, who had been brought up on surveying, looked on from behind.

It did not take more than two days' work for me to realize it was no child's play, or the work a matter of a few days. First I am compelled to say that H.M.S.

Chaba was a punt and, being one, failed to develop much speed, and, for the same reason, took an immense amount of muscle to send her from point to point on her scientific errand. As my part was to throw out the line, gather it in, and record the readings of the log, I am free to confess that on the second day of this exciting work I got the spool caught among some rocks about ten stations from camp. Pull, coax and manoeuvre as we would, we failed to loosen that spool and it remained wedged among great boulders fully eight feet below the surface of the lake. But one may not go on such an expedition and have it come to naught for so small an accident as that.

Wheeler, the boatman of the day (for I wore them out in turn), gazed long and studiously among the rocks, and at last I meekly and tremblingly said, "Now you are used to the water, Wheeler, don't you think you could dive for that spool? If you bring it up to me all sound, I'll give you the price of the spool."

"Done!" said Wheeler. He put me ashore; I guiltily felt of the water with my finger; it seemed to have a temperature of about 45° and I felt very sorry for the diver. Taking my sympathies and self-reproaches to the other side of the point, I awaited the signal which was to call me back to the boat. The quiet was all about me. I sat in a bed of moss and wondered if even an Indian had ever come to this special bit of shore before; watched a couple of sandpipers tilting, tilting — as sandpipers never seem to tire of doing — over the pebbles near me, and noticed a pair of ducks skimming quickly to the shore on the other side.

With thoughts on spools and careless people in general, I was suddenly aware that something was stirring just behind me. Of course, it was some of the little folk of the forest, so I rose gently to see what was watching me. Not more than eight feet away, at the top of the bank, sharpening his claws (as a cat does) on a spruce tree, was a marten. He turned to stare as though I were the intruder, paused in his work and deliberately turned to look me out of the place. I did not budge. This did not suit him; he spit at me like an angry family cat and made a threatening move as though to come on and insist I "get out of there."

I said, "You impertinent little rascal, clear out yourself, I am big enough to choke you." He stood still and seemed to digest my remarks, then decided the enemy was too large for him to tackle, and sauntered slowly away with a perfect air of "Who's afraid of you? Not I!"

Then I heard a call — "I've got the spool!" and I waded back through the moss and underbrush to see Wheeler, none the worse for his dip, brandishing the spool and full of how he dived with his "eyes open and got it on the first dive," while I was equally excited over having met a marten, and actually having held converse with him.

As moving day was to come along shortly and as Jack had seen fresh signs of goats on the green meadows of the Opal Hills, he decided we would have a picnic the following morning, taking a lunch with us, and rowing as far as Duck Cove, a beautiful indentation on the north shore of the lake about two miles from camp. It was a great nesting place for the many varieties of duck which inhabit those waters, and we had strong hopes of obtaining a few duck eggs, as well as allowing Jack to take his rifle and see if there were not a little fresh meat loitering round, waiting to fill our larder. For my part, I wanted to see what grew on those wonderfully vivid green patches which could be seen so far away. There should surely be some rare plant sunning themselves on those tempting slides.

As the *Chaba* glided silently into the quiet cove, ducks rose from all about us but, hunt as we would, not an egg was to be found. After lunch on the shore, we turned our attention to the hillside, Jack viewing it with a pair of binoculars. As it was "only a quarter of a mile over to them," we all set bravely forth. We walked and walked, crossed game trails, followed game trails, saw any amount of tufts of wool left on low bushes by the passing goat, waded through deep moss, climbed and struggled, switched mosquitoes out of eyes and ears, and sputtered them out of our mouths when we opened the same to grumble at the"quarter of a mile." After a good half hour's fight and climb, we reached the open meadows. They were worth the struggle, though my poor sister, having no hobs in her wornout shoes (she was still in borrowed plumes, her delayed duffle-bag not having yet reached her from Edmonton), was decidedly discouraged with her own back-sliding. When it came to the real hill, she was forced to give up; Jack went one way with the small boy looking for goat, and I climbed around looking for plant specimens. An hour passed, then back came the discouraged hunters. "Lots of signs, but not a goat in sight."

We all sat resting, one talking hobs, one flowers, two the contrariness of goat, when Jack suddenly looked far aloft and said, "I see a goat! By Jove, we must have him, Paul!" The rest of the family remonstrated that it was no time to drag a small boy along over that awful hill, but

Jack said, "I was a kid myself once, come on bring your *22.*" And away they went, the big man dragging the willing but small legs after him. The tremendous exertion caused the small hunter to cough violently; we could hear him when his wee body was a mere speck high up among the rocks. But Jack never let go his clutch on the small hand. The hill was extraordinarily steep, they fell and rose again, and the noise of the coughing and stumbling should have long sent that goat to the right-about. Instead it seemed to fascinate him and, though he drew out of sight several times, his curiosity caused him to look over the ledge once too often.

The two hunters were fully a half mile from us in an air line when I saw Jack kneel, saw a puff of smoke, and then, while the boy was left to recover his wind, Jack was off up the rest of the hill to the skyline. Had he shot him? No such good luck. But we rose and strolled round in that direction to make sure. Keeping an eye on the hunters, in a few moments we heard a shout from a childish voice, and then far, far up we saw a white body bounding down, careening, turning, flopping. It was our fresh meat. Still clutching his little *22*, his small legs flickering on the down-slope, the small boy joined us and the goat at the foot of the hill, saying, "We did pretty well, didn't we?" and proudfully stood with his *22* beside the dead goat while a picture was taken to prove what a *22* in certain hands could be made to do.

The poor goat was a yearling. Pushed out of the home circle before his wits had grown to match his legs, he had proved too young to deal with the wiles of the world and so filled the pot for us many times over before the last shred of him was finished. As for the small boy, after that everything was a mark for the *22* — chipmunks, gophers, discarded tin cans — though very soon orders became strict that he should confine himself to the cans as his aim was becoming a little too skilful and the small neighbours about camp were running too close chances for their lives.

The day came when we could dally no longer. It was cloudy, with rain imminent, but "science" could not be balked by rain, so H.M.S. *Chaba* was to show what she could do. She "did" a little more than two thousand pounds and looked capable of "doing" much more. Saddlery and all other extras were made into an enormous bundle, well lashed together, and swung high on a great tripod to keep them safe from the pestiferous little porcupine which is the greatest nuisance to the camper in the summer.

As we saw our worldly possessions poised on the shore awaiting a strong arm and a good deal of man-oeuvering to place them in so small a space for the voyage, we wondered where *we* were to come in. But we went, as also tents, blankets, food, cookstoves and pipe, axe, cross-cut saw, duffle-bag, cameras, and finally the five constituting the most important element of the outfit. From previous observations we knew we had at least ten miles to row to a fresh campground, the waters were wide, and the wind came in gusts down the great valley. The clouds thickened, the waves roughened; it was going to be anything but a pleasure trip. Huddled in our buckskin coats, with sweaters under and rubber coats over them, we were persuaded only by the diary-maker that it was really the 27th of June, so bitter were the erratic blasts which constantly struck us.

With the load high out of water acting as a huge resistant to the strong wind, the work needed herculean efforts, and the men were soon drenched with perspiration. We knew it had to be kept up for hours, and often wished we might change places for a "spell," just to warm our chilling blood; but there was no such thing as climbing over the obstacles behind which we were wedged, so we sat and endured it. I pointed out the scenery as it should be, but it had to be taken on faith for soon a slight drizzle set in, then the rain came down in sheets. The men, already wet, could get but slightly wetter; the small boy burrowed under the rubbers with one eye out and was only heard from occasionally when his small voice piped up, "Wish I could use the *22*, there go five ducks."

Toward the end of the fourth hour of that miserable row, Wheeler asked my sister if she could sing. I venture to say that even Nellie Melba, knowing how, would have declined under the circumstances, but the sister was game to the end. We had tried to tell funny anecdotes, we had tried riddles, so in the downpour and the wind and the cold I heard her start with a rather hoarse voice — "Pull for the shore," (a subject chosen probably on account of the trend of her thoughts). It was a brave feat and such an apt selection that I thought it worthy of a smile, but the men kept on solemnly rowing and I was forced to subside. Then we saw the new campsite coming into view, and so cheered were we by the prospect of a landing that Wheeler volunteered to sing for us "The Ship That Never Came Back." Its sentiment was fearful, there were fifteen verses, and there were so many interesting people who "never came back," that the listeners were glad when we came near enough to shore to stop the harrowing details, as the ending of each verse brought us roundly to the point where we ourselves might end if the *Chaba* failed to make port. The tepee and its fire, the cozy cooktent and supper were more than usually appreciated that night.

The campground chosen will, in the course of time, become a favourite one. It lies under the shadow of Mounts Unwin and Charlton, at the mouth of Samson Narrows, and is a large alluvial fan formed by the stream coming from Mount Maligne. Later we called that stream Sandpiper Creek as its shores were a favourite nesting place for the teetering little sandpipers so numerous in that country; and no matter when we walked down to the stream's edge there were always plenty of aspiring mothers to be seen teaching their children to balance and dip, balance and dip, just as the grownups themselves, till it made you tired to watch them. We brought a couple of the babies in one day and photographed them in the dishpan which had previously been lined with moss. It was not a natural picture; they appeared still, something I think a sandpiper never can be.

And now, having reached a new haven, and with a burning desire to get on with the measuring, we were to find other disposition of our time made for us than what we had planned. It kept on storming. Day in and day out it poured, it blew. We would try a row in the boat, only to be glad to come to shore again for fear even that steady old punt of ours would capsize in some of the hurricanes which swept down upon us without warning. On one of these tours of inspection when it really seemed as though the clouds *were* lifting, we found a nest of ten duck eggs. Of course we captured them and, as the rain again settled down on us, we started for home. A great argument took place as to whether they should be used for omelette or sponge cake. The household was divided. Then someone said, "Perhaps they can't be used for either, let's test them. I believe if they float, they're no good, but if they sink, they are all right." For my part I thought if they sank in that lake, they would be of small use to anyone. There and then in the cold downpour (to such idiocy had our long inactivity brought us) the punt was stopped, and each egg set floating. *They all floated!* We still persisted in carrying them home, but said less about omelette or sponge cakes. A few of the eggs were used, a few of them were promptly buried, and the resultant cake had a taste which only a camp appetite could excuse.

Day followed day; we made marvellous dishes in the cooktent, we played cards till sick of the sight of them;

two of us made a sortie up Sandpiper Valley to get pictures of Mount Maligne one morning when it looked as though the clouds had moved off permanently, and came back soaking wet with no pictures. It was terribly discouraging.

Fourteen days of inaction had gone by, spirits were at their lowest ebb. We had retired for the night, going off to sleep as usual, watching the rain dropping through the tepee wings, and putting our fire out. Some time later I woke; it was pitch dark, and a curious little noise arrested my attention — probably the cause of waking at all. Something seemed to jump onto the top of the tepee and then slide gently down, only to go back and repeat the performance over and over again.

At last I said, "Carrie, are you awake?"

"Yes," murmured a sleepy voice.

"What do you suppose is making a trapeze of this tepee?"

"Don't know, some sort of beast."

We couldn't sleep for thinking of it, and then I grew wide enough awake to realize I was pretty cold and it was snow which, unable to stick on the steep sides of the tepee walls, would mass itself and take a slide. That fact settled, we soon slept again, and knew no more till Jack stuck his head into the tepee in the morning, having just dug his way over from his tent to ours with the frying pan.

There seemed little more to expect in the weather line, and yet the very next day, as it cleared up a little and we went to the lower end of the lake with Jack to have a look at his horses (it is as far as the horses can be taken), we had an exhibition which none of us cared to see repeated. Within five miles of the mouth of the lake we pulled ashore to the point where H.M.S. *Chaba the First* had been built; here four of us were to remain, have a look at the old camp of 1908, and await Jack's return.

We were eating lunch when Jack suddenly paused with a piece of raisin pie half-way to his mouth, looked intently out to a point of the lake where he must soon go, and gasped, "By Jove, I wouldn't be there for a thousand dollars! Look!"

We looked. Fully two miles away from us, in the centre of the lake towered a waterspout, rushing headlong straight up the lake, then dying away as suddenly as it came. How high was it? We could not tell. So far away were we and the spout so well-defined that two hundred feet seemed a very modest estimate. I never liked that lake in a storm afterward; I was constantly wondering what might have been the result if we had met such an obstacle three years before when shoving the unwieldy raft along. We all watched Jack start for the end of the lake in a good deal of trepidation a few moments later. On the return voyage, while holding the rudder, I insisted on keeping well into shore, in spite of the fact that Jack thought enough of the *Chaba's* virtues to think she could stem such a waterspout. I hadn't finished measuring the lake, and certainly wasn't going to have those investigations cut off by such nonsense.

The next day the long-looked-for duffle-bag came on the scene, brought in by special messenger; letters from the outside world were read, and a fresh piece of beefsteak added to the general excitement. New garments were put on by the proudful owner of the duffle-bag, the weather cleared, the compass and log went forth for the day, and the following day we started for the new campground, a new station for investigations — the head or southeastern point of the lake.

It is this upper end of the lake which is so fine, even under trying conditions, but that day it was ideal. Not a ripple marred the surface of the glass-like lake excepting those made by the dipping of the oars or the scuttling of an occasional, low-flying, frightened duck. The mountains obligingly turned themselves up-side-down in the water; the many lovely waterfalls, duplicating themselves in the mirror, fell up as well as down; even the avalanches started by the hot sun met their own reflection halfway. We passed the last narrows, slowly crept out into the broader part of the lake where the black Ramparts pointed to the end, looked up to the great buttresses of the Thumb, and sighed a long sigh at the wonderfulness of it all. Even the small boy was silenced by the splendour of the scene for the time being, and then the little voice uttered what the solemn face had portrayed for some time, "It's all right, isn't it, Aunt Mary?" A pause and then, "I suppose I am too little a boy to have a mountain named for me," and another long pause and sigh.

"No," I said, "I think if you stayed a very good boy for the rest of the trip and not —" (mentioning a few lapses of good behaviour chronic to small boys), "we might call that mountain Mount Paul," pointing to the one just west of the Thumb. "But remember this, that if you fail to keep your part of the bargain, off comes the name, and it's a long distance to the top of that mountain to take off so small a name." He promised, but the name had to be removed twice; however, it was on there when we left. So I hope it may remain for many years to come, to mark the visit of the first white child who navigated those waters.

The camp at the upper end of the lake was as interesting as any of the other camps, with the added attraction of good weather as long as we stayed. We had heard that the Stoney Indians said they had reached the head of the lake, via a pass from Brazeau Lake, so our chief aim was to try and ferret out the pass by which they came. But pass we found none, neither a sign of the presence of horses or poles for tepees. The weather was so good there that it was almost too good. Instead of freezing, we baked and sizzled in the heat on the few expeditions we made. The finest trip at the head of the lake we found when exploring the valley from which flowed the stream that fed the head of the lake.

Having been rowed to the mouth of the stream, we skirted the great rock walls of Mount Warren, bent our steps to the right as did the stream which we were following, wandered on and on, counting the falls that threw their snowy streamers from every mountain side. So enraptured became the small boy that, when he saw a specially fine fall coming from the back of the Thumb, he stretched forth his little hand and said rather sentimentally, "I name thee the Veil of Tears. Not v-a-l-e, Aunt Mary, but v-e-i-l." It was enough to make older hearts than his sentimental, and it didn't matter much how it was all spelled.

The valley ended by receiving the name of Pixie Valley, so full was it of rocks at the upper end which looked almost human as they glowered down upon us working our intrusive way into their silent haunts. We found no pass through which even an Indian could have led his steed, and he can lead him through some queer places, so headed for camp and supper which we found as the sun went down.

The mosquitoes had fled with the sunshine; high on the Pixie Hills sunshafts were dying fast; the mountain goats, which had been sunning themselves or feeding all day in sight of us, were slowly meandering out of view — to some sheltering rock no doubt; the Monk's Head, a splendid buttress of Mount Warren, looked purple in the evening shadows; the Sunshine Falls, which on all sunny days busily tossed a dainty thread fully a thousand feet downward before striking the rocks on the slopes of the Thumb, had gone to sleep; even the avalanches had ceased their restive plunging; and we five were alone in the great quiet amphitheatre, almost whispering for fear of marring the wonderful scene. The small boy and his mother strolled away among the pines, just to be a little more alone I suppose, and I lay idly beneath the trees watching them and wondering how many more boys of his size would

Mount Charlton at the head of Pixie Valley

enjoy every throb of the evening's pulse as he was doing. A little later they came wandering back again, arm in arm, sentiment and poetry fairly treading on the heels of the child, his eyes glued to the surrounding mountains, his face bathed in a rapt expression. Suddenly there was a wild whoop, a great leap, and a grand scurry, then a sufficient recovery of poise for him to yell, "Where's the *22*, I almost stepped on a porcupine!" and I concluded there was no use worrying that the wilderness was going to make him old before his time — it needed but a porcupine and a *22* to prove that he was still "boy."

The last day came when we could no longer say there was surveying to do at the head of the lake but could safely affirm that the food supply was growing meagre; and as ten miles on the north shore, near the exit of the lake, was still untouched, it behooved us to pack up and move on. The day was fair beyond words; every detail of

the whole scene called us to stay; but it was not wise, and there were others coming who would need the boat at the lower end of the lake, eighteen miles away. Jack packed up the kitchen and diningroom and cellar, we folded our blankets and air beds while the small boy, now expert, neatly put the big tepee into a small compass; in an hour, like the Arabs, we were silently stealing away, with every heartstring taut to stay. O it was so beautiful! The wind, behind us in the start, proceeded to play its usual trick in a few minutes and soon became head on, making a hard, hard pull of eighteen miles when it might have been play with a pack-mantle sail.

We ate a good lunch about half-way down; then the wind having increased to uncomfortable proportions, we were forced to hug the shore, crawled at a snail's pace, and about suppertime drew up at our old campground on the north shore of the lake and climbed out, every muscle protesting at having been kept so long in durance vile. The horses, which had not seen us for several weeks by this time, showed every sign of being glad to have us back, though the salt that was always to be had for the asking was no doubt a strong drawing card.

The last few days of our stay on the lake were packed with play. One morning seeming to be specially propitious. Jack came in with five horses and we made a climb to the Bald Hills, the low range lying between Maligne Creek and the mouth of the lake. For a mile or more, we were bothered with fallen timber; after that, though very steep, we could push along almost anywhere, and at last came out on the great bare hills, obtaining fine views of the lake and surrounding country. It promptly grew cloudy of course, and no good pictures to be had, but we were growing accustomed to such disappointments. The flies and mosquitoes were exceedingly bad, and the day very hot. Next morning it was hotter, but as there were still several miles to survey and half of the family wanted to climb the Statue, which is a rugged, prominent peak lying between Mounts Unwin and Charlton, we were off up the lake while the morning mists were still hovering over the green water.

I hadn't an atom of envy in my heart as I watched the climbers start for the Statue, much preferring my cooler job of reading the log from station to station while Wheeler did the rowing. Hot? Well after the days of freezing I had forgotten it could be so hot at such an altitude (about 5600 feet) and such splendid ice-houses (glaciers) all about us. It reminded me of a story my sister told of an old Irish woman. Seeing her on a hot day with a big shawl over her shoulders, they asked her why she was so wrapped up, and she replied, "To keep out the heat, Mu'um." The sun was so scorching that day, that I put my buckskin over my shoulders "to keep out the heat," and when forced to turn and read and then throw the log back into the water, my hands were almost scorched by the heat of the boards of the boat, not to mention sticking fast to the melting pitch, the "calking" as Jack called it. But evening and the shadows and the cool winds from the glaciers came at last; we returned to pick up the climbers who had a nice supper ready for us; then all stowing ourselves away, we started on the last row of the summer on fair Lake Maligne. They told us of their successful climb — no mean little walk as the aneroid read 8200 feet at the top, and they had had considerable scree and ice work, using axes and rope. Reaching the Statue, they found the rock too weathered to climb to the top of it, so placed their flag (a bandana handkerchief) as high as possible, took some photographs, and then descended to the homely duty of getting supper for the "surveyors." Quite a come-down.

It grew darker and darker; Wheeler who had rowed over twenty-eight miles that day began to show signs of weariness, the sister took the oars from him. He tried the mouth-organ for a short time; I was glad when he put it in his pocket, it marred the *silent* music of the lake. Darker and darker became the way; the shimmering silver on the water disappeared; two tiny, red clouds in the west (like little night-lights) turned gray and went out; a loon called derisively after us; a few belated ducks went scurrying by, as though they knew they "would catch it" when they got home; we ceased to sing or talk. There was just the dip, dip of the oars; the silent passing of the spectral trees on the shore under whose shadow we rowed that we might hold our course — the last voyage.

A little bump, a grating of sand, and at 10:45, with the last readings of the last log and compass clutched tightly in my hand, we stepped ashore weary, yet longing, and groped our way to the ghostly-looking tepee — a big work accomplished.

Over the return I draw a veil. All went well, but it was a loosening of the grasp we all had learned to love. Each day was a "farewell" to some spot which for the moment had been our very own. The wedge had been driven in; in another year the secret places would be secret no longer.